Idriss Déby and the Darfur Conflict

ALSO BY ÉSAÏE TOÏNGAR

*A Teenager in the Chad Civil War:
A Memoir of Survival, 1982–1986* (2006)

Idriss Déby and the Darfur Conflict

Ésaïe Toïngar

McFarland & Company, Inc., Publishers
Jefferson, North Carolina

LIBRARY OF CONGRESS CATALOGUING-IN-PUBLICATION DATA

Toïngar, Ésaïe, 1968–
    Idriss Déby and the Darfur Conflict / Ésaïe Toïngar.
    p.   cm.
    Includes bibliographical references and index.

    ISBN 978-0-7864-7084-6
    softcover : acid free paper ∞

    1. Déby, Idriss. 2. Sudan—History—Darfur Conflict, 2003– 3. Chad—Foreign relations—Sudan. 4. Sudan—Foreign relations—Chad. 5. Chad—Politics and government—1990– I. Title.
DT546.484.T65 2014
967.4304'4092—dc23   2013039866

BRITISH LIBRARY CATALOGUING DATA ARE AVAILABLE

© 2014 Ésaïe Toïngar. All rights reserved

No part of this book may be reproduced or transmitted in any form or by any means, electronic or mechanical, including photocopying or recording, or by any information storage and retrieval system, without permission in writing from the publisher.

Front cover image: Sudanese Darfur survivor Ibrahim holds human skulls at the site of a mass grave on the outskirts of the West Darfur town of Mukjar, Sudan, Monday, April 23, 2007 (AP Photo/Nasser Nasser, File)

Manufactured in the United States of America

McFarland & Company, Inc., Publishers
   Box 611, Jefferson, North Carolina 28640
   www.mcfarlandpub.com

Acknowledgments

I acknowledge with gratitude the informants who continue to supply news of events in Chad, Sudan, the Central African Republic, Gabon, Cameroon, the two Congos, Rwanda, Burundi, and Uganda. This book could not have been written without their contributions, yet for their own safety I cannot name them.

In the course of writing this book, I have been sustained by the courage of the African people. People in the heart of Africa have suffered greatly, enduring the treachery and violence of tyrants in their cities, deserts, and jungles. Now I find myself in the heartland of the United States, my personal safety threatened more by winter ice on the windswept interstate than by madmen with automatic weapons. This book is dedicated to those who endure in Chad, Sudan, the Central African Republic, and elsewhere in the region, grieving the death and poverty created by political and economic mismanagement. As the mighty protagonists struggle, you have died in great numbers and you grieve your dead.

Chadian children, you were ripped from your parents, kidnapped into rebel bands and armies without training. You have been wounded, maimed, and killed for no worthwhile cause. We grieve for you. This book is dedicated to you and your loved ones.

Brahim Solguet and Adoum Abakar Moustapha, you were among the rare young Chadians who found a way to fight peacefully against the injustice in Chad. You were tragically assassinated. We still do not see your dream realized. This book is dedicated to you and to other young Chadians who are still struggling for peace, justice, equity, and freedom.

Abas Koty, Laoukeïn Bardet Frison, Kétténodji Moïse, and Youssouf Togoïmi, you were forced by circumstances to carry guns to defend yourselves or democracy in Chad, like many other Chadian leaders. Unfortunately, you were all assassinated or tortured and killed because the current regime in Chad could not let you succeed. This book is dedicated to you, to honor your sacrifice.

Ibni Oumar Saleh, you used words as your weapon to fight for democracy in Chad. You never bore arms against any government in Chad, as the regime of Déby itself knows. But when Déby's relatives and other rebels launched an attack on Déby in N'Djaména, you were one of those arrested, tortured, and assassinated by Déby's regime. This book is dedicated to you, your comrades, and your family, in the name of every service you gave to your beloved country.

Dobian Asngar, Jacqueline Moudeïna, Delphine Djiraïbé, and others, you have been menaced and many times barely escaped assassination. This book is dedicated to your sacrifices for the rights of voiceless people in Chad.

Ngarleji Yorongar, though imprisoned more than 14 times, you never stop fighting for justice in Chad. Today, your body maimed by so many beatings, you continue to protect thousands of Chadians who might have joined the ranks of the 70,000 of our people who have fallen victim to Idriss Déby. This book is dedicated to you and other leaders who follow your path.

This book is dedicated also to people of faith in Chad, living and dead. Foreign missionaries, devoted Animists, religious Chadians and their leaders, whether imams, pastors, or priests, have been murdered by the current regime of Chad.

To my lovely wife Brigitte Toïngar and wonderful children Jeany, Joyce, Josiana, Joseph, and Judith Toïngar, I dedicate this book with unconditional love and pride. My special, lovely family, thank you a thousand times for your support. I stole time from you to write this book, to denounce greed and cruelty on the other side of the Atlantic. Children, your mother and I were voiceless people there before we escaped as refugees and gave you life in this peaceful and wonderful country, the United States of America. We have joy with you here, but our hearts break when we see what is going on in Chad, Darfur, and the sub-region. May the suffering end before you are grown.

I would like to thank Dr. Karen Agee of the University of Northern Iowa for helping to make this book readable in English. My wish is that the voiceless people in Darfur and neighboring regions will someday read this book and know their sorrows are shared by English-speaking people of the world.

Table of Contents

ACKNOWLEDGMENTS v
PREFACE 1

1. Chad, Sudan and Darfur 5
2. Idriss Déby Struggles to Maintain Zaghawa Power 9
3. Bour, Survivor of Zaghawa Attack 31
4. Déby's International Counterfeiting Operation
   Revealed 39
5. Chad's Black Gold 45
6. Deadly Betrayal in the Oil Fields of Sidegui 57
7. Darfur's Troubles Begin with Déby 64
8. Chad, Sudan and Rebels 70
9. A Leader in Deception and Corruption 77
10. A Skeptical Look at "the Usual Suspects" 84
11. Birth of the Janjawiid (Militiamen with Horses) 94
12. The Voiceless Children 107
13. They Called Each Other "Younger Brother,
    Older Brother" 115
14. The Fall of Bangui 127

15. Misperceptions 139
16. The International Criminal Court 152
17. Proposition for Peace in Darfur and the Sub-Region 165

Appendix A. Interview of Hassan Fadoul Kitir by Alwihda 173
Appendix B. Chad Discovers Oil 185
Appendix C. Groundbreaking Ceremony at Komé Oil Field 188
Appendix D. World Bank News Report, June 6, 2000 193
Appendix E. Dreaming of a Kingdom of Zaghawas 198
REFERENCES 201
INDEX 216

Preface

Idriss Déby Itno, current president of Chad, is the unacknowledged cause of much of the trouble in Central Africa. He has been accused of high crimes: ethnic violence against the people of Chad; instigating two wars in Sudan; removing the democratically elected president of the Central African Republic; assistance in the removal of the democratically elected president of the Congo Republic; involvement in war in the Democratic Republic of Congo during the regimes of Mobutu Sese Seko and Laurent Kabila; maintenance of an international counterfeiting operation; and theft of diamonds and property all over the region.

Despite Déby's known or suspected murders, depredations on neighboring countries, and drug and counterfeiting conspiracies, he retains power. The French government seems to trust in him to keep down rebel groups and maintain control of the country and thus protect French economic interests in Chad and the region. Indeed, despite pleas to France and the European Union from outraged Chadian tribal leaders and despite insurrection and attempted murder by his own family, Déby is considered by some to be a man of justice and democracy in Chad and a leader in French-speaking Central Africa. As former U.S. ambassador Herman Cohen (2006) put it, the French government sees limited options in Chad: Déby's oppressive regime on the one hand or "Somalia-style chaos" on the other.

The government of France under Jacques Chirac (president 1995–2007) and Nicolas Sarkozy (president 2007–2012) continued to support Déby with French military and political assistance. Although Déby has not fulfilled his promise to expand democracy in Chad, he continues to protect French business interests in Africa. Relations between France and

Chad may have been strained since President François Hollande in 2012 asked about possible human rights abuses in Chad; specifically, the disappearance of Déby's political rival, Ibni Oumar Mahamat Saleh, in 2008. However, Hollande sought Déby's collaboration with Operation Serval in Mali in January 2013, furthering France's military support of the Déby regime.

Is Déby really vital to Western interests in the heart of Africa? This book attempts to uncover what truths we can about Idriss Déby, considering that he has likely committed crimes against humanity and even now wields destabilizing influence in the region. This book concludes, as do many knowledgeable individuals, that much of the responsibility for the Darfur crisis must be borne by Déby.

There are some understandable difficulties in gathering data, documenting incidents, and detailing events referred to in a book like this. Crimes in Darfur and the Central African sub-region are especially sticky when committed by those with political power and military clout. Unfortunately journalists, civil rights leaders, and political critics of the government in Chad are harshly oppressed (Rolley, 2008). They cannot be consulted for this book and are available neither to denounce nor to explain events described here. The private press does report anti-regime opinions on important issues, including the government's misuse of oil revenues, destruction of the environment, and attacks on tribes viewed as hostile to the regime, but in response the government calls the authors of these articles "the 'grave-diggers' of lucrative oil deals with foreign investors," and journalists tend to self-censor to avoid legal action by the state (Committee to Protect Journalists, 1998, para. 4). According to the UN refugee agency, UNHCR, "Freedom of expression is severely restricted, and self-censorship is common" in Chad. "In response to the 2008 coup attempt, the government imposed a new press law, Decree No. 5, on February 20 [2009]. It increased the maximum penalty for false news and defamation to three years in prison, and the maximum penalty for insulting the president to five years" (UNHCR, 2009). In August 2010, Decree No. 5 was lifted and replaced with a new media law introducing prison sentences, fines, and publication bans for "inciting racial, ethnic or religious hatred and condoning violence," and the repression continues (Amnesty International, 2013).

Journalists suffer more than accusations and lawsuits. In the past several decades, critics of Idriss Déby have been subject to imprisonment, poison, torture, or assassination by the regime. Among these critics, journalists especially have been targeted. At least 90 percent of journalists working in Chad have been harmed in some way, deported, or killed. Victims include Maxime Kladoumbaye and Djérabé Déclaud (Békoutou, 1992); Néhémie Bénoudjita (Yorongar, 1999); Yaldet Begoto Oulatar, Dieudonné Djonabaye, Sy Koumbo Singa Gali, and Tchanguis Vatankah (Committee to Protect Journalists, December 1998); and even four French journalists (Tempest, 2008; Kaloga, 2007). Interested readers are directed to websites of the Committee to Protect Journalists, www.cpj.org, and of the Association pour le Respect des droits de l'Homme à Djibouti, www.ardhd.org.

A 2006 report by the Committee to Protect Journalists (CPJ) analyzed the state of the press in Chad in 2005. The report was given to Déby and also made available to the world (at http://www.cpj.org/attacks05/africa05/chad_05.html). Most chilling is the description of Déby's "assault on the media" as "rooted in Déby's attempt to remain in power" (para. 2). Because Déby canceled the constitution limiting his rule and now claims power for life, these assaults on Chadians' freedoms of speech and the press are not likely to decline in the future. As a result, books like this one must rely on whatever documentation can be gathered outside the communication channels Déby controls.

CHAPTER 1

Chad, Sudan and Darfur

Chad and Sudan have suffered perpetual instability since their independence from Europe about 50 years ago. Chad was controlled by France for more than 100 years and gained nominal independence from French Equatorial Africa in 1960. Sudan had already gained independence from Egypt and the United Kingdom in 1956. Since 1962, Sudan has supported numerous warlords, insurgents, and revolutionaries against the government of Chad. According to Herman Cohen, former U.S. assistant secretary of state for Africa, Chad's government now finds itself in danger because of the fighting in neighboring Sudan (Cohen, 2006). The civil war in Chad that officially ended in 2010 is closely related to the Darfur crisis, and "the convergence of the two crises" means they cannot be settled independently of each other (International Crisis Group, June 1, 2006).

Chad and Sudan Linked by History

In fact, the fates of Chad and Sudan have been closely linked for many years. A number of tribes have traditional territories spanning the mostly unmarked border of the two countries and have ties to relatives in both countries. Both states are geographically and culturally similar, with Christians and Animists in the south pursuing agriculture and forestry and Muslims grazing cattle in the arid north. There are differences between the countries, though. Chad's first democratically elected president, Tombalbaye, was a southern Christian, and so was his usurper in 1975, Felix Maloum Ngakoutou Beïndi. Sudan, by contrast, has never been led by a Christian president. In fact, in both Chad and Sudan, Muslims have taken power and now rule by means of the violence of their mercenaries.

The despots of Chad and Sudan rule also under the aegis of the French military. France helped Hissène Habré, Idriss Déby's predecessor in Chad's presidential palace, to gain power in Chad in part because Habré actively opposed a rival's plan to accept Libya's oversight of the country in the late 1970s and early 1980s. Both France and the United States helped Hissène Habré to drive the Libyans out of Chad in the late 1980s. Then, when Habré's murderous schemes against his people were eventually revealed, the French supported Idriss Déby's rebellion against Habré. Why then are France and the United States having second thoughts about supporting Déby? Ambassador Cohen himself asserts that Déby must go, "for the sake of the region" (Cohen, 2006).

Chad and Sudan Linked by Idriss Déby

Idriss Déby is said by some not to be a Chadian at all. He has had a lifelong and complex relationship with the rulers of Sudan. According to Chadian opposition leader Yorongar le Moïban and Jean-Marie Darmian, Déby's superior officer and then biographer, Idriss Déby was born in the town of Kornoy in the Darfur region of Sudan, his father's area, but was raised in Chad, in the region of his mother's relatives (Yorongar, 2007; Darmian, 2007). Déby himself claims to have been born in Chad's capital, N'Djaména (Yorongar, 2003), and also had a third birth certificate attesting to his birth in the town of Fada, in Biltine, a prefecture in northeastern Chad. Regardless of the location of his birth, it is agreed that he was raised for some years in the Central African Republic and received military training as a helicopter pilot in France when he was a young man (AfriquEducation, 2004).

When Déby returned to Chad in late 1980, he joined Hissène Habré's rebellion against General Félix Maloum Ngakoutou Beïndi (Idriss Déby Itno, n.d.). Maloum's officers had overthrown the democratically elected president, François Ngarta Tombalbaye, with the help of French soldiers, while Maloum was in prison. Maloum was installed as unelected president, but Hissène Habré, Idriss Déby, and others strove to keep the power of Chad in the hands of Muslim men and opposed Maloum's rule.

This begins the story that interweaves the modern histories of Sudan and Chad. Three times the rulers of Sudan helped Déby to take ever greater control of Chad. The horrors of civil war and genocide in Sudan are well known to many readers. It is not so well known that these atrocities are mirrored by those in Chad. The evidence indicates that the same man is responsible for death and destruction in both countries and throughout Central Africa (Debos, 2008).

Twice Déby came to power with the help of Sudan. Shortly after Tombalbaye was overthrown in 1975 by Abdel Kader Kamogué, a disaffected colonel, Maloum was removed from prison and put into power by Kamogué and the other young officers. Hissène Habré and Goukouni Weddeye continued their rebellion against the new government of Maloum, but eventually Habré fled to Sudan and then negotiated with the government of Chad and became prime minister of that country in 1978. In that year, Déby was in charge of Hissène Habré's fighters in western Sudan, secretly preparing them to support Habré's coup d'état. With Sudan's help, Habré and Déby launched the civil war that brought Habré to power in 1982 (Posthumus, 2000).

Sudan helped Déby a second time to gain power in Chad when Déby took shelter there in the spring of 1989. He had failed in his attempt to overthrow his former leader, Hissène Habré. As Omar al-Bashir gathered leadership power in Sudan, he also supported Déby to gather the forces and materiel he would need for a coup against Habré, which took place in December 1990. With al-Bashir's assistance, Déby was able to take N'Djaména after only three weeks of decisive fighting (Posthumus, 2000).

Arab Africa's Interest in Chad

Nor was Déby the only Chadian rebel leader who found steady support in Khartoum. The Muslim Brotherhood of Sudan provided direct and indirect support for the Front de Liberation Tchadienne and then the Front de Liberation Nationale Tchadienne (FROLINAT) when they attacked the government of Chad in turns under its first president, Ngarta François Tombalbaye (Prunier, September 7, 2007; Nolutshungu, 1996, pp. 58, 96). As mentioned, during the time of Felix Maloum Ngakoutou Beïndi, the ruling family of Sudan helped Hissène Habré and Déby, the leaders of the Committe Central des Forces Armee du Nord (CCFAN), to destabilize Chad in both 1978 and 1982 (Posthumus, 2000; Prunier, September 7, 2007). Chadians avowing an interest in making Chad a Muslim country seem to have gained support from Sudan, in the past and in the present day.

Like Muammar Khadafi in Libya, leaders of Sudan sought to create Muslim hegemony over the entire region of Africa. As Gérard Prunier puts it (September 7, 2007), Libya's leader, "bloated with oil money and feeling he ran a country which was too small and unimportant to satisfy his vast geopolitical ambitions, had set his sights on Chad as the first stage of creating an Arab-dominated empire across the Sahelian region" (p. 1). With the Arabs came an attempt to re–Islamize this region of Africa. Bishop

N'Garteri of the diocese of Moundou in southwestern Chad expressed his concern in 1993 over forced conversions and church burnings (Survie-France, n.d.). Sudan's recent support of rebels against Idriss Déby, even the 2008 attacks on N'Djaména, continue this theme. According to Jedrzej Piasek, a Polish missionary priest serving in southern Chad's Doba diocese, Muslim rebel leaders have claimed that Chad is to be a Muslim country. He quotes one rebel leader as saying that he does not want priests and consecrated religious workers in the country. "The first thing he will do after winning the civil war is expel all missionaries" (Catholic World News, February 5, 2008).

When Hissène Habré finally overthrew the government of Goukouni Weddeye and became president of Chad, he did attempt to convert all Christians and Animists to Islam. Though he killed many who resisted conversion — and although many other Chadians did convert simply to save their lives, get access to food, or gain positions in the government — Hissène Habré was not able to convert the Chadian Republic to an Arab (Islamic) country. Chad was proclaimed in September 1982 to be "secular and indivisible" (Nolutshungu, 1996, p. 179). The leaders of Sudan, who apparently were not happy with Chad's Hissène Habré at least in part because of this failure, seized the opportunity to replace him with his former lieutenant, Idriss Déby.

Déby in Attack Mode

One would like to think that those with power in Khartoum would not have brought Déby to power in Chad had they known the consequences. In fact, however, in 1989 Sudan supplied Idriss Déby with military and civilian personnel, intelligence agents, supplies, and ammunition to overthrow Hissène Habré (Nolutshungu, 1996, p. 251; Yorongar, 2007). After a few months of deadly war between these former companions in arms, Déby won the war with the strong arm of Sudan and pronounced a democracy in Chad. In his first speech as president of Chad, on December 4, 1990, Déby proclaimed, "I have brought you neither gold nor silver, but liberty!" (See Idriss Déby Itno's biography on Afrique-express.com.) Despite these bright words, those who knew him and his predecessor well saw no real change from the vicious murders and ethnic violence of the past, expressing their hopelessness with the adage, "The body may have changed, but the head is the same."

CHAPTER 2

Idriss Déby Struggles to Maintain Zaghawa Power

A few days after his speech declaring democracy in Chad, President Idriss Déby began killing to consolidate his power and eliminate rivals ("Idriss Déby Itno Biography," Afrique-express.com). First a member of his inner circle was accused of poisoning and killing individuals from other tribes, despite the fact that these men had fought side by side with them from Darfur to N'Djaména. Captain Demtita Ngarbaroum, a southern officer in the Chadian army, was kidnapped, tortured, and then killed (Verschave, 2000, p. 152). On October 13, 1991, Déby accused Vice President Abbas Maldom and the army under his command of conspiring to overthrow him. Tribe by tribe he accused his former companions of disloyalty, attacked the "disloyal" groups, and arrested, tortured, and killed the leaders. In January 1992, the vice president of a Chadian human rights organization (Ligue tchadienne des droits de l'Homme) was assassinated. A month later, one of the most competent senior administrators, Mamadou Bissou, was killed by Déby's fighters (Verschave, 2000, p. 152).

After the death of Mamadou, the local insecurity spread across the country. By this time, Chad's army had swollen from about 35,000 under Hissène Habré to about 50,000 troops as Déby consolidated his power. New recruits included members of the Zaghawa tribe of Déby's family as well as tribesmen of his chief commanders. Déby merged his own forces with Habré's army to create a new national Chadian army, FANT (U.S. Department of State, 1992). In the intervening years, thousands of Chadians have been killed for no known reason, and more recently Déby turned against two nephews, Timan and Tom Erdémi, and many other relatives (Nolutshungu, 1996, pp. 249–253; Verschave 2000, pp. 151–153).

Hissène Habré is believed to have killed at least 45,000 people with the stalwart assistance of Idriss Déby. Once Déby became president, he showed no reluctance to continue the strong tactics. (One of Déby's lieutenants was Djamtato, a man from the South. To spare him grief, Déby summoned him back to N'Djaména on some pretext before launching his attack on Djamtato's home region.)

Once in the presidential palace, Déby claimed himself innocent and Habré an evil ruler who had had to be removed. However, Chadians began to understand the true nature of their new leader. They started crying for the days under their former ruler, saying it is better to cooperate with an evil one knows than an angel one does not (Madonet, 2004).

Zaghawas Rule

All Sudanese — and especially the Zaghawa tribe who accompanied Déby to N'Djaména — became the masters of the country. Some tribes from northern regions had at least a chance to escape theft, torture, and murder, because they have physical characteristics that are more or less the same as those of the Zaghawa. People of the South, however, are visibly distinct from the nomadic tribesmen. Not one of them could escape (Verschave, 2000, pp. 151–153; Allazam, 2006).

Cohen (2006) says that Déby was able to maintain strong control only until 1998, because at that time other northern tribes became increasingly disaffected. As President Déby concentrated resources and power among the Zaghawas, the other ethnic groups — constituting more than 95 percent of the Chadian population — were marginalized.

The Empty Treasury

According to Bardet (2008), the treasury was empty when Déby made himself president of Chad. Hissène Habré, after twice sending soldiers to Tiné (on the Sudanese border) and losing them in battle, marshaled his military leaders for one final assault at Tiné. Barely escaping capture and certain death, Hissène rushed back to N'Djaména. There he took time to clean out the national treasury before escaping to Cameroon with his cash-stuffed luggage (Bardet, 2008).

Idriss Déby then came to power with no state funds and a need to reward his supporters. He quickly turned to private companies, including the primary manufacturer, CotonTchad, and many other enterprises in

Chad, as documented by Jean-Prosper Boulada, president of the United Front for a Democratic Alternative in Chad (FU/ADT) (2003). At that time, Haroun Kabadi was the CEO of CotonTchad and of Huilerie-Savonnerie, producers of cotton and cottonseed oil and related products. The manager of the Huilerie-Savonnerie plant was Timan Erdémi. (Timan is the nephew of Idriss Déby who more recently rebelled against his uncle and today leads a political-military movement called RaFAD, Rassemblement des Forces Armées Democratiques). Madonet (2004) reports that Timan and his boss, Kabadi, have stolen all the company's money to give to Déby, which left the company valueless and caused its financial collapse. The two men were rewarded for their loyalty with important government positions in lieu of those they had held at CotonTchad. Since that time, the company has not been able to recover and continues to struggle financially. Because it has been a few years since the company had money to buy cotton from farmers, Déby now provides counterfeit FCFA francs to the company for purchasing cotton. Chad's farmers suffer now that they are paid for their crops in worthless money (Madonet, 2004; Kitir, 2003).

A claim can be made that Déby's economic depredations to maintain power have had the unintended consequence of collapsing the entire economy to profit his regime, family, and tribe, the Zaghawas of Chad and Sudan. With their economic and political power, Déby and his protectors could take action against real or supposed challengers without guilt or repercussions (Nolutshungu, 1996, pp. 249–253; Yorongar, 2007).

Zaghawas Plunder Chad

Opposition leader Yorongar, in an interview with AfriquEducation (Madonet, 2004), and rebel leader Albissaty Saleh Allazam, at a press conference in Dakar, Senegal (Allazam, 2006), charged that the strategy of taking the resources of Chad and removing them to Sudan was quickly organized by the officers of Sudan and their mercenaries, with the complicity of Déby and his regime. They report that for the first six months after Déby took office as president, there were regular military flights from N'Djaména to Sudan (more precisely, to Darfur). No agent was allowed to inspect the cargo loaded onto planes by Zaghawa forces. Later revelations show that the planes were filled with supplies and money that the Zaghawa and the new leaders of Chad had misappropriated from Chad and sent to Darfur.

Why would supporters of Déby's regime send goods and funds out of Chad? There is speculation that Zaghawa tribesmen of both Chad and

Sudan had a shared interest in one day establishing a separate kingdom in Darfur. Or perhaps they thought to make all of Sudan and Chad their Zaghawist kingdom (HelBongo, 2008). A later chapter on the continuing crisis in Darfur will provide more information on this speculation.

Déby's regular mercenaries from Darfur — and their tribesmen who followed them after their victory over Hissène's forces — were sanctioned by their patrons to attack anybody who had something that they thought they could use in Darfur. With the blessings of the ruling tribe in Darfur, then, the Zaghawa started robbing the population of Chad at gunpoint. They focused their attention especially on the people in the towns (who were most likely to have portable goods) and those in the area where anti-government fighters had arisen. When they had taken all the vehicles and valuable goods they could find by breaking into homes and threatening people with death should they resist, they rounded up the cattle, camels, sheep, and goats to take back to Darfur (Verschave, 2000, pp. 152–153; Allazam, 2006). Numerous articles in both Ndjaména's biweekly newspaper, *N'Djaména Hebdo*, and the weekly *Le Temps* attest that the despoilings continued for years — and in fact continue to this day.

Most often the Zaghawa seemed to be well informed about whom they could rob with impunity. People from the southern regions of Chad who had moved to N'Djaména lived primarily on the south side of town. The Zaghawa steered clear of the Muslim neighborhoods on the north side, where reprisals would be more certain. They apparently knew that those living on the south side — primarily Christians and Animists — had no influence with the government and no power to protect themselves. The police officers, police military officers, and other authorities, sworn to protect civilians against any injustice and to ensure their security, had no power now. These officers were generally well educated and friendly to all, but the leadership of their units had fallen to illiterate and hostile Zaghawa from Chad and Sudan. In this author's experience, all the police could do was to offer advice to southerners in the city to stay inside and avoid confrontation with the Zaghawa tribesmen. If officers knew an attack was planned or even in progress, they had to wait until the Zaghawa had left the area before rushing to the scene to compile reports and restore public safety (U.S. Department of State, 1994, 1996).

Kouladoumbaye Maxime, a nephew of the author, was working for the government at the time, as a journalist for the newspaper run by the political party of Idriss Déby. He had ridden his motorcycle to visit his girlfriend in another section of town. On his way back home, less than half a mile past the police station, he was shot. Though the police heard the shooting, they stayed where they were, giving the armed band time to steal the motorcycle and get away. By the time officers reached Kouladoumbaye, he was still alive and could have been saved if airlifted to a hospital in France. As he was only an employee of the government, however, and not a member of the ruling tribe, they had no incentive to expend funds for his life, and he soon passed away (Békoutou, 2000).

Most raids occurred between 6:00 P.M. and 6:00 A.M. In N'Djaména, groups of fighters would arm themselves with Kalashnikovs and drive their military vehicles to Moursal or Chagoua, suburbs populated with people from southern Chad. Fighters hid themselves behind trees or piles of bricks from bombed houses and waited for someone to pass by in a vehicle that could bring money in Chad or Darfur. (See Allazam, 2006; Madonet, 2004; and newspaper reports from 1991 through 1998.)

Fighters would generally be dropped off individually along the road by someone in a vehicle. Each fighter wanted to check out the area beforehand, so he concealed his weapon beneath the folds of his *jalabiyah*. When night fell, he would conceal himself along the road where he had a good vantage point. So as not to be recognized, he would wrap his head before coming to the hunt. The fighter kept his finger ready on the trigger of his weapon to shoot in case someone were to pass with a motorized vehicle. The real prize would be a car or truck, which just about any of the fighters knew how to drive. A motorcycle was worth money in Darfur, but not every fighter knew how to operate one. (If a fighter had gone all night having captured nothing of value, he would ambush a bicyclist heading to work at dawn. Very few fighters were skilled riders of bicycles, so they would wait for their ride to pick them up in the morning and load the bicycle into the vehicle.) Fighters went out on ambush every evening until they had accumulated many cars, motorcycles, and bicycles. These and many other goods would be loaded onto trucks or even cargo planes for Darfur. Business in the bars must have been slow, because people risked their lives if they went out during the evening (Verschave, 2000, pp. 151–153; Békoutou, 2000).

Nor were homes safe havens. Some people were attacked at home and in the presence of their wives and children. Every day people talked about someone who had been killed or robbed the night before. The fact that no arrests were made lends support to the suspicion that theft, robbery, and murder were permitted by the highest authorities in Chad. The same scenario plays out even today, though less frequently: during the February 2008 attack on Déby's regime, Zaghawa fighters belonging to the rebels of Sudan led by Dr. Khalil Ibrahim Mahamat pursued a Chadian named Djato. These fighters were Sudanese "rebels" who had come to rescue Déby during the final attack of February 2008. In their Toyota, they pursued Djato on his motorbike until he reached his house and dashed inside. According to Djato's family, the fighters chased after him even into his house, shot him, and then loaded his motorcycle into their vehicle and took off.

Failure of French-Supported Military Reorganization

Nightly murders had continued for at least four years when an administrator named Mianbé was murdered by Zaghawa fighters in the capital city in 1993 (Nolutshungu, 1996, p. 251; Allazam, 2006). In fact Mbaïlaou Mianbé was one of the Chadian administrators with great knowledge and long experience who had been charged with reducing the size of the military and ensuring its members' qualifications to serve. The mission of reducing the size of the army in Chad must have seemed an easy one to French officers there, who simply gave instructions to Chadian military and civilian administrators to muster out those unfit to serve. However, the task was extremely difficult and complicated for Chadian administrators. Most of them were of southern tribes and thus were viewed by even illiterate Muslim fighters as their slaves. Without the decree signed by Déby, these skilled and educated southerners would not have been able to carry out their responsibility to eliminate from the military all those who were unfit. Although he had to sign the decree under order of French authorities, Déby was not pleased to do so, nor were the other Zaghawas pleased.

Then as now, the army was a familial league of Zaghawa tribesmen. According to Saleh Kebzabo, leader of Chad's UNDR party, even the uneducated and criminally insane serve as soldiers, officers, and administrators (2005). The veracity of Kebzabo's statement might be questioned on the grounds that he serves as senator and leader of an opposition group, but his assertion is supported by Bichara Idriss Haggar, a Zaghawa who served as a senior administrator in Déby's regime, now self-exiled in Canada (Haggar, 2003, p.183).

Mianbé, as chair of the commission to review military fitness (Secrétariat Permanent à la Réinsertion de Militaries Déflatés), reviewed the evaluations of service fitness that had been prepared by military administrators. It was the responsibility of the administrators to determine if each soldier was qualified to serve, to receive training, or to be discharged with severance pay. Many of the men who had served Déby for many years (as soldiers during the rule of Hissène Habré, as forces during Déby's rebellion against Habré, and in the army during Déby's presidency) were listed to be retired from service. The names of those fighters and soldiers came before Mianbé, who signed the list. The leaders of different units then were to discharge those judged not fit for service.

Déby was in a bind, under pressure from the European Union to reduce the size of his army and on the other side pressured by his relatives, the Zaghawa fighters, to respect his commitment to them (made when they were in the rebellion in Darfur, Sudan). Critics have charged that Déby was behind the assassination of Mianbé, who was in fact not personally responsible for determining fitness for service but only for carrying out the judgment of military administrators. Apparently Déby tried to cool down the fury of some Zaghawas who had been discharged by saying he was innocent and it was Mianbé and others who had dismissed them from service.

Early in the morning, presidential guards arrived in Mianbé's neighborhood in the capital and waited silently for him. Unaware of the lurking danger, Mianbé entered his car with his driver Laoukeïn Noël around 8:04 A.M. and headed to work (Bérassidé, 1993). His pursuers followed the car in their military Toyota pickup. When Mianbé reached de Gaule Avenue, his route to downtown N'Djaména, he apparently sensed danger. His driver tried to elude pursuit by pulling off at a gasoline stand onto a secondary street. The Toyota followed, passed quickly, and lurched to a stop in Mianbé's path so that his driver had to stop suddenly to avoid a collision. Mianbé ran for refuge into the tiny shop of a tea and barbecue seller, but he was too late to save himself. Two of his three pursuers stepped out with their Kalashnikovs and opened fire. Mianbé took seven bullets from the two fighters and fell down dead. The tea seller, a man named Atim, ran out to see what was happening and took a bullet in the shoulder. The gasoline seller was also shot. Atim was taken to the hospital by a kind stranger but collapsed and died a few hours later. The gasoline vendor also died. The murderers stayed at the site with the corpses for a while before returning to the presidential palace (Bérassidé, 1993).

After the death of Mianbé, which had been preceded by the murders of Joseph Beidi and many other educated men from the South, the southerners in N'Djaména were in shock. The body of Mianbé was taken to the residence of his relative, Naïmbaye Lossimian. Community leaders from southern Chad — even some who had cooperated with Déby's regime — including women, men, and many young people, came to wish Mianbé good-bye. Grieving people filled Naïmbaye's house, yard, and entire neighborhood. People wept both for the death of one of the best administrators in Chad and for themselves, too. They knew that what had happened to so many southerners could happen to them at any time.

One of the women, named Bourkou Louise, was stricken with the deepest grief by the assassination of Mianbé. When she saw General Kamougué Abdel-kader (the former military leader in the South in the late 1970s and early 1980s) coming to say good-bye to his former administrator, Bourkou Louise approached Kamougué in tears. She held one of Kamougué's legs and wept continuously, asking where were the men now like her brother Mianbé and like other brothers in the past. The weeping of the women and especially Bourkou's cries of grief and helplessness shamed many men there.

Déby sent his defense minister, a man from the South named Loum Hinaïssou Laïna, to attend the wake and represent his government beside the body of Mianbé. This seemed like mockery to some of the participants, that Déby would send to the funeral the minister responsible for public safety and security. A few arrested Defense Minister Loum for betraying his people and took him away to an apartment to kill him. Fortunately for Loum, men like Dangdé Laoubélé and Mianbé's brother, Bidi Néatobeye, who were well respected because of their determination not to work with Déby's regime, after a few hours convinced the young captors to release their hostage. Red Cross International took Loum into protective custody.

Zaghawa Violence Against Southerners in N'Djaména

A few days before Mianbé was killed, a conference in N'Djaména had convened many young people of Chad. Those participating in the conference from the southern region of Logone Occidental who heard about Mianbé's murder and attended his wake said they would no longer let themselves be killed. They had a quick meeting and created a committee of self-defense. They went out into the streets of south N'Djaména to protest the death of Mianbé and gather other young people (Bérassidé, 1993).

Zaghawas and their allies knew that people of southern Chad were apostles of non-violence. They often said, "You can kill their loved ones in their presence without feeling any danger of reprisal." Often when Zaghawas and their allies killed people, they laughed mockingly at those who wept and bewailed the death of their loved ones.

That day, the wind changed direction. When the young people of Logone Occidental led their comrades on a march of discontent, two presidential guards, Saleh Annadif and Issa Adam, wrapped their heads in scarves to conceal their faces and rode a motorcycle through the street toward the marchers to see what they would do. Saleh and Issa were attacked by the crowd, knocked from their motorcycle, doused with gasoline, and set on fire. The charred, dead bodies were later found by the Guards.

The Presidential Guards were shocked by the deaths of these two young men and in revenge vowed to kill anyone who tried to bury Mianbé's body. In response to the Guard's massing of armaments around the area, the young men of the area met and resolved to march again, in defiance of the Guards, and to confront the heavily armed troops even though they themselves had no weapons. The Guards were withdrawn, though, and no more deaths occurred on that day.

The next day the marching resumed on the main street of south N'Djaména, but when the Guards rushed up in heavily armed vehicles and started shooting, the crowd dispersed. Several unarmed, peaceful marchers died that day (Bérassidé, 1993).

As another example of the atrocities carried out by Déby's followers against southerners in N'Djaména, here is the tragic story of two brothers, narrated to the author by a school friend (whom we will call Abdelkarim to protect his identity) who grew up with the young men. The younger brother followed his soldier brother from Darfur to N'Djaména and asked the fighter to get him a motorcycle. Most of the Darfur boys who had brothers in the army in Chad had motorcycles, cars, and many other fine goods. The mercenary fighter asked his brother if that were all he wanted, only a motorcycle. The fighter, knowing how easy it is to be generous with other people's goods, said that should be no problem. He gave one of his Kalashnikovs to his brother and coached him in the basics of shooting the weapon.

Late in the evening, he took his brother to Moursal and placed him in a well-hidden spot, with instructions to shoot any person who passed on a motorcycle. As soon as the motorcycle and rider fell to the road, he should pick up the bike and ride it home. He left his brother at the place of ambush and went back to where he lived with his family. The boy spent all night along the road without seeing anyone with a motorcycle whom he could kill. Finally, early in the morning before people went to work, just when the boy thought he would have no luck at all, a motorcycle did come along, and even slowed down near his place of concealment. Immediately he shot the rider, picked up the motorcycle, and raced to his brother's home. His sister-in-law greeted him and asked him about her husband. The boy said that her husband had shown him where to set up an ambush and then had returned home, hadn't he? His sister-in-law said that her husband had left home shortly before to pick him up, since apparently he had not had any luck last night. And what was the boy doing with her husband's motorcycle? It was at that moment that the boy realized he had killed his own brother.

Zaghawa Violence Across Southern and Western Chad

In the other towns, the situation became desperate. Perhaps events in N'Djaména were mitigated because of the presence of diplomats from abroad, requiring that Déby keep the peace or at least try to prevent incidents from coming to light. Elsewhere in the country, such as in the towns of the Sara people of the South, taking away people's property and then killing or torturing the owners was an all-too-common situation (Allazam, 2006). The fighters seemed to operate with impunity. Vehicles and other goods that the Zaghawa collected by force from the population were taken to the military police station or military camp. Vehicles were often taken directly to N'Djaména and then to Darfur. Some people could see their vehicles sitting openly in camp, not even locked away in a compound, but they could not reclaim them without risking their lives.

A resident of Moundou in southern Chad fell victim to the Zaghawa. A man we will call Nadjitessem to protect his identity for this publication encountered a military vehicle with at least five fighters as he drove his motorcycle home after work. They stopped him and collected his Honda 125. There was no use for him to ask for help from his neighbors or the people at his house, because nobody could help him against five armed men. He was glad to have been asked to surrender his vehicle only, and not his life. Had he resisted, he might have been shot on the spot or perhaps taken away for torture and then thrown into the river.

A few days later, people who knew Nadjitessem's motorcycle informed him that they had recognized it in the military camp. Because he was well known in Moundou, someone close to one of the fighters begged for the release of Nadjitessem's vehicle and returned it to him. At that time, the former ambassador of Chad to the United States, Soubiane Abdallah, was the prefect in Moundou, and all those things happened under his supervision.

Déby Recruits Supporters in Sudan and Libya

When Idriss Déby had failed in his first attempt to overthrow Hissène Habré, he had to run to Sudan to escape Habré's firm reprisal (Marchal, 2006). According to Goukouni Weddeye, the elected president of Chad who had been ousted by Hissène Habré and was fighting in northern Chad to regain power with Libya's assistance, a man named Adoum Togoï, one of Goukouni's senior officers in the GUNT (Gouverment d'Union Nationale de Transition) coalition, had ambitions for himself. Togoï offered to Libyan leaders (who were always looking for an opportunity to oust Habré) to act as interlocutor between Libya's Khadafi and Chad's Déby, to talk Déby into joining forces with him. In the beginning, the Libyan leaders apparently saw Togoï as the man to replace Habré in power in Chad. But once Togoï introduced Déby to Libyan officials, Togoï lost influence, and Déby became Libya's candidate for the Chadian presidency (Correau, 2008).

Abandoning Goukouni's GUNT and Togoï's new movement, the Libyans promised support for Déby's MPS (Mouvement Patriotic du Salut). Most of GUNT's forces and their commanders joined Déby, perhaps simply to return home to Chad. It was through the Libyans that Déby obtained at least 300 Toyota pickups and a variety of equipment and weapons. Among the leaders of the soldiers that Déby recruited in Libya were Generals Ngarou Kerim and Nadjita Ngororo, Colonels Subiane and Djibrine Dassert, and many other officers (Kebzabo, 2005).

While in Libya, Déby encountered other refugees and former soldiers from Chad. In fact, thousands had left Chad for Sudan and Libya in the previous few years. Some had been victims of Habré's policies, and others were victims of Déby's own actions. Nevertheless, Déby was able to convince many of the soldiers that their future lay with him. If they helped him gain power in Chad, he would restore democracy and bring peace. He gathered troops from many countries of West Africa, as well.

In 1998, Colonel Ngarboubou shared with this author several stories of the political situation in Chad while they were in Lagos, Nigeria, seeking United Nations (UN) refugee assistance. Colonel Ngarboubou had been third in power of the Adjirai tribe and had helped Déby to consolidate power in Chad. According to Colonel Ngarboubou, Déby had gone mad with power; when awakened by a dream in the palace, he would attack and kill his nearest bodyguard in a frenzy of fear. Later (in 1999) Colonel Ngarboubou was courted by rebels against Déby but in the end was enticed by Déby's agents to return from Nigeria to Chad's capital. After a dinner at the presidential palace, Colonel Ngarboubou died, it is believed, from the effects of poison.

Déby Undermines the Hadjiraï

During the rule of Hissène Habré, a leader of the Hadjiraï tribe, Idriss Miskine, served as Habré's representative for foreign affairs, as he had served him during the rebellion that brought Habré to power. On a visit to Paris, the French attempted to entice Miskine to replace Habré in power, but Miskine told them he could not betray his leader and president. On his return to Chad, Miskine informed Habré of the French attempt to challenge his regime. Not wanting to have near him someone who had an opportunity to take power, Habré had Miskine poisoned at dinner in the palace (Nolutshungu, 1996, p. 234). Many of Miskine's tribe held positions of responsibility in the regime, however, so a strategy had to be devised to prevent their exacting vengeance for this murder. Habré ordered Déby to despoil the region of the Hadjiraï people, Guéra, located in southeastern Chad (Nolutshungu, 1996, p. 234). Commander-in-chief Déby may have recognized the Hadjiraï as rivals and competitors for power and took this opportunity to clear the way for his own ambition. Some of the Hadjiraï—such as Maldom Bada Abbas, Ngarboubou, Khèffine, and Koddi—took up arms and tried to resist, but troops under Déby and Djamous forced them over the border into Sudan. There, some of them were arrested by the government of Sudan, which at that time did not welcome Chadian rebels on its border (Nolutshungu, 1996, p. 234).

After Déby's failed coup against Habré, he escaped across the border into Sudan, which welcomed him, since his father was a native of the area. Déby needed to gather troops to recommence his insurrection, so he spoke with the Hadjiraï being held prisoner. They could either die in prison or join his cause. All of them chose the latter option and were released from their Sudanese prison to fight for him against the government of Hissène Habré (as described to the author by Colonel Ngarboubou in 1998).

Although Maldom and his followers and many troops joined their persecutor Déby to overthrow Hissène, ten months later, after helping Déby to take power in N'Djaména, Maldom and his tribe became the first victims of Déby. Déby surprised the Hadjraï in the month of October 1991 with a deadly attack against their tribe in N'Djaména. One explanation for Déby's treachery may have been a secret plot by his tribe to control power. Another explanation may be that because Maldom helped Déby achieve the presidency, he was number two in the MPS. When Déby became president of the Republic of Chad, Maldom wanted to be named president of the MPS. Rather than share power, Déby decided to destroy not only Maldom but also his tribe. Whatever the explanation, hundreds of Hadjiraï lost their lives. Their homes, businesses, titles, and goods were now at the mercy of Zaghawa fighters. Maldom was fortunate; he was arrested alive and released later through the intervention of the French ambassador to Chad (Nolutshungu, 1996, pp. 249–250).

Déby Suppresses Other Tribes

Three months after annihilating the most influential tribe in the MPS, Déby turned his attention to other critics, including those who were fighting for human rights. The famous lawyer and vice president of the Chadian League of Human Rights, Joseph Beidi, was assassinated near his home (Nolutshungu, 1996, p. 251; Verschave 2000, p. 152). People said that Beidi had been stalked and killed by Idriss Déby himself, who left the body by the road and returned to his palace, with some of his bodyguards driving at a discreet distance behind him. Popular opinion may well be true: a few days later, people saw Beidi's car at the palace. And the investigation into the assassination of Beidi progressed only to the point of examination of the killer's fingerprints on the door handle of Beidi's automobile. The Justice Department suddenly closed the file on the death of Beidi, attorney and vice president, without comment (Allazam, 2006).

The people of Moundou did not forget, however. They later achieved a moral victory over Déby and avenged Beidi. A few years after the death of Beidi, when Déby visited Moundou, the celebration committee's organization was infiltrated by citizens still shocked by the loss of their loved ones by Déby's order. To make sure that Déby was "touched" by their sentiments, they took two different actions (Laoukoura, 1994).

At the celebration, a young girl presented Déby with a smile and a calabash of flowers. It was later that his inner circle of friends at the assembly place of Moundou found that a picture of Beidi had been placed in the calabash beneath the flowers. Later during the celebration at the "independence place," two doves were given to Déby to throw into the air as a sign of peace—but the two doves could not fly and fell to the ground. It was intended as an insult and warning to Déby, for the birds' wings had been broken.

People worried that Beidi had been killed simply because he was a man of truth and wanted to denounce injustice in the country. Following his assassination, many people in the South were anxious; what happened to the Hadjiraï could happen to them. As a result, a large group of soldiers formed around Kétté Nodji in southern Chad for self-protection and for rebellion (Lanne, 2004).

In those years of 1991 and 1992, it was not only Mamadou Bissou, Beidi, and the Hadjiraï people who were victims of Déby's attempt to maintain power. There were also hundreds of Chadians, real or supposed members of a rebellion called the "Mouvement pour la Democratie et le Development," who were illegally kidnapped from Nigeria and deported to Chad. Those unfortunate individuals, who had sought peaceful democracy and economic development for Chad but had found it necessary to escape to Nigeria to save their lives, were brought back to their native country, tortured, and executed in the prison of Chad's National Security Agency. Hundreds of other people were also butchered in the region of Lake Chad for seeming to challenge Déby's regime (Bardet, 2008).

In early August of 1993, the people of Ouaddaï had their turn to suffer. This was the region in northeast Chad where Déby spent some of his teen years — and where, according to Yorongar and many other Chadians, young Déby had killed a fellow student in a knife fight after an evening at a dance club, back when Tomalbaye was president. Yorongar (see www.Yorongar.com) asserts that punishment for this murder would have prevented Déby from completing high school had a well-placed relative not interceded, taking Déby off to Bongor in southwest Chad to complete his schooling.

Now that Déby was in power, apparently he held a grudge against the region. Déby's fighters waited until many people of the region of Ouaddaï brought their goods to the weekly market at Gniguilim, and then surprised the poor villagers by suddenly firing on them. At least 82 people were killed and 170 wounded. Among the wounded were many children and pregnant women (Alwihdactualité, March 23, 2001). Forty-eight hours later, on August 6, 1993, the people from the region of Ouaddaï living in N'Djaména organized a peaceful demonstration in the capital against the atrocities in Gniguilim by Déby's fighters. Déby sent his Presidential Guards, with orders to kill these unarmed people at the demonstration. At least 190 people were killed and 300 wounded (Alwihdactualité, March 23, 2001).

Déby Moves Against Rivals Within His Own Tribe

In October 1993, Déby targeted Colonel Abbas Koty, his brother-in-law and co-founder of the MPS movement, one of his first companions in the offensive against the regime of Hissène Habré. Colonel Koty had first been commandant-in-chief of the National Chadian Army under Déby, then defense minister, and finally minister of public works and transportation before he fell afoul of his brother-in-law. When Koty was attacked by Déby's men, he resisted with the assistance of his movement, the National Council for Recovery (CNR). Muammar Khadafi of Libya, ever alert to events in Chad and, as always, involved in playing rebels and despots against each other across Africa, reconciled the two brothers-in-law in August 1994. Koty naïvely returned to N'Djaména with Déby after their reconciliation in Libya, and two months later he was assassinated by Déby's Presidential Guards at the residence of a friend, Bichana Digui. Koty's body was taken to the palace by his killers and shown to Déby as proof that Abbas Koty was dead. Déby ordered his fighters to take the body to Moursal, to be buried near the National Police School. Four years later, it was Bichana Digui who was assassinated in the middle of the day in the heart of N'Djaména. Thereafter, hundreds of the partisans of these two men were detained under the worst conditions, tortured, and killed (Verschave, 2000, p. 153; Nolutshungu, 1996, pp. 250–252). According to Amnesty International (October 16, 2001),

> Torture techniques used under Hissein Habré reappeared under Idriss Déby. In 1996, among the most common tortures described by both victims and witnesses, involved prisoners having chili powder inserted in their nostrils, eyes, and mouth; prisoners being forced to drink huge quantities of water, then being beaten; people being tied up in the *arbatachar* manner, and sometimes being tied to the back of a vehicle and dragged several hundred metres, and people who had been subjected to psychological torture and had received death threats during their interrogations [Amnesty International, 2001, p. 36].

More Attacks Against Suspected Rebels in the South

In the meantime, Kétté Nodji Moïse, one of the founders of MPS, was not spared. Kétté and a few of his followers from the South, shocked by the assassination of Beidi, escaped N'Djaména and went over to the rebellion in the South. Déby used this as a pretext to attack the rebels led by Kétté. In January of 1993, Déby ordered his Presidential Guards to the province of Oriental Logone, where Kétté's people lived. There they killed at least 246 innocents, burned 22 villages, and stole all their goods (Amnesty International, October 16, 2001).

On April 5, 1993, Déby's Presidential Guard massacred 104 civilians in the county of Bodo, more precisely, in the villages of Kobiteye, Bekolo, and Kouh. All their goods were taken to the big towns in Chad and sold or used by Presidential Guards in N'Djaména (Amnesty International, October 16, 2001).

At the same time that the people of Oriental Logone were being murdered and their property stolen, the populace in the Lake Chad region were suffering the same fate. Déby's army spared neither friend nor foe, South nor West (Amnesty International, October 16, 2001).

On the tenth anniversary of 1984's Black September, Déby sent his

Presidential Guards into Oriental Logone to exterminate the remaining people of that region. The people were hunted down and killed in villages and in the bush. The situation of the people in the Logone region (including both Oriental Logone and Occidental Logone) was now even worse than it had been in 1984 and 1993 (Amnesty International, October 16, 2001).

The hunt for prey in Logone did not stop. It continued on October 30, 1997, when Déby sent his fighters to decimate the rebels of the Front d'Action pour la République Fédérale (FARF), with whom he had just signed an agreement of peace. Hundreds of civilians belonging to or merely suspected of belonging to FARF were summarily executed. Also entire villages through which FARF troops had passed or were suspected of having passed were subject to group punishment, including rape, theft, and burning of property by government troops. Any remaining villagers in the area fled to the countryside (Amnesty International, 1997; Amnesty International, March 19, 1998).

Some of the victims of this attack against the FARF were bound hand and foot before being pushed into burlap bags, which were tightly tied and thrown into the Logone River in Moundou. It was a horrific tragedy in Moundou. A human-rights report describes the attack on Moundou in this way:

> In the hours and days following the first exchange of gunfire on 30 October, members of the security forces combed Moundou and extrajudicially executed, or arrested and then tortured and ill-treated, many unarmed civilians who[m] they suspected of being FARF members. Dr. Merci Danyo was arrested on 30 October. He was beaten, tied up, and put in a plastic sack; there has been no news of him since his arrest. Dominique Djekoula, Alain Doumran, Mathias, and Gaston (other names not known), members of the FARF, were arrested in Deli, a village near Moundou, on their way back to Moundou from the capital, N'Djaména; there is no further news of them. Alain Baltimore, two mentally ill patients, and members of the family of Desiré Laonoji, the executive secretary of the FARF, were all extrajudicially executed by the security forces. Two wounded civilians were taken from the hospital; one was returned to his family and died shortly afterwards, but the other is still missing. Two human rights activists were taken hostage but managed to escape [Amnesty International, 1997, para. 4].

The FARF leader, Laoukein Bardé Friston, recognized the ambush too late to save many of his men. Most had no weapons, because they had come to Moundou to be issued their equipment and orders as they joined the regular army. Though Friston escaped the sharpshooter assigned to kill him, most of the former rebels who had come in peace were shot as they assembled in his compound in town.

Who was responsible for this atrocity? Soubiane Abdallah has been named as the butcher who coordinated these actions against the population of the South (Amnesty International, May 20, 1996). He later served as Chad's ambassador to the United States, 1998–2004, and was received in Washington as the representative of the Republic of Chad. As ambassador, Soubiane Abdallah said he wanted to develop democracy in Chad. He asked other countries to help him achieve his program of democracy. In fact, at the time of the murders, he was the prefect in Moundou and had coordinated the troops sent from N'Djaména to do the killing (Amnesty International, March 27, 1998; December 11, 1997).

Even before he came to Moundou to kill the residents, Soubiane had been internal minister for the entire country of Chad, the chief administrator responsible for all affairs inside the country, including appointment of prefects (governors), control of police and military police, and management of border disputes. Sent by Déby to serve as prefect to Occidental Logone, he apparently was charged with eliminating opposition and rebellion (Amnesty International, 1997). Under his personal instruction, the fighters killed many innocents, and hundreds of other people were arrested and tortured.

Among the people arrested and tortured was Yorongar le Moïban, leader of a political party in opposition to Déby. Yorongar le Moïban reports being arrested and tortured by Soubiane, Déby, and other fighters at least 13 times before and after his election as president of Chad in 2001. Déby refused to leave the presidency, and Moïban could not gain the protection of the French embassy to Chad, so he was denied the office to which he had been elected (Madonet, 2004; Verschave, 2000, p. 174).

From November 1997 to March 1998, the Presidential Guards expanded their terror in both Oriental Logone and Occidental Logone. There were assassinations of public officials and murders of women, children, and farmers every day in the towns and villages.

As but one example of these horrors, in Goré the chief of the canton, Gaston Mbaïnaïbey, was invited with 15 of his village chiefs by the subprefect of Benoye to attend a meeting. The canton chief arrived with his delegation on March 11, 1998, at the area of appointment. Suddenly three military vehicles appeared with armed fighters. The fighters tied Gaston Mbaïnaïbey and his village chiefs together with strong rope. They took them to the southern border of Logone and shot them by the river, except Gaston. He was taken back to Goré, placed in his chair of authority, and shot dead by the soldiers (Barthélémy, 1998; Verschave, 2000, p.151; *Alwihda*, 2003).

Déby Takes Action Against Youssouf Togoïmi and the MDJT

Some members of Déby's administration were horrified. Youssouf Togoïmi, a native of Zouar (in northern Chad, near Déby's own people), had occupied different ministerial positions, including justice minister, defense minister, and internal minister, from 1990 to 1997. Youssouf Togoïmi had negotiated the peace treaty with the FARF on behalf of Déby's government. When Déby sent the special unit to violate that treaty, kill the rebels, and massacre the people, Togoïmi was not happy and regretted having negotiated with the FARF. He was shocked at the deaths of so many innocent Chadians in Moundou. Togoïmi was known as a just man and a fair judge. It was difficult for him to comprehend that Déby had intended this outcome. Some months later, Déby made a secret deal with the president of Niger, Maïna Bal Nassara, to hand over a Niger rebel leader currently in Chad in exchange for Niger's turning Mahamat Fadil over to Déby (and certain death). Togoïmi was at that time the internal minister and was informed only that his counterpart from Niger would come with a message from Maïna to Déby. Togoïmi welcomed the internal minister of Niger at the airport in N'Djaména and took him to the presidential palace to meet with Déby, where the bodyguards stopped Togoïmi at the door. Togoïmi quickly surmised that Déby was planning something inappropriate. Knowing that the Niger opposition leader, waiting at a hotel for what he thought would be a friendly meeting with Déby and Togoïmi, was really to be arrested and flown to Niger, he immediately got word to the opposition leader to escape. Humiliated for the second time, Togoïmi resigned from his job in the administration (Djonabaye, 2002; Aubert et al., 1998). A year later, he decided to join the rebellion against Déby and created a movement in northern Chad called Movement for Democracy and Justice in [T]chad (MDJT), on October 12, 1998 (Djonabaye, 2002).

After Togoïmi rebelled against Déby, he faced violent attacks. He resisted Déby's forces and wreaked havoc on them, inflicting terrible losses. Angry about the surprisingly strong resistance of Togoïmi's forces, Déby gave order to his fighters to destroy the towns and villages of Togoïmi's people, despite the fact that not only Togoïmi but Déby himself had family connections there. Déby's troops tortured and killed people living in that region. All their cattle were taken away. The water wells and springs were poisoned. All road crossings were mined with explosives. The huts and palm trees were burned in Bardaï, Zoumri, Wour, and Yebbi-bou. Youssouf Togoïmi, a man who offered hope to Chadians, hope of a change for justice and democracy, died in Libya of suspicious causes on September 24, 2002. Unfortunately, Déby's non–Zaghawa soldiers fell victim to their own actions. Many of them died when Déby was not able to supply them with drinking water from N'Djaména by airplane. When they had depleted their reserve water, they drank from the wells and springs that their own troops had poisoned (Yorongar, 2000).

In April 1998, Chad had signed international conventions on the protection of prisoners of war; nevertheless, on Déby's orders, Laoukeïn Bardé, leader of the FARF rebellion, was arrested and taken to Moussoro, a Déby stronghold north of N'Djaména. He was tortured under inhuman conditions, and then he was burned alive (Madonet, 2004; Kpatindé, 1999).

Besides the MDJT, other suspected rebel groups were also targeted. On September 6, 2000, Kétté Nodji, leader of the CSNPD, was arrested through complicity of people from his region and taken to N'Djaména. Some sources said that Déby himself tortured Kétté Nodji for several days before Kétté finally died (Madonet, 2004). In January 2001, Mr. Yahya Labadri, one of the leaders of MDJT, and 12 other fighters were arrested, presented to the press as prisoners, and then privately executed (Alwihdactualité, April 19, 2001).

In April 2001, Mr. Koki Sougui Abakar and Mr. Ali Teguil were arrested during the war in Wour. This was when the MDJT was fighting against Déby's forces. After the government presented the names of these two men as rebels on national radio, the two men were executed. There were so many hundreds of cases like this in Chad that they have not all been documented (Alwihdactualité 16, 2001).

Attacks on Refugees Fleeing Chad

When Idriss Déby took power from Hissène Habré, he created a wave of emigration from Chad. Besides those who were arrested, tortured, and killed in Chad, there were also others who fled Chad in the hope of safety outside the country. Hundreds of them were kidnapped and sent back to Chad, betrayed to Déby by his accomplices in countries of their exile. In 1992, as has already been mentioned, more than 200 individuals who had escaped Chad to save their lives were sent back to Chad by the government of Sani Abacha of Nigeria, and most of them were tortured and killed by Déby despite the fact that Déby had assured Abacha that he would jail and question the men but not kill them. Goukouni Guet was among the men returned to Chad and murdered. (Both the Abacha administration and Amnesty International noted and widely published this betrayal.

Abacha did not send exiles back to Chad after that.) Similarly, Bichara Chaibo, who had escaped to Togo when Habré fell, was returned to Chad by the government of Togo. Colonel Mahamat Fadil was sent back to Déby by Niger. Both Chaibo and Fadil were tortured and killed (Bardet, 2008).

Violence Against Leaders and Groups

The repression continues, of course. Anybody in Chad who tries to talk about injustice or human rights violations under Déby's rule is subject to arrest, torture, and assassination. This was true for young Adoum Abakar Moustapha, president of the Collective of Youth Associations and Movements of Chad (CAMOJET), who was assassinated in the middle of the night on September 11, 2006. Adoum Abakar Moustapha and his colleagues had gathered in N'Djaména to discuss ways to solve the problems of war and injustice in their country. The police, not finding any other way to stop the association, hired a secret agent to toss a grenade into the house of Adoum Abakar Moustapha in the middle of the night. The blast killed him. Politicians, journalists, and human rights organizations have expressed concern (Manga, 2006). (See Amnesty International's annual reports for Chad, available online.)

Attempts to Ensure Unconstitutional Succession Despite Drug Scandal

Early in 1991, word was spreading in Chad about Déby's involvement with the drug trade. It was said that Déby and members of his government were involved in corruption. They were buying and selling cocaine and marijuana, some said. Others argued that Déby wouldn't involve himself in drug dealing, though he might buy some drugs to give to his fighters and the teenagers that he was using to fight against the rebel Movement for Democracy and Development (MDD). A few years later three special advisors to Déby, two of his close friends, and Déby's eldest son were arrested in Germany and France for trafficking in cocaine and falsifying international currencies over the previous few years. Circumstantial evidence points to Déby as the leader or at least accomplice of these crimes (Verschave, 2000, pp. 151–174; Alwihdactualité, March 23, 2001).

In late 1997, a presidential advisor of Déby named Djamal Adoum Aganaye was the first to be indicted on drug charges. He made an official trip to Dusseldorf, on a diplomatic passport, where he was to be welcomed by a relative, Her Excellency Aganaye Bintou, Chadian ambassador to Germany. Customs agents found 130 kilograms of cocaine in his suitcases labeled "Republic of Chad." According to the police, it was the most significant quantity found in any European Union country in ten years (Verschave, 2000, pp. 151–174).

Déby's son was arrested nearly ten years later. Brahim Déby, Idriss Déby's eldest son, served as advisor on infrastructure during his father's presidency. On June 1, 2006, he was arrested in Paris for having in his possession marijuana, cocaine, and an illegal weapon. For many years, Brahim had been suspected in Chad of involvement in the drug business but was not caught until 2006 (Heurtaut, 2006). In May of 2006, Brahim Déby was escorted by one of his friends, Daoud Wardougou, across the river that separates N'Djaména from Koussouri, Cameroon. They were headed for Cotonou in the Benin Republic with four suitcases full of money. Two days later, Daoud was back in N'Djaména, and Brahim continued on his way to France. When he showed up at a night club near his residence with a hostile attitude and a pistol tucked into his belt, someone in the bar called the police. In the melee, Brahim's pistol fell onto the floor (Eolas, 2006). Brahim's friends who were with him that night were clever enough to phone his residence and warn friends there that the apartment might be checked by police officers. By the time police arrived, his friends had taken steps to conceal signs of illegal activity, but police officers were still able to find more than 250 grams of marijuana, two grams of cocaine, and many suitcases full of money (Heurtaut, 2006).

The people of Chad had murmured against Brahim for some time. In 2005, Déby successfully won a fight to extend his presidential term beyond the constitutional limit. This fueled suspicion that he would attempt to serve as president for life, which panicked disaffected members of his tribe and family (Cohen, 2006). As one option, should he not obtain a life term in office, speculators said that Déby might choose a successor from within his family and continue to rule from behind the scenes. None of the rest of Déby's family is speaking with the president after he held a secret meeting outside the capital in 2005 at which he said he wanted his son — the sunglasses-clad Brahim — to take over the presidency. Since that meeting, Chadians refer to "Déby's dysfunctional family," and now other relatives have taken up arms against Idriss and Brahim Déby (Yorongar, 2005).

Indeed, when Brahim's father named him as his heir to the presidency, even Déby's inner circle began to panic. The son seemed even less presidential than the father. For example, Brahim was said to have given powerful backhand slaps to classmates at school and then to people in bars, in night clubs, on the road, and even at the presidential palace without respect for social rank. Even some family members were victims of his violent disrespect. Worse yet, perhaps under the influence of cocaine or marijuana, Brahim is reported to have shot and killed neighbors and even his friends with the weapons he carried. Nevertheless, after his arrest in Paris and his demotion by his father, Brahim was released from French custody and returned home to Chad. Idriss Déby had made a telephone call directly to French president Jacques Chirac (Loalngar, 2006; Nadingar, 2006).

Apparently Brahim's instability was one of the main reasons that the twin nephews of Déby took up arms against him (Cohen, 2006). Well educated and certain that only an elected president can keep power in Chad after Déby's death, these nephews hoped to forestall Déby's naming Brahim his heir. Should one of Déby's sons be named the next ruler of Chad by unconstitutional means rather than a fair election, power in Chad (and the oil wealth that such power brings) would leave the Zaghawa tribe (Cohen, 2006).

CHAPTER 3

Bour, Survivor of Zaghawa Attack

The power of Zaghawas over other tribes in Chad and particularly over the Sara people of the South has grown greatly since Déby came to power. According to the author of one biography, Déby has favored his tribe over all others (Idriss Déby Itno Biography, author unknown, Fund for Peace, 2007). The Zaghawas have not been punished for attacks on Chad's citizens despite numerous instances of violence. Reports from Chad indicate that the Zaghawas injure, torture, and assassinate members of other tribes with impunity (Verschave, 2000; Garro, 2008). One of their victims, Bour Nadoum, managed to survive an attack in 1993.

Following the Épervier Plan

In 1992, Christian Quesnot, chief of staff to French president François Mittérand, was sent by Mittérand to N'Djaména to give six conditions for maintaining French soldiers in Chad. Those conditions were known as the Épervier Plan. France demanded (1) a significant reduction of forces in Chad, (2) organization of a Sovereign National Convention for truth and reconciliation, and then (3) formation of a new government of transition to democracy, (4) unconditional liberation of political leaders held in prison, (5) recognition and application of human rights, and (6) restoration of control of government finances by qualified personnel (replacing Déby's system of nepotism) (Tchadoscopie, 1996).

In 1992, just six months before the start of the Sovereign National

Convention, Mittérand wanted to provide economic assistance to the people of Chad. But France also wanted to review the economy of the country and be certain of a balance in the treasury as a precondition for providing help (Tchadoscopie, 1996). This was a serious issue for Déby and his tribe, who were accused by opposition leaders of using the treasury of Chad as their personal piggy bank (Verschave, 2000, p. 154). Because Déby had already been warned by President Mittérand a few months before to get his affairs in order, he allowed his former prime minister Joseph Youdeiman to find a qualified person to fill the head customs position, which at that time was the highest post in the financial area of the administration. (Customs officers are not in Chad's Justice Department or Homeland Security, as in the United States, but serve as assessors of taxes on goods crossing Chad's borders. Most taxes never make it to the capital.)

Youdeiman and his finance minister, Mayodine Sallah, went through the archives and investigated possible candidates they might put in charge of customs to meet one of the conditions demanded by Mittérand. Bour Nadoum was the most qualified by skill and seniority and was recognized as knowledgeable by French experts and senior Chadian authorities in the finance ministry. In fact, Bour had been recruited to customs work early in 1960 at the age of 18 and was one of the few Chadians to work among French customs officers in Chad. Having acquired a reputation for skill, at 22 years of age he was sent to Goz Beïda as assistant to the (French) head of the customs office there. By the time he was 36, he had served as chief of customs and brigade chief in several regions. When Hissène Habré started his civil war against the regime of Maloum Ngakoutou Beïndi, Bour fled for his life, returning to his native village, Béhomon. Very soon the authorities of southern Chad, cut off from the capital, saw the need to reestablish government in the South and nominated Bour to command all brigades in the regions of the two Logones (Oriental and Occidental) and Tanjilé (Nadoum, 2008; Nékim, 1993).

When Commander Galium and Captain Demtita won victory for Habré in the South, Bour was removed from his post of responsibility and served in lower positions until 1990. After the fall of Hissène Habré's regime, the director of customs sent Bour to Abéché as chief of customs and coordinator of customs offices in the region of Ouaddaï, which includes Tiné, André, Goz Beïda, Iriba, and Guéréda (Nadoum, 2008).

After 32 years of brilliant service to his country, Bour was in N'Djaména in summer 1992 for a three-month vacation when he was suddenly promoted by Finance Minister Mayodine to be national director of customs and was asked to take office immediately (Nadoum, 2008). No southerner (and no educated person) had held that post since Habré's revolution in

1979. Bour officially took office on June 14 and set about to strengthen the country's economy (Nékim, 1993).

Later that year, in December of 1992, Idriss Déby signed an agreement with the government of France to reform Chad's finances by setting up a Financial Mechanism of Support, which would oversee income from the treasury, taxes, and customs. The agreement would allow French experts to work in these areas and share power with senior Chadians in the Finance Ministry.

In accord with the agreement, a French financial expert was sent to co-direct Bour's section of customs. After eight months of service, Déby noticed a positive change in the public treasury. Unfortunately for Déby, his personal finances were suffering under this careful management, and after the Sovereign National Convention, all the country's finances might be structured so as to prevent his and his family's enrichment. Déby then nominated for general controller of customs the former director of customs under Hissène Habré, Djiddi Hissène (a nephew of Hissène Habré). Some sources report that Djiddi had only five or six years of formal schooling. Déby gave him ten Toyota pickups and 200 armed men. Djiddi and his armed force were officially installed in the headquarters of customs on March 13, 1993. From that date, public revenues started decreasing again (Nékim, 1993).

About a month after the nomination and installation of Djiddi, the Sovereign National Convention named the former prime minister, Fidele Moungar Abdelkarim, to lead the Government of Transition. Moungar was eager to fulfill France's requirements so that his government could get economic assistance for the benefit of Chad. Looking for qualified people to place in the financial ministry, Moungar chose Robert Royingam, an employee of an international finance institution, to be Financial Minister. Bour Nadoum was retained as director of customs. Those two leaders were highly qualified by their education, expertise, and experience to restore Chad's economy (Nékim, 1993).

Zaghawa Resistance to Reform

Unfortunately, Bour and Royingam could not accomplish France's requirements for the structure and function of financial institutions because the relatives and tribesmen of Déby who were working as "mobile fighter customs officers," so to speak, would not tolerate an ethnic Sara in command over them (Nékim, 1993). Though few Zaghawas had enough schooling to read their names, they were placed in high positions and reported only to Déby. Zaghawas in Chad's finance and customs posts did not care about finance ministers, nor did they have any patience with hierarchical chiefs in the Finance Ministry. Mobile customs officers, under pretense of performing some official service, in fact stole from the people. They confiscated goods they "suspected" of being contraband, but in fact they stole even property for which citizens had purchase papers. Anyone crossing into Chad or traveling within Chad was subject to sudden search and seizure (Nékim, 1993).

Despite Moungar's eagerness to show that good government could improve the economy of Chad, Déby was not ready to allow the new government to grow the economy. France became aware of Déby as the source of the problem, probably informed by French advisors in the Finance Ministry — more precisely, by the French expert who was assisting Bour as national director. Thoroughly frustrated by the crimes of Djiddi and his 200 "mobile customs officers" who enriched themselves and Déby, the French finance contingent resigned en masse and returned to France (Nadoum, 2008). Informed of this matter, French officials began to pressure Déby to annul the post of general controller of customs officers and to give all materials and authority to the national director, Bour, to do his job (Nékim, 1993). This put Déby in a difficult position, because General Controller Djiddi Hissène was his relative and close friend and had more power than the director of customs officers. In addition, Djiddi Hissène was needed to ensure that goods and taxes were taken either to the presidential palace or to the homes of regime leaders rather than to the treasury. Déby dared not cancel that key post; nevertheless, he was required to do so to satisfy France's conditions for aid and prevent the country's financial collapse (Nékim, 1993).

Djiddi Hissène was called to the office of Finance Minister Royingam in the presence of his staff, including some senior customs officers. Royingam informed Djiddi that his post was canceled and that he would need to present his resignation and assess the contents of the treasury warehouses by a deadline only a few weeks in the future. Despite the fact that he had already been informed unofficially by Déby, Djiddi was furious with Royingam and lashed out at him, saying Royingam had humiliated him in front of Royingam's female secretaries, whom he called Royingam's prostitutes. Royingam immediately ordered everybody out of his office. Royingam's staff had to use utmost diplomacy with Djiddi to get him into the office of the general director to resolve other issues related to his "resignation" (Nékim, 1993).

Djiddi was reportedly furious to have lost his post, in part because it brought in millions of CFA (Central African francs) per week for his own use, and he was not likely to obtain such a sinecure again. Another frustration was that he knew nothing about finance or records and had to inventory all the warehouses and report to Bour. At that time, 37 military police officers were sent to the warehouses by Moungar to prevent any loss of goods. Djiddi was unable to write the report or do the inventory because of his limited education and expertise. Two days before the inventory deadline, Djiddi issued an ultimatum to Bour: pay Djiddi's fighters before Djiddi left office and give them their bonuses (10 percent of all the goods they brought in), or the consequences would be dire. Bour apparently told Djiddi to address his request to the Finance Ministry, which was in charge of paying government employees (Nékim, 1993).

The Attack on Bour

On June 14, 1993, Djiddi and his fighters, known as Karang-Karang, surrounded the building where Bour, his four bodyguards, and two secretaries were working. At 11:30 A.M. they shot bazookas and lobbed grenades into the building. Bour wisely restrained his bodyguards from counterattacking the 200 fighters outside. Bour and his six staffers hid in the corners of the building for better safety in case the structure collapsed. They expected these to be the last minutes of their lives (Nékim, 1993). Bour struggled to the telephone to beg for help from the presidential palace, from National Army Headquarters, and from many other nearby locations, but no saviors were prepared to intervene (Nadoum, 2008).

It was nearly three hours before the defense minister, commander-in-chief of the army, high authorities of public security, Presidential Guards, and military police arrived to demand an end to the attack, on order of the prime minister. By that time, the attack was already over. Bour and his staff were lucky not to have been killed or even wounded. Their building, though, was riddled with damage from the Kalashnikovs, grenades, and bazookas of Djiddi's men (Nékim, 1993).

Déby was in Europe that day. The Presidential Guards were able to rescue Bour and his staff from their hiding places and convey them in the president's armored vehicle to their base near the palace, where Bour was welcomed by high army officers, including the defense minister himself. Despite the presence of these high authorities at the base, some of the Presidential Guards treated Bour like a prisoner, slapping and punching him. Fortunately for Bour, a commander of the Presidential Guards named Dremi was there. He ordered his fighters to stop mistreating Mr. Bour and took him to the police commissioner's office near the base. Knowing the mentality of his fighters, Dremi was not certain enough of Bour's safety even at the commissariat, so he asked Lieutenant Sam Manang (of Chad's equivalent of the CIA) to come and rescue Bour for the second time. Manang took Bour and the others to a military police camp (or gendarmerie) for their own security. They were kept there for a week before they were transported to court to tell their story to a judicial authority and then taken home (Nékim, 1993).

Two Fighters Killed in the Attack

After his attack on Bour, Djiddi discovered that two of his fighters had been killed in action. Djiddi accused Bour of shooting his two fighters, an allegation that Bour denied. Although he and his staff had been attacked, Bour said, none of them had shot even one bullet. Because Djiddi and his fighters had completely surrounded the building before the attack, the two fighters — Taher Hamat and Issa Oumar — were probably killed by bullets from the weapons of their comrades. Hamat and Oumar were Zaghawas and had family ties to Déby (Nékim, 1993).

Bour reports that he thought Djiddi had probably sent Hamat and Oumar to the first floor of the building to shoot down on them; during the attack, Bour and his personnel saw bullets coming down vertically from the first floor as well as laterally from different sides. Bour contended that Hamat and Oumar received wayward bullets from their own companions when they tried to get down from the first floor to open the main gate of the customs offices (Nadoum, 2008).

When the Presidential Guards learned that two of their comrades had been killed in the attack on Bour, they were desperate to assassinate Bour. For some reason, Dremi now cast aside his earlier protectiveness and joined his fighters to "deal with" Bour. When Dremi heard that Bour had been released from protective custody, he took his fighters to the Supreme Court and ordered the general prosecutor to return Bour to prison. Dremi gave the court 24 hours to find Bour and take him back to prison, or Dremi would shoot up the court (Nékim, 1993).

The following day at 11 A.M., Presidential Guards went to the Supreme Court building to see if their ultimatum had been carried out. The court was empty. The Guards found no prosecutors and no justices but only a few police and military police officers assigned to maintain order at the court (Nékim, 1993).

Informed of Dremi's threat to the prosecutors, Prime Minister Fidele Moungar contacted the commander-in-chief of the army who, in turn, called Dremi to the prime minister's office to deal with the problem. Dremi accepted the "invitation" to discuss the issue but denied having menaced the general prosecutor. Déby, who was still in Europe, had been informed about the situation but said the entire issue was nonsense and not worth his bothering about (Nékim, 1993).

When Déby returned from his trip, though, and was advised of the events that had transpired, he immediately accused Prime Minister Fidele Moungar, who officially represented him as president in his absence, of having attempted a coup d'état. Déby claimed there was no reason for Moungar to have sent military police to protect the goods in the customs warehouses. Further, Déby stated explicitly that Djiddi Hissène would not be legally charged for his attack on Bour's office. He added that "Moungar must put out the fire that he has started" (Nékim, 1993).

Déby's reaction stirred his fighters to continue with their attacks on Bour. Moreover, the relatives of Hamat and Oumar ordered the prime minister to remove Royingam from the Finance Ministry and Bidi Valentin from the Internal Ministry. The parents of the dead Guards, Hamat and Oumar, demanded that Bour pay a *dia* (Muslim death indemnity) of eight million CFA. Prime Minister Moungar urged Bour to resolve the problem amiably with the young men's parents by paying the *dia* demanded. The prime minister was criticized by some for making this request, because *dia* had been canceled by the new law code created during the Sovereign National Convention that had named him prime minister (Nékim, 1993).

Bour's response was that he had been on the job and in service when he was attacked by Djiddi and the fighters. Despite that, he had not reacted to their attack with violence. The two men had been killed by their comrades' bullets. Why then should he pay the *dia* when he was not the one who had killed the two fighters? In addition, Bour said, by law of both the former constitution and the new code, when an accident occurs to an employee of the government in service, the government will be responsible for the consequences and pay compensation. Thus the government would need to acknowledge its responsibility for the consequences (to Bour and his colleagues) of the attack launched by Djiddi (Nadoum, 2008).

After first resisting, the government eventually agreed to pay the eight million CFA rather than require payment of Bour. When the parents of Hamat and Oumar received their money, they still were not satisfied and demanded that Bour personally pay two million CFA more, or something would happen to his relatives. Pascal Yoadoumnadji, who later became prime minister, volunteered to pay the fine on Bour's behalf (Nékim, 1993).

Attacks on Bour Continue

Bour was replaced by another individual as head of customs. The government gave Bour two military police officers to protect him in his private residence. On January 21, 1994, a Toyota pickup filled with fighters launched another attack, this time on Bour's residence. One of Bour's two military police and his private driver were killed. That day his backyard was full of visitors, as usual. Many would have been killed but for a Zaghawa named Saleh Abderahim (Nadoum, 2008). Saleh Abderahim and Demou Dogui, customs officers from the North whom Bour had mentored in their careers, were there to visit Bour. It was Saleh who came out of Bour's villa and stood with his hands up in surrender, calling to the attackers in the Zaghawa dialect, "The man that you are looking for (Bour) is not here. So please do not kill the children." The attackers trusted this man of their tribe and immediately returned to their base. That same night, Saleh helped Bour to escape to an undisclosed location (Nadoum, 2008).

A military police station about 150 meters from Bour's home did not rush to the aid of Bour's family when his home was strafed. The license number of the attackers' Toyota was written down and taken to the station, but nothing was done. Because of this betrayal of law and protection, because even the police could not protect Bour from the Zaghawas, his relatives gathered and urged him to leave the country. Bour had to leave 11 children and the rest of his family to go into exile on January 24, 1994 (Nadoum, 2008).

The lives of Bour's children were also in danger. At that time the two elder sons were at university, four were in junior and senior high school, and the others were in primary school. The children knew they must leave Chad also. They escaped into neighboring countries to save their lives. Without money or a home, their lives were wretched. Needless to say, they could not continue with their education (Nadoum, 2008). Since Bour left Chad in 1994, he has received no financial support from the government of Chad, a country that he had served with loyalty and commitment for more than 34 years.

Djiddi Hissène tells people that he knows where Bour is living and refrains from killing him out of respect for the country where he has found sanctuary. Djiddi has never been disciplined by Idriss Déby for his attacks on Bour.

CHAPTER 4

Déby's International Counterfeiting Operation Revealed

Chad uses a currency common to at least 15 countries in Africa. The countries formerly colonized by France share the FCFA, which is the franc of the Communauté Financière Africaine (African Financial Community). Counterfeiting FCFAs jeopardizes not only the currency of West Africa and Central Africa but also the currencies of many other countries that exchange with these areas, and thus weakens trust in those nations' financial systems. Idriss Déby, president of Chad, is accused of having counterfeited not only FCFAs but also dinars of Bahrain and dollars of the U.S. and Canada. In so doing, Déby may be the only president to enrich himself and impoverish others by counterfeiting so many currencies, and yet he remains in power (Verschave, 2000, pp. 151–174).

As an adage says, every day cannot be Sunday. Déby had been able to cover his crimes until the year 1998, when his counterfeiting and drug schemes unraveled. The story takes us to France, Ivory Coast, South Africa, Bahrain, and back to Chad. It was only after 1998 that Déby's earlier and concurrent crimes were found out and put on display. In August and September of that year, articles appeared in newspapers in Chad (*N'Djaména Hebdo*; Oulatar, August 1998); Niger (*Le Citoyen*, September 22, 1998); and even France (J. Juliard in *Le Canard Enchaîné*, September 9, 1998; V. Bolloré in *La Lettre du Continent*, September 24, 1998; *La Lettre du Continent* #310 & #313; and L. Valdiguié in *Le Parisien*, September 30, 1998). By the following summer, even Paris' *Le Monde* published the story (Tuquoi, June 28, 1999).

The Counterfeiting Operation

In 1998, the Chadian Development Bank fell victim to a counterfeiting scheme that stuck them with tens of millions of fake bills. The website of the Movement for Democracy and Justice in Chad (MDJT) and Chad-Forum (ChadForum.com, a website hosted by a Chadian refugee in the United States) carried news that the fake money had been produced in an unnamed neighboring country. These seem to have been the first news sources publicly to connect the president of Chad with falsification of international currency (Kpatindé, 1999).

How did the counterfeiting operation begin? According to a citizen of Ivory Coast by the name of Armand Grah, Idriss Déby made a deal with him to falsify some bills in FCFA as a trial run in 1995-1996 (AfriquEducation, 2006). Through that arrangement, seven billion FCFA were printed in Europe. Though the European country was not named, the expert counterfeiters employed were French. According to Grah, Déby prudently wanted to avoid bringing those bills directly into Chad and therefore wanted to work with an Ivorian to bring the bills from France to the capital of Ivory Coast, Abidjan (AfriquEducation, 2006).

How could Déby bring so large a load of money from Abidjan to N'Djaména without arousing suspicion? According to news sources (e.g., Cameroun Link, 2006, and AfriquEducation, 2006), Déby sent his presidential airplane to Abidjan on the pretext of a medical emergency — sending the traditional chief of the region of Léré to the hospital of Abid in January. In fact, the real purpose of the flight was to get the presidential plane to Abidjan and then return with the false bills to Déby. Déby had need of such counterfeited funds, to use them as he had in previous years, that is, to sequester legitimate FCFAs from the Chadian treasury in his residences and to spend the fake money for his expenses.

Unfortunately, according to Grah, the counterfeiters, who were highly skilled French specialists, were not satisfied with the level of remuneration proposed by Déby for their work. The false bills were taken to another, secure, French-speaking country in Africa (Cameroun Link, 2006; AfriquEducation, 2006). Apparently Armand Grah was unhappy about the payment dispute between Déby and his comrades, the French counterfeiters. He manifested his dissatisfaction to Déby in N'Djaména. Because Déby did not want the news to get out, he quickly ordered his military to put Armand in jail to keep him quiet. In prison, Armand was asked to make a choice between his life and a promise not to implicate Déby in the counterfeiting scheme (Cameroun Link, 2006).

Armand chose not to end his life. He accepted Déby's terms, which included writing a letter of confession claiming that he alone had thought up the counterfeiting scheme. Déby's government sent the letter to Luc Furhmann, the French ambassador in Chad. Armand was then released from prison on September 23, 1998 (Cameroun Link, 2006).

Bad Bills in Chad

In 1996, workers in Chad started hearing about some falsified bills and unfortunately received payment in counterfeit bills. At first no one knew the source of the fake money. Some of the shopkeepers in various towns heard about the counterfeit bills and tried to make sure that customers paid in genuine FCFA bills but could not always distinguish the fakes (Alwihdactualité, March 23, 2001).

Bankers, however, seemed to know which bills were counterfeit. When someone with counterfeit money went to the bank, the teller would accept that money and pay back good bills, letting the customer know that the bill brought in was false. It is not clear why banks made this money-losing exchange. Bank officials also explained to curious customers how they were able to distinguish true bills from false: all the false bills shared the same serial number (Alwihdactualité, March 23, 2001). Apparently BEAC (Banque des États de l'Afrique Centrale) officials in N'Djaména eventually informed the central BEAC bank that Déby was behind the falsified bills, which had deleterious effects on regional currency. BEAC officials did not publicize the issue. Though it is an international institution of at least five countries, it failed to take the action needed to halt counterfeiting the currency of the sub-region. Not one of the authorities of those countries criticized Déby's criminal behavior.

In the same year, 1998, Déby was accused of distributing fake FCFA bills to CotonTchad, the leading Chadian marketer of cotton fabric, to buy the raw cotton from farmers. In payment for their cotton crop, the farmers received worthless money. They could not purchase seed for the following year with counterfeit money, nor could they pay medical bills, buy supplies, or feed their families.

On May 23, 2000, other fake FCFA bills, along with some fake U.S. and Canadian dollars, were taken to the Cameroonian town of Koussouri, across the border from Chad's capital city. The bills were transported by the commander of the Presidential Guard, Youssouf Boy, who is a brother-in-law of Déby (AfriquEducation, May 16–31, 2006). It is suspected that Déby hoped to enrich his bank accounts outside Chad without a paper trail to trace the money. Because officials of the government of Cameroon knew that Déby and his followers were involved in drugs and counterfeiting, the authorities there were suspicious of diplomatic vehicles passing through their territory. At the same time, they would certainly have hesitated to rupture relationships with the government of Chad. Cameroon purchases Chadian petroleum — worth at least $20 million USD every year (World Bank, 2006) — and supplies many bilingual French-English-speaking specialists, engineers, chemists, and technicians to Chad. Nevertheless on this occasion the Cameroonian officers stopped the car of the commandant of the Presidential Guard. He was accompanied by one of Déby's bodyguards. In the car the officers found many suitcases packed with fake dollars and FCFA, and they arrested Boy. Reports say that he was released after a telephone call from Paul Biya Yaoundé, the president of Cameroon (AfriquEducation, 2006).

Fadoul Tells His Story

According to Verschave (2000, pp. 151–174), a sharp critic of Déby's regime, and also as confirmed in a report by the human rights organization Fédération Internationale des Ligues des Droits de l'Homme (Rapport, 2000), in the summer of 1998 Déby had printed in Argentina nearly 25 tons of counterfeit 20-dinar bills of Bahrain. One-third of the money was skimmed off by Ibrahim Baré Maïnassara, the president of Niger, who had been informed of the transport over Niger's airspace. His air force made the plane land in Niamey so that he could take a "campaign donation" promised by Déby without troubling his friend Déby to bring him the cash.

Two-thirds of the bills continued their flight to the international airport of N'Djaména and were driven with an escort of Déby's Presidential Guard directly to Déby's palace. Where did Verschave get his information? A former confidential friend and special advisor of President Déby, Hassan Fadoul Kitir, was a key figure in the counterfeiting operation. When the plot was discovered and Fadoul knew Déby would make him take the blame, he flew to France and was arrested. Fadoul said at his arrest that he had anticipated their interest in him and was ready to talk. He explained the entire scheme and how it caused the collapse of the Bank of Chad. He also spoke of falsification of Bahrain's dinars, equivalent to at least two billion French francs ("an amount so huge that authorities in the emirate, fearing the destabilization of their currency, had to urgently withdraw from circulation all denominations of 20 dinars and request assistance from the FBI," according to the International Federation for Human Rights [2000]).

Fadoul's testimony opened the eyes of some French groups to the politics of former-French Africa.

In December 2000, Fadoul was under investigation of the French police. He was for a while under their judicial control as well. Before he left France for his current residence in Burkina Faso, the country north of Niger, Fadoul was interviewed by the French newspaper *Le Journal Figaro* and told the story. He later was interviewed by Radio France International (Daoud, 2002) and told his story more recently in five episodes played on Bakchich television (and available online at Gay, 2009). The drama and scandal of his tale, from his first contact to his betrayal by President Déby, is worthy of an adventure novel or dramatic film. Fadoul explained that he and his confederates had tried many times to exchange the counterfeit 20-dinar bills in the banks of Belgium and France but had failed. The banks of those countries soon discovered that the money was false and worthless; immediately France and Belgium released international arrest warrants against the network of counterfeiters and especially Fadoul. But Fadoul said it was Déby, not he, who was at the center of the counterfeiting operation. According to Fadoul, Déby had paid $2.3 million USD to a printing house named Ciccone in Argentina.

According to several sources (among them online news commentators of *Bakchich*, *Alwihda*, and *AfricaTime*), Déby defrauded the Chadian Development Bank of more than $4 million USD by this counterfeiting scheme. Unfortunately for Déby, Fadoul was outsmarted by a Nigerian money changer, who gave them a check made out to Déby, which Déby cashed at the Chadian Development Bank. When the bank attempted to draw on the (British) Barclays bank account of the money changer, it discovered that no account existed. The money changer had his payment and was safe from British reprisal in Nigeria. Déby got — and instantly spent — the millions of dollars. The Chadian Development Bank was out of funds.

When Fadoul, the advisor and close friend of President Idriss Déby, traveled to France to surrender in Paris and testify that he was just following Déby's orders in the counterfeiting scheme, the French police — wanting to hush up the matter — said they had no need of his testimony. In frustration, Fadoul Kitir spoke to the press in Paris on March 16, 2001, and a transcript of his testimony was published on the *Alwihda* website that same day. Although Fadoul is only one of several who accuse Déby of these crimes, he provides an interesting and ironic behind-the-scenes commentary on his relationship with Idriss Déby, his former good friend (Alwihd-actualité, March 23, 2001). Why should we believe Fadoul's version of these events? It would be difficult to think of any other pretext for him to have traveled to Argentina in the official jet of the President of Chad.

Furthermore, records of the flights into and from Niger have been documented, implicating the president of Niger in skimming from the funds and the involvement of Saudi Arabia. Fadoul could not have taken the presidential jet filled with counterfeit money to Nigeria without Déby's permission and authority. Finally, Idriss Déby endorsed the check cashed at the Development Bank of Chad, and his signature is visible on the check. (See Appendix A.)

Togoïmi Tells

The interview of Fadoul Kitir by *Alwihda* was of course not the only source of information about Déby's counterfeiting operation. Though the business was hushed up in Chad and in France, some authors were able to get word out about secret deals and betrayals. See François-Xavier Verschave's book, *Black Silence* (*Noir Silence*) and Yorongar LeMoiban's book, *Le Procès d'Idriss Déby*. Journalist Francis Kpatindé of *Jeune Afrique* interviewed Youssouf Togoïmi in June 1999. Togoïmi was by that time a rebel leader of the Movement for Democracy and Justice in Chad, but he had served in Déby's administration in several positions, as justice minister, defense minister, and internal minister, over a period of more than five years. In Kpatindé's June 8, 1999, interview, Togoïmi revealed Déby's election fraud, assassination, drug, and counterfeiting crimes (Kpatindé, 1999). His knowledge and authority made him a powerful witness against the president, before his death in Libya.

As the secret was revealed with more and more evidence that Déby had caused a major economic crisis for his own country's bank and for financial institutions in other countries, the problem of counterfeit dinars became less an issue of finance and more an issue of politics. There is some embarrassment for the French government, which supports Déby. Not until November 2009 was Fadoul Kitir convicted in Paris of fraud and counterfeiting 140 million Bahrain dinars, the equivalent of 270 million euros (Meunier, 2010). At that time he was sentenced in absentia to five years in prison. See Appendix A for a translation of Hassan Fadoul Kitir's interview with *Alwihda* on March 16, 2000.

Chapter 5

Chad's Black Gold

Chad, which used to have the respect of other nations, is now considered one of the most corrupt countries in the world (Transparency International, 2010). Of the 180 countries surveyed in Transparency International's Corruption Perceptions Index, Chad ranks 175th. In recent years, Chad's government has been listed among the top ten and even top five most corrupt in the world. Chad tied with Bangladesh in 2007 as the most corrupt trade nation in the world (Workman, 2007). Ironically, part of the reason is Chad's rich oil resources. Former U.S. ambassador Herman Cohen (2006) traces the history of Déby's difficulties in Chad and Sudan — that is, the history of the current Darfur crisis — back to oil discoveries in southwestern Chad that made control of Chad lucrative.

Searching for Oil Wealth in Chad

When François Ngarta Tombalbaye became Chad's first president on August 11, 1960, he took action to grow Chad's economy. In 1962, he invited a French oil company to search for oil and mineral deposits in Chad. From 1962 to 1965, the Bureau des Recherches Pétrolières made an unproductive search for oil. Another French company, ORSTOM, took over from 1965 to 1967, with similar results (Aubert, Brana, & Blum, 1998; Béguy, 2002).

On the evidence of a letter to French president Georges Pompidou from Chadian president Tombalbaye in 1969 (see Appendix B), the French oil companies apparently claimed they were abandoning Chad because they had found nothing in their resource surveys. President Tombalbye did not despair, though. In fact, he had information that Chad's oil reserves were quite rich and easily accessible and that France wanted to keep Chad's resources in reserve until they were needed later. In 1969 he turned to an American company, Continental Oil Company (Conoco), giving it permission to search all of Chad. Conoco conducted a thorough search by airplane and helicopter in and around Lake Chad and the prefectures of Oriental Logone, Moyen Chari, and Salamat. The results were good: one of the richest petroleum regions of Africa lay under Chad's soil (Aubert et al., 1998; Béguy, 2002).

In 1971, notice of Chad's petroleum reserves attracted the Dutch company, Shell, which became a 50 percent shareholder of Conoco. Conoco gave hope to Chadians and particularly to President Tombalbaye (known after the cultural revolution of 1970 as Ngarta) by drilling test wells and striking oil in Doba in September 1973. On December 18 of that year, Ngarta inaugurated the first oil well at Nya, close to Doba, thanking God for this blessing and saying, "Our wish is that the first oil wells should be fruitful in bringing forth our rich natural resources. The realization of this hope should allow us to place more and more milestones along the road of our development" (Djimrabaye, 2005, p. 5; Béguy, 2002). In Ngarta's presidency, Western oil companies were greatly interested in Chad's oil fields and wanted to participate in their development. Chevron, a U.S. corporation, entered into the consortium in 1974 by purchasing a 25 percent share. Even after Ngarta was assassinated on April 13, 1975, Esso (also known as Exxon/Mobil), another U.S. company, entered into the business in 1976 by purchasing a one-eighth share and then increased its holdings, giving Esso and Shell 37.5 percent each (Djimrabaye, 2005, p. 5; Béguy, 2002; Djimrabaye is an especially good source of information on this topic).

In 1972 another oil field was discovered in Sedigui, but the quantity that could be extracted was too little for serious export development, Ngarta was told, so he was advised to use the Sedigui oil field for domestic consumption. Three years later, after Ngarta's assassination, Chad lost the stewardship of its elected president, and there was still no refinery for petroleum production in Chad. The government was still only studying the ways and means to build a refinery in N'Djaména to process the Sedigui oil, planning for which advanced only at the speed of a chameleon, as the Chadian saying goes. Conoco pulled out of Chad early in 1979, when Hissène Habré initiated civil war against Ngarta's successor, the strongman Maloum Ngakoutou Beïndi, on February 12. All the activities of oil exploration and production were stopped, and refinery operations were stillborn (Aubert et al., 1998; Béguy, 2002).

In 1982, when Hissène Habré had taken control of the country, his government attempted to revive the project of the Sedigui oil field, but it seemed that the violent and unsettled conditions were not appropriate for the project. It was almost six years later in 1988 that Esso signed an agreement with Habré's administration to research, explore, and transport hydrocarbons. One year before the end of Habré's regime, Esso launched another study on the Sedigui project and confirmed its usefulness to produce electricity and gasoline for domestic and regional consumption.

Funding a Pipeline to Cameroon

Habré was soon forced out of the country. December 1, 1990, brought the end of Habré's reign of terror. The oil studies and negotiations resumed when Déby seemed to have the country under his firm control. Oil search and drilling equipment moved from Sarh (in Moyen Chari) to Komé (in Oriental Logone) to continue exploration of that area, which earlier had been confirmed as a ready site for drilling. Early in 1992, Déby forced Chevron to sell its share of Chad's oil rights to Elf, a French company (Aubert et al., 1998; Béguy, 2002).

The consortium now included Exxon (U.S.), Shell (Holland), and Elf (France) and undertook new negotiations with the World Bank and Déby's government. The World Bank was interested in funding the project, and at the end of July 1992, the oil companies signed an agreement with the governments of Chad and Cameroon to build a pipeline to pump Chadian crude oil through Cameroon to the Atlantic.

Oil companies seemed reluctant to invest great sums of money in a country wracked with terror and violence under Déby, however, and did not quickly move to construct the pipeline. Involvement by the World Bank would provide greater financial security for the project than private investment alone. On February 8, 1996, Chad and Cameroon signed a bilateral agreement for the construction of the pipeline. Many non-governmental organizations (NGOs) in Chad, Cameroon, and France were involved in the pipeline project in an attempt to alleviate the consequences of the pipeline on the people and the environment (Jaillard, 2007; Djimrabaye, 2005, p. 7; Béguy, 2002).

Déby's government, eager to finalize a deal, on August 5, 1996, announced Law 96/13 ratifying the bilateral agreement with Cameroon to build a pipeline and Law 96/14 to transport crude petroleum by pipeline to Cameroon. In 1998, there was a reevaluation of the covenant of 1988 that Habré had signed with the oil companies. The revised covenant seemed to tie the Sedigui oil field to the Cameroon oil transport project, effectively eliminating oil production for domestic consumption in Chad, which continued to import oil at high cost from Nigeria (Jaillard, 2007; Djimrabaye, 2005, p. 6; Béguy, 2002).

In November 1999, Elf and Shell abandoned the oil project in Chad in favor of an oil field discovered in Angola with fewer risks and more potential profits. At the time, Exxon remained interested in Chad's oil and sought new partners to share the risk, but the Sedigui part of the project was shelved (Jaillard, 2007; Djimrabaye, 2005, p. 7). On November 16, 1999, the government of Chad accused France of engineering Elf's departure. Déby's regime mobilized the population of N'Djaména to protest Elf's withdrawal from the oil consortium, and protesters burned the French flag (Djimrabaye, 2005, p. 7; Béguy, 2002).

On April 3, 2000, there was a reconstitution of the oil consortium, with a 65 percent share held by American companies — Exxon/Mobil (40 percent) and Chevron (25 percent) — and a 35 percent share held by Petronas, a Malaysian company. On June 6, 2000, the administrative council of the World Bank approved the Chadian oil project, on the condition that there be financial transparency. Also, some portion of the oil revenues would have to be used to reduce poverty in Chad.

On October 18, 2000, an official ceremony marked the beginning of the installation of the Chad-Cameroon pipeline. The ceremony was organized in Komé and presided over by the two presidents, Idriss Déby of Chad and Paul Bya of Cameroon (Jaillard, 2007). See Appendix C for speeches of the officials present at the ceremony in Komé (Esso, 2000–2003). Two days later a similar ceremony was organized in Kribi, Cameroon.

The distinguished speakers at the pipeline ceremony in Komé trilled that Chad's oil would bring joy and prosperity to the country. Joy perhaps came briefly to the inner circle and extended family and tribe of Idriss Déby, who constitute less than 1 percent of the country's population. Déby has worked patiently to obtain the oil wealth of Chad, whether for himself or the country. First there were the many years of negotiations between his regime and the oil companies. Then he had to work through several years of negotiation among the oil companies to determine how to finance the operation. After that came discussions between his government and the World Bank. Finally his administration was to receive millions of dollars from investors around the world, and the World Bank was about to close the deal (Prunier, 2007).

Opposition from Human Rights Groups

Déby was buoyed by support from France and world investors but then confounded by hostility from non-governmental organizations, civil rights organizations (e.g., Human Rights Watch), religious parties, and opposition political parties in Chad. Swayed by their arguments, the World Bank reconsidered its earlier support and was about to refuse to finance the project requested by Déby's regime. Leading the opposition were Yorongar Ngarlejy, the deputy Federalist of Beboudja; Dobian Assingar, the president of a human rights organization in Chad, the Ligue tchadienne des droits de l'Homme; and Delphine Djiraïbé, the leader of the Chadian Association for the Promotion and Defense of Human Rights. They said they represented the people of Chad in opposition to Déby's agreement with the World Bank and oil companies to extract the oil. In a meeting with World Bank officials in Washington, D.C., Assingar and Djiraïbé demanded that, before receiving World Bank financing for his oil project, Déby cease his crimes against humanity, guarantee basic human rights for the citizens, and pledge to utilize oil profits for the benefit of Chadians (Jaillard, 2007; Aubert et al., 1998).

Yorongar, who had long been suspicious of Déby's motivations, explained in a letter to World Bank officials the actions of "the tyrant" and the horrendous oppression of Déby's regime. Yorongar went further, predicting the consequences of financing an oil project in Chad so long as Déby held power: extracting the oil and piping it out of the country would not decrease poverty in Chad but rather would increase it — and increase also the regime's bloody reprisals against the peoples of southern Chad. The NGOs in Chad confirmed Yorongar's contentions in their own testimony to the World Bank (Aubert et al., 1998).

Serge Michailof was the negotiator designated by the World Bank to work out an agreement on the Chad-Cameroon pipeline project. In a documentary (*A qui profite*, 2007), Michailof reported that in late 1990 an unnamed U.S. Treasury official called him into his office during negotiations on the project. The official was interested in the World Bank's financing of oil projects in Chad but was concerned about charges of corruption and human rights violations against Déby. The U.S. official asked Michailof to guarantee that if the World Bank financed the project, oil revenues would be used to help reduce poverty in Chad. He insisted that Déby's regime not receive World Bank funds unless procedures were in place to make the funds transparent so that the World Bank could keep track of how the money was used (Jaillard, 2007).

Michailof responded that many fail-safe procedures would be in place to keep World Bank investment money from falling into the wrong hands. First, the legislature of Chad had passed laws requiring financial transparency for all oil revenues, and that legislation had been signed into law by Déby himself. In addition, a watchdog body had been created: the Collège de Contrôle et de Surveillance des Ressources Pétrolières. This oversight group was made up of civilians, human rights workers, and others who would on principle watch carefully to make sure oil funds were used at least in part to benefit the people of Chad. In addition, the World Bank itself, though impressed by these initiatives from Chad, would of course maintain full control of the funds. Revenue was to be held in escrow at a British bank. Ten percent of all incoming revenue would be deposited in an account in a secure European bank to be used for "the new generation"—saved until the oil ran out and a future generation needed to find another source of energy. Another 5 percent of the revenues would go directly back to the region from which the oil was taken, since the land belonged to the people of the prefecture known then as Oriental Logone. The rest of the petroleum profits would go to alleviate misery in all regions of Chad. These moneys would be used, for instance, to provide potable water, build hospitals, and construct much-needed infrastructure (Jaillard, 2007). The president of the World Bank, James D. Wolfensohn, was eager to use Chad as a model for similar projects to be undertaken in Africa. Africa would at last be developed, not colonized or corrupted as in the past (Uriz, 2002; Jaillard, 2007).

Michailof was undoubtedly sincere in his trust of these measures to control the flow of oil payments. Unfortunately his faith was misguided. As is now clear, the U.S. Treasury official who sought Michailof's guarantee was right to be suspicious, probably from experience in other countries that oil wealth tends to go not to the people but into the private Swiss bank accounts of the country's dictator and his inner circle (Jaillard, 2007).

World Bank Doubts About Further Development

After a thorough investigation into the complaints of NGOs, human rights groups, and others, the World Bank was having second thoughts about financing oil projects in Chad. In 1999, the World Bank voted not to fund further projects in the country after the initial Chad-Cameroon pipeline. A dissenting minority argued that it was possible to enrich the people of a poor region by helping them to sell their natural resources. The majority opinion of the World Bank, however, took the position that oil and development do not mix (Jaillard, 2007).

This is not to say that only Déby stood to benefit from the pipeline. The oil companies in Chad stood to gain magnificently because they had successfully negotiated a contract with Déby that gave them 50 percent of the revenue from Chadian oil. Only in Chad do petroleum companies receive so great a portion of the profits. According to former Elf Aquitaine official Loïk LeFloch-Prigent (in Jaillard, 2007), oil companies receive between 5 percent and 15 percent of the revenue elsewhere in the world, with 85 to 95 percent going to the country of origin. Why would Déby be so generous to the oil companies and sign a contract so unfavorable to Chad's interests? One opinion is that he needed the deal and the oil wealth to retain power, and therefore was willing to "marry the devil," as the Chadians say, and obtain whatever contract he could.

When various Chadian civil rights and human rights organizations made an appointment to meet in Washington, D.C., with World Bank president Wolfensohn to argue against financing the pipeline project, representatives of Déby's government insisted on attending the meeting. Delphine Djiraïbé, who would later win a 2004 Robert Kennedy Human Rights Award for her advocacy for "social, economic, and environmental rights in Chad and for World Bank accountability and corporate responsibility in the disbursement of oil revenues" (Robert F. Kennedy Memorial, 2007), was part of the delegation of NGO leaders who had planned the meeting with the World Bank to offer evidence about Déby's human rights record. Djiraïbé gave permission for the Chadian government's delegation to be present at the meeting (Jaillard, 2007).

Delphine Djiraïbé's comments in a later documentary on oil development in Chad (Jaillard, 2007) reveal how Déby was beginning to manipulate the World Bank: "We were not at all incovenienced that the delegation of [Déby's] government came and 'assisted' in the meeting that we had requested," Djiraïbé reported. "But when that delegation arrived, the meeting took on a completely different aspect, one that we could not understand. Attacks, insults, and so on came from this delegation built of all pieces" (Jaillard, 2007). By this last phrase, Ms. Djiraïbé implied that Déby's delegation had been hastily cobbled together with people who would parrot the government's line. She also implied that the delegation was less than trustworthy. In fact, the delegation had been constructed of representatives from contrived and non-existent societies and organizations, a pretense to convince the World Bank that there was broad support across Chad for the oil pipeline. It has been said by some (Jaillard, 2007) that Déby gave out envelopes to individuals to serve on the delegation and that these envelopes contained not only instructions and "talking points" but also money.

Frustrated that the World Bank was apparently planning to refuse to finance the oil project in Chad primarily because his regime was known as one of the several "criminal regimes" in Africa, Déby came to Washington in person to meet the authorities of the World Bank. To judge from a news tape of the discussions (Jaillard, 2007), Déby grew increasingly distraught during the meeting. He and his delegation left the meeting room looking abject.

Déby returned to Chad without World Bank funding for the Chad-Cameroon pipeline project, so he needed to change strategies. According to the documentary on Chad's oil development (Jaillard, 2007), Déby "brought into play billions of dollars" and was able to sway the opinions of enough decision makers in the World Bank to receive funding within a few months. What Déby did or said to achieve his goals is unknown. "It is surprising to think the World Bank would put so much trust in a government that came to power on the back of a violent coup d'état and for the first six years in existence exhibited many of the same repressive patterns that have plagued the country since 1965. The word of the current president was all the assurance the international community had, and that sufficed" (Cash, 2009, p. 13). What is known is that French president Jacques Chirac traveled to Washington in March 1999 and met quietly with World Bank leaders, including the president of the World Bank, and immediately the loan to Déby was approved (Verschave, 2007, p. 160).

World Bank Approves Pipeline Loan

A World Bank news release (ESSOChad, 2000; see Appendix D) announced the loan in celebratory tones:

> The Board of World Bank Group today overwhelmingly agreed to support the Chad-Cameroon Petroleum Development and Pipeline Project — an unprecedented framework to transform oil wealth into direct benefits for the poor, the vulnerable and the environment. In addition to the financing, the package of support includes a first-of-its-kind program to direct new revenues to support economic and social development programs in Chad, which is one of the world's poorest countries.

The report intimated that President Wolfensohn still harbored misgivings yet had faith that Déby would use World Bank funding to benefit the people of Chad:

> The Chad-Cameroon project reflects an unprecedented collaborative effort [among] the Bank Group, the consortium of private companies and the two governments. While some may still have doubts, I believe that the hard work of specialists from the Bank Group, the private companies and the two countries, combined with the strong participation of civil society within Chad and Cameroon and around the world, have made this a better, stronger project. The real challenge is about to begin. We intend to pursue it, with our partners, with the same openness and thoroughness we have brought to the process so far. (EssoChad, June 6, 2000)

Oil for Guns

Unfortunately, neither openness nor thoroughness seems to have been brought to the process, and the people of Chad are poorer than before. How did this happen? Instead of using the first $25-million oil bonus to pay government employees who had not received their salaries for many months, or to relieve starvation, Déby used the entire fund to buy two helicopters, several tanks, many weapons, and other military equipment. Déby defended these purchases as necessary for defense of the country and its oil fields from outside aggression. In fact, however, he used his new military power to support rebellion in Darfur. The small arms were given to the rebellion of Darfur against the regime of al-Bashir in Khartoum, Sudan. The two helicopters were taken to Faya Largeau to shell the anti–Déby rebels of Youssouf Togoïmi. Unfortunately for Déby, the rebels made a surprise raid in Faya and destroyed the two helicopters (Jaillard, 2007; Yorongar, December 3, 2004). The funds intended to alleviate the suffering of Chad had been entirely wasted (Jaillard, 2007; Djimrabaye, 2005, p. 7).

James Wolfensohn, who trusted that the agreements between Déby's regime and the World Bank Group would be honored and that the oil revenues would be strictly accounted for and used only to reduce poverty and sickness in Chad, seems to have realized too late that with many African leaders, signatures on paper do not matter much. Those who had opposed the project — the human rights advocates who had argued that Déby was not to be trusted — seem to have scored the first point (Jaillard, 2007; Toussaint, 2006; Friends of the Earth, 2001). After the World Bank announced its decision, Yorongar, the senator from Beboudja and coordinator of the Federalist parties, was interviewed in France. He explained that he, Djiraïbé, and others had tried their best to reason with Mr. Wolfensohn (Yorongar, 2004). They knew Déby could seem to accept any condition imposed by the World Bank and then disregard it. Yorongar ended by grimly warning that by approving the oil pipeline project, Mr. Wolfensohn and the World Bank would have the blood of Chadians on their conscience (Toussaint, 2006; Aubert et al., 1998).

Meanwhile FIDH (the International Federation for Human Rights) published on their website (www.fidh.org/tchad/chaden.htm) an open letter to Mr. Wolfensohn and other officers of the World Bank Group:

> The fight against poverty — which is your main mandate — should not be dissociated from the establishment of democracy. As you are aware, the Chadian people not only suffer from misery but are also the direct victims of Mr. Déby's government repression. In an area where oil will soon flow, blood continues to be shed. The [T]Chadian National Army (TNA), which

was involved in the fight against the rebellion of Moïse Kétté, has continued to commit grave human rights violations against the population [Madonet 2004].

On behalf of civil society organizations, human rights groups, peasant farmers, and NGOs, Delphine Djiraïbé said, when news of World Bank funding was announced, that she and others had informed the World Bank Group that Déby's government was a disorganized and corrupt regime. She pleaded that the World Bank should delay, to allow the people of Chad to prepare themselves for the work of extracting oil and using the oil wealth wisely. The government, too, should use the time to eliminate its human rights abuses and plan the project carefully, she said, because at that time the government was not yet ready to manage that kind of project. The project should not be implemented until the regime was ready to use the money for the purpose intended (Jaillard, 2007).

There was a call to stop the project until concerns could be addressed. Mr. Dobian Asngar, president of the Chadian League of Human Rights, said that there had been arbitrary arrests, repression, and violence against political opponents in Déby's election and that oil revenues had already been diverted to purchase military arms. "How can the World Bank endorse a project that reinforces the violence of the regime of Idriss Déby?" (Friends of the Earth, 2001).

When informed of Delphine Djiraïbé's request to hold off funding the pipeline until concerns could be addressed, Mr. Wolfensohn retorted that such a delay would not be necessary, nor would it be useful since the poor of Chad would benefit from employment on the pipeline construction project. Wolfensohn's argument was that the waiting of the past ten years had already taken its toll on the people of Chad (Uriz, 2002; Jaillard, 2007).

The World Bank Group hoped that the development of Chad's petroleum reserves would serve as a model for the rest of Africa, even where strong democratic governments were not in place. Unfortunately such optimism was misplaced. In countries like Gabon and the Congo Republic, whose leaders are accused of hiding away their oil revenues in Swiss banks and elsewhere, at least conditions are stable and people have food to eat. In Chad, not only is the country's economy collapsing, but also people are dying of starvation and warfare, despite the fact that their "black gold" is on the international market (Uriz, 2002).

What about the board established to oversee oil revenues in Chad? The Collège de Contrôle et de Surveillance des Ressources Pétrolières (CCSRP), the mission of which is to control oil revenues, was established in 1999 by Chad's parliament to make certain that oil revenues would be used to reduce poverty in Chad (CCSRP, 2007). Unfortunately, the Collège has never been able to control oil revenue. "While the Collège can influence the budgeting process, reject ill-founded expenditures and investigate the execution of projects it approves, ultimately its ability to ensure that oil revenues are used for poverty reduction depends on the willingness of the judiciary to prosecute cases of misuse, fraud or corruption that the Collège may uncover" (Gary & Reisch, 2005, p. 2).

Some members of the Collège who tried to put the law into practice have been threatened with death, and some of them have in fact barely escaped assassination (Jaillard, 2007; Voice of America, 2007). Today the CCSRP exists in name only. One member, Mahamat Ben Barka, ran away and joined the rebellion in the Darfur region of Chad. Another member of the Collège, Dobian Asngar, asserted in a news documentary,

> It is not my pleasure to carry this piece of scrap iron [a pistol] all the time, but if I do not, I will be shot down. So I have to insure my own security. I have said that the law on managing the oil revenue — the law that some people have taken as a model — is no more than stabbing one's sword in the water. A law without application is worthless. Failure of this law is failure not only for CCSRP, but also for the World Bank Group that has given its approval and the countries that voted to allow the World Bank Group to give its agreement for the project [Jaillard, 2007].

A few weeks before James Wolfensohn welcomed his successor, Paul Wolfowitz, to the World Bank Group presidency in 2005, Wolfensohn was interviewed by a French journalist who asked if he had doubts about financing the oil pipeline project in Chad. Wolfensohn responded that although there are always doubts, in this case the risk was low, because the World Bank had signed an agreement with the government of Chad about how the oil revenues would be used to benefit the people.

Oil Makes Chad Poorer

Unfortunately, as in other areas of Africa, the Chad-Cameroon pipeline made the life of local residents more miserable than before and provided an undemocratic ruler with dangerous amounts of wealth (Nguiffo & Breitkopf, 2001). Without financing of the pipeline by the World Bank, Déby would not have had the funds to destabilize Darfur and instigate civil war in the Central African Republic and in Sudan. "Today, the hopes that Chad would manage its new oil wealth have been shattered. The innovative oil revenue management law — designed to ensure transparency and funnel money to health, education and other social needs — was significantly modified in 2006, allowing the government to spend more money on arms and other needs.... Using a state of emergency (in spring 2008), the Government of Chad has suspended even its weakened oil revenue law" (Gary, 2008).

While Déby was actually funding rebels in Darfur and causing ethnic massacres in eastern Chad and western Sudan, he urged the World Bank and the international community to note the troubles along his border. Claiming that he would need to use some of the oil revenues to secure the borders and protect his people from the Janjawiid and other Sudanese mercenaries, Déby ordered attacks on neighboring countries. Revenues that were supposed to remain in the bank for future generations were instead spent to oppress the present one. And funds designated for the people instead empowered Déby's dictatorship (Polgreen, 2005; Prunier, 2007).

In the interval of just one year, Chad received about $500-million USD for oil passing through the Chad-Cameroon pipeline. The entire population of Chad is less than nine million, seven million of whom live on less than one dollar a day (Gary & Reisch, 2005, p. 1). Yet those with government jobs went unpaid for many months at a time and did not receive even their basic salary of $20 to 500 per month. Worse yet, the people of Chad's cities and villages lack electricity, potable water, hospitals, and other necessities (Jaillard, 2007; Djimrabaye, 2005, pp. 7–12). Measured by UN human development indicators, Chad is seventh from the bottom in the world (Human Development Report, 2010). Conditions in Chad now are so dire that, far from benefiting from oil revenue, the people are even more wretched than before. Of course, Déby and his friends seem to be doing well financially.

CHAPTER 6

Deadly Betrayal in the Oil Fields of Sidegui

Déby's intention was to create his own oil company that would build a refinery in N'Djaména to serve the Sidegui oil fields (Nolutshungu, 1996, p. 249). Negotiations between Déby and Esso concerning the oil fields of Sidegui took five or six years. Finally Esso withdrew and left the project to Déby. Serge Michailof, who represented the World Bank in the talks, knew what Déby's intentions were. Michailof said that the World Bank and Esso wanted to work together with Déby on the Sidegui oil project; unfortunately, Déby wanted to work on the project by himself. Royal Roland, Esso's representative in Chad, more diplomatically confirmed what Michailof had said. Roland said they had discussed the oil fields of Sidegui for several years with Déby's regime. At the end of their discussion, Esso preferred to leave the project to the government because it was not likely to produce large profits for the company (Jaillard, 2007).

Déby's Oil Company

Unfettered by outside interference now, Déby could process the oil of Sidegui in his own refinery and for his own profit, since the World Bank and foreign oil companies had no interest in those fields. Unfortunately he did not have enough money at that time, and the oil of Komé/Doba (the fields of Komé, Miandoum, and Bolobo whose development had been funded by the World Bank and Exxon/Mobil) was not yet in the international market to produce sufficient capital. Eager to see himself among the richest African leaders (Madonet, 2004), Déby and longtime ally Adouma Ali Ahmat convinced Acheik Ibn Oumar Yusuf (Assaid Idriss), a member of Sudan's parliament and one of that country's wealthiest men, to be their partner in the refinery project (International Federation for Human Rights, 2004). Acheik came to an agreement with Déby and Adouma. The three men created the Chad Petroleum Company. Acheik invested 40 billion FCFA in the project. Unfortunately, the project was unsuccessful. A Sudanese company did receive a contract to install the pipeline from Sidegui to N'Djaména, but barely a quarter of the pipeline had been installed before a powerful windstorm blew up and destroyed what had been built to that point (Madonet, 2004).

The destruction of the aborted pipeline and refinery of Sidegui-N'Djaména turned the project in another direction. Acheik noticed not only that the construction had been damaged but also that his investment, all 40 billion FCFA, had disappeared. As a CEO of the project, Acheik demanded clarification and certain details on the project so they could change strategy. Apparently, the project was already bankrupt (Madonet, 2004).

Déby Eliminates His Business Partners

Adouma Ali was one of the top 50 military officers and secret agency officers whom Sudanese strongman al-Bashir had given to Déby during the latter's rebellion and fight for the presidency of Chad. Adouma Ali served as a key player on the refinery project and was from the same region of Sudan as Déby and Acheik, the Darfur region. Déby had used him to convince Acheik to provide capital for Déby's Chad Petroleum Company. Perhaps only Déby and Adouma knew what had happened to Acheik's billions (International Federaton for Human Rights, 2004).

During that period, Déby, Adouma, and others stirred up the rebellion in Darfur. And Adouma Ali's name was among the list of 50 military and secret agent officers that al-Bashir wanted back in Sudan. He asked Déby to extradite the men to Sudan for questioning about their involvement in the Darfur rebellion against him (International Federaton for Human Rights, 2004; N'Diékhor, October 5, 2003, p. 3).

Had Déby extradited those 50 men back to Sudan at al-Bashir's request, today we might not have what the world calls the "trouble in Darfur" and the continuing strife in that sub-region of Central Africa. Déby said to the authorities of Sudan that he would send the officers back home, but unfortunately he did not send them back. Al-Bashir's regime seems to have suspected Acheik of supporting the rebellion in Darfur, as well as Adouma, because Acheik was from that region, was related to Déby by marriage, and had led oil-company negotiations with Déby's elder brother and Adouma in Saudi Arabia. Acheik was also a deputy to the parliament of Sudan, however, and needed to be questioned carefully about his loyalties. What happened next is in dispute among Déby's regime, opposition leaders in Chad, and human rights organizations in Chad.

According to official sources, Adouma was due to be returned to Sudan with the other officers, but for some reason he had a falling-out with Acheik and killed him. Acheik died of bullets fired from Adouma's pistol. In retribution for this heinous crime (since Acheik had been an important member of the parliament of Sudan and an advisor to Déby in Chad), Adouma was tried for Achiek's murder and executed in Chad (International Federaton for Human Rights, 2004; N'Diékhor, October 5, 2003, p. 3).

The condemnation of Adouma to death for murder did not follow accepted procedures of Chadian and international law. The International Federation for Human Rights (2004) and Amnesty International strongly condemned the execution:

> Four of those executed in N'Djaména, Mahamat Adam Issa, Adouma Ali Ahmat, Abderamane Hamid Haroun and Moubarack Bakhit Abderamane, were sentenced to death on 25 October 2003. They had been convicted by the Criminal Court in N'Djaména of the murder of a Sudanese Member of Parliament and businessman, Acheik Ibn Oumar Idriss Youssouf, on 25 September 2003. The case was highly sensitive not only because of Acheik Ibni Oumar Idriss Youssouf's status in Sudan, but because he was also reported to be close to family members of Chad's President, Idriss Déby. He was also director of the Chad Petroleum Company.
>
> On 5 November, lawyers and national and international human rights groups, including Amnesty International, expressed concern over reports that President Idriss Déby had denied presidential clemency to the four men named above even though their limited appeals procedure had not been exhausted, and their cessation plea was still pending at the Supreme Court. If upheld, the cessation plea would have sent the case back for retrial.
>
> The executions were carried out despite serious procedural and legal flaws, particularly for the four men executed in N'Djaména. Their executions took place in blatant violation of international human rights treaties, to which Chad is bound, and of Chadian domestic procedures. The convictions of the men appear to have been based on statements extracted under torture. Executions carried out after unfair trials amount to arbitrary executions in violation of the right to life guaranteed in Article 6 of the United Nations International Covenant on Civil and Political Rights (ICCPR) and Article 4 of the African Charter on Human and People's Rights [Amnesty International, 2003, p. 1].

The unnatural hastiness of the capital trials and summary executions naturally raised questions about whether Déby's administration was attempting to silence Adouma for some reason. The International Federation for Human Rights noted that Adouma's relatives hired a lawyer to seek evidence and defend him against the murder charge, but the attorney was never permitted to meet with Adouma, either before or during his trial (International Federaton for Human Rights, 2004).

Some sources claim that it was not Adouma, in fact, who killed Acheik, but rather two presidential guards close to Déby, who acted on orders of Déby. The two murderers were said to be Déby's nephew and a brother-in-law of that nephew. In support of the claim that Acheik was killed by Déby's regime rather than by Adouma, it has been noted that Acheik's driver on the day of his death was assigned to him by Déby. Further, Acheik was living in one of Déby's villas in Farcha at the time of his death (Ngarnim, 2005).

A police officer (*commissaire*), son of Togou Djimé, was an eyewitness to the murder and could have provided useful assistance to the government in its investigation (Ngarnim, 2005). He was nearby when the murderers came to kidnap Acheik. Unfortunately, he was killed immediately after Acheik's death. Why was this *commissaire* killed? Suspicion grew that Déby did not want him to reveal the truth about what had happened to Acheik (Ngarnim, 2005).

A number of sources make convincing arguments that Déby and his internal minister orchestrated the assassination of Acheik and then accused Adouma of having killed him. Adouma could be arrested and quickly sentenced to death for the murder, whether or not he was in fact the murderer (Madonet, 2004; Bénadji, 2003, p. 3).

According to the biweekly national newspaper *N'Djaména Hebdo*, Adouma did not in fact shoot his good friend Acheik. Acheik's killers used a gun and silencer belonging to Adouma, but the operation had been ordered by Déby (Que lumière, 2003; La mort d'Adouma, 2003). Under Déby's regime, killers tend to eliminate high authorities or personalities while the president is traveling outside the country. Once again Déby was in France when Acheik was assassinated and then was in the air returning to Chad on September 25, 2003, when Adouma was arrested by authorities in N'Djaména on the charge of murdering his friend (International Federation for Human Rights, 2004).

Adouma claimed to be innocent of the murder of Acheik and tried to defend himself, but he no longer had authority or power. He was jailed and condemned to death. From his jail cell, once he realized how serious his situation had become, he tried to get in touch with other influential

Zaghawas to reveal to them the truth, but access to communication with others was denied to him. Adouma tried to meet with lawyers so he could reveal to them the truth about the death of Acheik, but he was not permitted to meet with an attorney. Adouma was taken to court on October 25, 2003, tried, and sentenced to death. On November 6, he and others were taken to the racetrack and publicly executed (International Federation for Human Rights, 2004; Amnesty International, 2003).

Why were others executed with Adouma? They seem to have been men already condemned for various crimes elsewhere in Chad, brought to the execution for no clear reason. One explanation has been that since the condemnation, sentencing, and killing of Adouma were so rushed, Chad's Supreme Court did not have time to twist Adouma's "crime" into a terrorist act or other threat to national security. Putting him to death before consideration of all appeals, however, would be perceived as the regime-ordered execution it was. To confuse national and international observers, the justice system in Chad took actions that now are seen as very unjust. Six men who had been sentenced to prison terms for various crimes were gathered from their various prisons to be killed with Adouma. Thus, to keep Adouma's death from particular notice, the authorities killed others with him, creating an egregious multiple murder (Amnesty International, 2003; International Federation for Human Rights, 2004).

The Zaghawa platoon ordered to execute Adouma and the other prisoners took the victims to the racetrack to see their last sun. By mistake, the execution squad included a man named Nelde, who was a southerner rather than an ethnic Zaghawa. Right before the execution, Adouma tried again to shout that it was Déby who had ordered Acheik to be killed. Despite the horrendous torture he had suffered to tear out his tongue, he was still capable of making himself understood. One of the Zaghawas among the fighters in charge of executing the prisoners apparently realized that Nelde comprehended what Adouma was trying to say. He turned his weapon on Nelde, and Nelde dropped to the earth, dead (Madonet, 2004). Family members interviewed by an International Federation for Human Rights mission stated that "Adouma, up till the end, did not believe, because of the privileged relationship which he had long held with the President of Chad, that he was going to be executed. He would therefore have withheld essential information in the hope that the Head of State would grant him clemency. The gendarme wounded by the 'stray bullet' would thus have heard this information from Adouma which had not to be passed on at any cost" (International Federation for Human Rights, 2004).

Thus both Acheik Ibn Oumar and Adouma Ali lost their lives doing business with Déby. The 40 million CFA francs that Acheik had invested in the refinery project and the $20-million USD that he transported in a suitcase from Sudan to Chad, according to Yorongar, had gone to Déby (Madonet, 2004). Six prisoners died by firing squad to cover up the double murder. Nelde, too, was killed because he was not supposed to know the truth about the death of Acheik.

Déby's Ingenious Solution

Although some of the plot twists in this strange case of murder and intrigue seem almost too strange to be true, they are verified by the International Federation for Human Rights (FIDH), which is an international non-governmental organization dedicated to the defense of human rights as defined by the Universal Declaration of Human Rights of 1948. For more than 70 years, the FIDH has undertaken missions in over 100 countries and has experience from more than 1,000 international missions. Their report (number 404) confirms that the deaths of both Acheik and Adouma were part of a devious plot by President Déby. When asked by al-Bashir to return the 50 advisors and make sure they were not inciting the rebels in Darfur against Sudan, Déby tried to continue to support the Darfur rebels against al-Bashir while simultaneously seeming to do al-Bashir a favor by removing Adouma, and at the same time eliminating the need to repay Acheik's Sudanese business investment in the refinery project (N'diékhor, March 31, 2003).

Why did Déby not return al-Bashir's 50 officers? Extraditing the men to Sudan would have weakened Déby's regime. Without the Sudanese mercenaries who protected him, Déby's power would collapse in just a few weeks. But how could Déby stall al-Bashir and his demand for extradition? First, instead of deporting the officers, Déby would put to death a man whom the regime in Sudan had suspected of leading the rebellion in Darfur (Adouma). Al-Bashir would be forced to show his gratitude to Déby and would no longer suspect Déby of fomenting rebellion in Darfur. In addition, Déby would obtain compensation from al-Bashir because Déby arranged the death of a man who wanted to disrupt Sudan (Adouma) and another (Acheik) who might have similar designs and who might be protected from al-Bashir by his political position in Sudan. According to Ngarnim Idriss, a Chado-Sudanese living in Karthoum, the assassinations of Acheik and Adouma netted Déby $17-million USD in reward money from al-Bashir (Ngarnim, 2005).

By killing Acheik and Adouma, Déby would have more influence on the rebellion of Darfur than before. Adouma had been a man of unique leadership and influence in Darfur because of his Zaghawa and Sudanese connections. (Al-Bashir had commissioned him to act as an intelligence officer, to help Déby overthrow the regime of Hissène Habré.) Now Déby could take control of Adouma's men and use them for his personal ends. In Darfur and eastern Chad, the "rebels" were really mercenary soldiers who served in Darfur at Déby's command. They could be moved quickly to N'Djaména if needed there for Déby's security, and also to eastern Chad to put down local rebellions against the president.

Some of these groups of "rebels" in Darfur have now broken with Déby after certain misunderstandings and frustrations. According to them, Déby was and is the source of trouble in the sub-region (Doumnandé, 2006).

CHAPTER 7

Darfur's Troubles Begin with Déby

A number of sources blame Chad's president, Idriss Déby, for the current troubles in Darfur. Julie Flint, an independent journalist, and Alex de Waal, a British writer and researcher on African issues, have written that the beginning of the Darfur rebellion should really be dated to July 21, 2001, when a group of Zaghawa and Fur tribesmen met in Abu Gamra and swore oaths on the Qur'an to work together to defend against government-sponsored attacks on their villages. Financing, transport, and weapons for this league reportedly came from Déby (Flint & De Waal, 2008, pp. 76–79, 85; Tanner & Tubianna, 2007, pp. 12–17).

Déby Blamed for Causing Darfur Crisis

According to Yorongar, a deputy leader of the Federalist Party, an opposition party in Chad, Déby himself created the rebellion in Darfur and officially baptized it in Tiné on December 1, 2002. Tiné is a town divided between Chad and Sudan, much as Jerusalem is divided between Israel and Palestine.

Doumnandé, a Chadian now living in the United States and maintaining a news website, wondered in late 2006 when the world would get around to admitting that, since 2004, Déby has been the prime mover of the Darfur crisis:

> For three years, the world has been ignoring or refusing to confront some of the originators of the war in Darfur, namely General Idriss Déby Itno

of Chad and part of his Zaghawa tribe. Everybody knows that he is behind the rebel groups fighting in Darfur. Everybody knows that he is funding them and providing all the material, military and logistical support to factions like the Justice and Equality Movement [led] by Dr. Khalil Ibrahim or the Sudan Liberation Movement via his older brother Daoussa Déby Itno and General Mahamat Ali Abdallah Nassour. Why this silent complicity with the Chadian regime? Does it come down to oil again? ... General Idriss Déby Itno is ready to sacrifice everybody, including his own populations. According to various reliable sources, General Idriss Déby Itno has even gone as far as acquiring the services of the Janjawiid militias to export the killing fields inside Chad, all to draw the international community to rally to his side [Doumnandé, 2007].

Doumnandé also claims that Déby is guilty of sins of omission and of commission: instead of using millions of U.S. dollars (Chad's first petroleum bonus money from Mondial Bank) to help his hungry people, Déby increased the sufferings of Chadians and the people of Darfur by creating a senseless rebellion in Darfur (Doumnandé, 2006).

Even Herman Cohen, former assistant secretary of state and ambassador for the United States, claims that "the horrendous Darfur disaster" began when Déby, "feeling increasingly isolated ... decided in 2005 to export his internal problems by sending Zaghawa fighters across the border into Darfur to rally their ethnic cousins into an armed rebellion against the government of Sudan," and "the government of Sudan responded with massive force that included genocide and massive refugee flows" (Cohen, 2006).

How can one small man have created so much trouble in Darfur? A number of sources tell us that Idriss Déby has fomented and now fueled the Darfur crisis for his own security and that of his tribe.

The First "Darfur Rebels"

It is generally agreed that the Darfur rebellion was begun by Zaghawas, members of Déby's tribe, to carve a Zaghawa kingdom from Chad and Darfur. How do we know, however, that the rebels' attacks on Sudan had Déby's blessing? According to the leader of a Chadian anti-government movement, Dr. Albissaty Saleh Allazam (Niang, 2006), the Darfur rebel Movement for Justice and Equality (MJE, now led by Dr. Khalil Ibrahim Mahamat) was founded by a Chadian Zaghawa, Tidjani Salim Djerou. Dr. Mahamat was a member of the Islamist Front of Sudan before he became a special advisor to Déby and a member of his inner circle. Ahmed Tagod Lisan, the foreign affairs deputy of MJE, was customs officer of

Chad (that is, one of Déby's closest advisors) who had been a student in Sudan (Niang, 2006). The following leaders of the rebellion in Darfur were all Chadian Zaghawas: Abdul Allah Bunda, Colonel Abdul Allah Abakar (killed in the battle of Abou Guimra), Colonel Djibril, Lieutenant Colonel Saleh Aguid (in charge of MJE's rebel trainees), and Commander Djirdi Abdallah of the Chadian National Army. On April 14, 2004, Lieutenant Colonel Bahraddine Djar Al Nabbi of the Chadian National Army was sent by Déby to Aldjinena — a Chadian town that shares a border with Sudan — to prepare an attack against Sudan. The long list of "rebels" killed by Sudanese soldiers during the first attacks includes members of the Chadian military. Finally, the commander-in-chief of that earlier rebellion in Darfur was Abdallah Abakar Bashar, a former officer in Déby's Republican Guard (Flint & De Waal, 2003, pp. 77–79, 85; Tanner & Tubianna, 2007, pp. 12–17; Allazam, 2006).

It is clear that Idriss Déby planned and ordered the attacks on Sudan to create a Zaghawa area independent of Sudan (Madonet, 2004; Hel-Bongo, 2008; Allazam, 2006). Moreover, the involvement of Chad's military has been continuous. For example, on December 12, 2005, Colonel Mahamat Ali Fakki, a commander of Chadian soldiers in the region of Wadi Hor near Darfur, joined the rebellion in Darfur with at least 150 Chadian soldiers to fight against the Sudanese.

When Sudanese and rebel groups were asked to make peace, the Movement for Liberation of Sudan (MLS) was the one rebel group that eventually signed a peace agreement in 2005, encouraged by the U.S. administration. Minni Arkou Minnawi, the leader of MLS, then traveled to the White House in 2006 and told President George W. Bush, "as long as General Idriss Déby Itno of Chad remains in power, there will be no peace, neither in the Darfur nor in Chad." Until Minni's signing of the peace agreement, he had received much support from Idriss Déby, and it is significant to note that 60 percent of the MLS rebels were members of Zaghawa tribes located in Chad rather than in Sudan (Fisher, 2006). (A photograph of President Bush shaking hands with Minni Arkou Minnawi during their meeting is no longer among the White House photos but is available on Wikipedia and at http://emm.newsexplorer.eu/NewsExplorer/entities/en/71558.html.)

Why would the rebellion be of benefit to Déby? According to Laurent Correau (2006), a French journalist for Radio France International, without the rebels of Sudan — MJE and MLS — the government of Chad would be in serious trouble. In fact, it has been those Zaghawa rebels in Darfur who have kept Déby in power. They helped the Chadian army repel attacks launched by a coalition of Chadian rebels against President Déby in April and December of 2006. Because of the military assistance provided by the Sudanese rebels founded by Déby, the Chadian rebels were not able to take control of Adré. Meanwhile, French forces protected Déby from a flanking rebel attack in N'Djaména (Correau, 2006).

There is other evidence to persuade the world that Déby was the main instigator of the rebellion in Darfur. At the time, it was puzzling that Déby chose to celebrate the 12th anniversary of his coming to power (on December 1, 1990) in the small town of Tiné rather than at the Presidential Palace in the capital. Now it is clear that he wanted to call together all the Zaghawa tribal leaders in Chad and Sudan and would not have been able to convince them to meet at his palace in N'Djaména in western Chad or even in Abéché, nearer to the border. Tiné actually straddles the border between Chad and Sudan. Documents Déby received from the traditional chiefs of Tiné would, if available, probably confirm that Déby sought to rouse up the Zaghawa leaders against the government of Sudan to create their own power center (HelBongo, 2008; Madonet, 2004).

People who are struggling to bring peace in Darfur and the entire sub-region of Central Africa might well start by asking Déby how to understand the fact that most of the founders of the rebellion in Darfur were from Déby's Presidential Guards, special advisors, family, or tribe. Is it credible that those people could have initiated the rebellion in Darfur without the involvement of Déby himself? Many Sudanese and Chadians may be skeptical if Déby denies involvement, but his direct involvement with the rebel movement against Sudan's government has not been demonstrated with hard evidence.

But indirect evidence abounds. According to an article in Chad's national news, the local runway near Goz Beïda, at the border of Sudan in Darfur, had not been used for many years. Déby suddenly renovated the decaying runway and stowed there some military materials purchased in Sierra Leone, right before the rebellion of Darfur. In a country where people do not earn even one dollar per day or have a simple oil lamp to use at night, President Déby spent hundreds of millions of dollars to buy weapons of war (Madonet, 2004).

Further evidence makes Déby's involvement in Darfur likely. It is believed that Déby sent more than 5,000 Sudano-Chadians as mercenary soldiers to overthrow the government of Patassé in the Central African Republic, succeeding on March 15, 2003. Most of these mercenaries were not involved in the fighting. It was their task to gather from the Central African Republic's army bases most of the military and civilian vehicles, weapons, ammunition, food supplies, and other portables and transport them to Darfur to supply the rebel troops there. Other Zaghawas transported goods to Moundou, the economic capital of Chad and a Zaghawa stronghold, where they set up a market for stolen war material (N'Diékhor, April 16, 2003b).

It is a law of physics that every action necessarily provokes a reaction. Déby had taken the Central African Republic rather easily, but by arming his Darfur raiders he was now waking a sleeping lion, al-Bashir, the leader of Sudan. Perhaps Déby began to fear that he himself would be devoured. Step by step Déby had provoked Omar al-Bashir. When Déby started attacking in Darfur and al-Bashir called him on it, Déby lied and said he was not in any way involved. When al-Bashir demanded the return of his advisors and mercenaries, Déby promised to return them to Sudan but then did not. When the Janjawiid (an Arab tribe) and others, oppressed by Déby's mercenaries, fled to Sudan for protection among their tribesmen, al-Bashir at first would not arm them against Chad. Nor at first would he arm the rebel leaders who sought his help to topple Déby. Although al-Bashir may be no saint, he did show remarkable patience and tolerance.

Sudan Reacts Against Déby's "Rebels"

Around noon on March 23, 2003, the area of Tiné just over the Chad border in Sudan was attacked by a group of Zaghawa tribesmen. That group was called the Darfur Liberation Front (DLF) and, it is now known, intended to "liberate" the region from Sudan's political control. The purpose was to create a Zaghawa kingdom straddling the border between Chad and Sudan. Apparently, the rebels swept down from the mountains of Ouaddai, Chad, with at least 17 heavily armed Toyotas. Sudanese forces retreated in surprise but were able to regroup and get reinforcements to help push the rebels out of town five hours later. The DLF pulled back to Chad with at least 11 of their vehicles and many other weapons (N'Diékhor, March 31, 2003).

Three days after that attack, the government of Sudan sent a delegation of eight or more authorities to N'Djaména to clarify that the deadly attack had been launched by rebels coming from Chad. Apparently the authorities of Sudan and Chad discussed the problem of security between the two countries. Among the delegation that President al-Bashir sent from Sudan were Internal Minister Abdérahim Mohamed Hissein, Darfur governor Ibrahim Souleymane, General Manager of National Security Salah Abdallah, Police Director Mohamed Ahmed Bahar; Sub-Director of Military Intelligence Abbas Abdelaziz; Chief of the Sudanese Intelligence Service Abdallah Mohamed Nourene, Chief of Police Communications

7. Darfur's Troubles Begin with Déby

Mohamed Said, and Police Executive Bureau representative Anwar Ahmed Mohamed.

According to the national newspaper, *N'Djaména Hebdo* (N'Diékhor, March 31, 2003), Darfur had been under rebel attacks since October 2002, and at least four Sudanese helicopters had been shot down over Darfur by rebel SAM 7 missiles. This led the news reporter to wonder how a group of 3,000 rebels could have obtained surface-to-air missiles.

The rebel movement in Darfur was tied to President Déby of Chad by family, as well. The DLF movement of rebel forces against Sudan was led by Dr. Diredj, a former minister of Marshal Ibrahim Abbud, president of Sudan from 1958 to 1964. Diredj is from the region of Darfur and has family ties to Idriss Déby. Dr. Diredj is the maternal uncle of a wife of Timane Déby, the older brother of President Déby.

CHAPTER 8

Chad, Sudan and Rebels

Chad, by its location in the heart of Africa, constitutes a crossroads between two power blocs with different visions. The people of the southern region of Chad are predominantly Christians and traditional believers (Animists). The rest of Chad's population, who live in western, northern, and eastern Chad, are predominantly Muslims and pseudo-Muslims. (Where wealth, influence, and even employment depend on religious belief, the religion of the rulers gains followers, if not believers.) If France had not colonized Chad, all the country would have been turned to Islam; Muslim slavers had great influence over early Chad. A door would have been opened for white Arab Muslims to launch—by force of arms or of preaching—the word of Islam to black African Muslims. Although today many white Arabs do not consider black African Muslims to be true Muslims, nevertheless they wish to spread their religion throughout Africa, and Chad under France became a bit of an obstacle to their mission (Mayadi, 1996).

Overthrowing Christian Tombalbaye

According to Sam Nolutshungu (1996), former professor of political science at the University of Rochester, the Republic of Sudan continuously created trouble in Chad before and after Chad's formal "independence" from France in 1960. Chad could be considered a "sovereignty under surveillance" of France and greatly under the influence of external forces (Nolutshungu, 1996, p. 11). Shortly after Chad's election of President Francois Ngarta Tombalbaye, who was Christian, a group of rebels formed the Front de Libération Tchadienne or FLT (the Liberation Front of Chad) and rose in opposition to Tombalbaye's government. The group was founded in Sudan by Ahmed Hassan Musa, an Islamic fundamentalist close to the Muslim Brotherhood. He was a leader of the General Union of the Children of Chad (Union Générale des Fils du Tchad) or UGFT. This was an Islamic traditionalist movement composed of Chadian exiles in Sudan. The adherents of UGFT were recruited primarily among people of the Ouaddaï region in eastern Chad (Nolutshungu, 1996, pp. 58–64).

In the first week of September 1965, Musa was ready to launch his first attack against the regime of President Tombalbaye, who had been supported by France since the late 1950s (and continued to be supported by France until 1970). At the same time he urged a revolution of the people against the government of Chad. Two months later, Musa would have more insurgents from Guéra and, more precisely, the population of Mangalmé. The villagers of Mangalmé revolted against the government early in November 1965 as a result of frustration among the Muslim peasantry with what was taken as government mismanagement and tax collection abuses. The prefect sent by the administration to explain the new taxes to the cattle growers had been murdered by the cattlemen. A deputy of that region and many other local authorities who went to Mangalmé to arrange a solution to the problem were all slain by the villagers of Mangalmé, and then the villagers fled to Sudan to escape reprisal by the government. Although Musa was in Sudan, he was able to reach most of the Muslims in Chad through the political power of Islam. The situation in Mangalmé brought to Musa's FLT even more insurgents (Nolutshungu, 1996, pp. 52–53).

The following year, Musa and Ibrahim Abatcha united their movements. Ibrahim Abatcha was a leader of the movement called Chadian National Union (Union Nationale Tchadienne), UNT. The two movements came together and created a new party known as the National Liberation Front of Chad (Front de Liberation Nationale Tchadienne), or FROLINAT. The movement had a committee of 30 officers, 15 from each group. Abatcha was secretary general. Apparently, though they shared the same goal, leaders of FLT and UNT did not share the same vision. A few months after they merged, FLT and UNT regained their separate autonomies. The FLT movement had its base in Sudan but operated on the border of Sudan and Chad (Nolutshungu, 1996, pp. 58–64).

President Ngarta Tombalbaye needed France's support to remain in power, but several political blunders with France and with his own people weakened his power. France apparently set some of his own French-trained generals against him, and Tombalbaye jailed them. In 1975 President Ngarta Tombalbaye was assassinated by young military officers.

General Maloum Ngakoutou Beïndi, who had been commander-in-chief under Tombalbaye, was released from prison by influence from France. He and his liberators created a party called the High National Military Council (Conseil National Superieur Militaire), the CNSM, which appointed Maloum president of Chad. The CNSM party was eager to bring Christians, Muslims, and others together as one nation. The armies of all rebel movements were invited to the negotiating table. In 1976, the FLT of Musa accepted the outstretched hand offered by the government of Maloum. FLT signed a peace agreement with the new regime (Nolutshungu, 1996, pp. 93, 95–96).

In the extreme north of Chad, Abba Sidick and Goukouni Weddeye had also led a rebellion against the government of Tombalbaye. Tombalbaye had attempted to bring Abba, Goukouni, and other northern insurgents to heel by sending Hissène Habré to make peace, not realizing that Habré would take his resources and join the insurgents. Once Hissène Habré had sided with Goukouni Weddeye, he made a name for himself as a well-educated and powerful leader. (He had studied political science in France.) Habré was appointed by Goukouni to the position of general secretary of the Northern Army Forces (Forces Armées du Nord, FAP), which skirmished with Tombalbaye's army. Goukouni Weddeye, who had only a grade-school education, ceded command of the northern troops to Habré (Rosen, n.d.; Collelo, 1988).

Though Habré and Goukouni agreed that the Christian Tombalbaye needed to be removed from the presidency, they did not agree on many other issues. One problematic question was what to do about Libya. Goukouni, who had established his base of operations in Libya, offered to Libya the strip of northern Chad called Aouzou, which is very rich in uranium and manganese. In return, Libya would help him in several ways, including building some mosques and Islamic schools in Chad. Hissène Habré did not agree with Goukouni that Aouzou should pass into Libya's control. Goukouni was well respected in Borkou Ennedi Tibesti (the territory along the border with Libya) because he was from the family of the hereditary chief of that region. Habré, despite his gift for public speaking and personal charm, did not have enough power to face Goukouni in that region. Habré left Borkou Ennedi Tibesti with about 200 fighters and fled to Sudan (Cornwell, 1999; Henderson, 1984).

During those years, Sudan and Egypt had political problems with Libya. Sudan was eager to have Habré in its territory with his 200 fighters. Habré and his team were allowed to train their rebel troops in Sudan. It was there that Habré apparently fortified his contacts with Sunni Muslims in Sudan and multiplied his connections in Europe (Nolutshungu, 1996, p. 95).

Habré Becomes Prime Minister, Attacks Christians

In 1978, three years after appointing Malloum president of Chad, the High National Military Council was making peace with many rebel groups in Chad and appointed Colonel Alphonse Kotiga to travel to Sudan and negotiate with Habré. After the negotiation, the CNSM offered Habré the post of prime minister. He accepted that position with a hidden agenda. When he had to deal with Europe, Prime Minister Habré made himself a supporter of the entire country of Chad. When he had to deal with Arab Muslims, he portrayed himself as a good Muslim. Even before becoming prime minister, Habré succeeded in convincing Muslim Arabs of his Islamic sincerity and desire to spread Islam throughout Chad.

Naïvely, the High National Military Council did not disarm Habré's fighters. Habré—who had gained his support from the government of Sudan and many other Muslims of Africa and the Middle East—started planning a civil war in the heart of Chad. Because he had skill in public speaking and was one of the best-educated Muslims in the country, he easily convinced Muslims fighters to launch attacks against Christians and Animists across Chad. Habré used his intellectual skills and his rank to convince the Muslim leaders of Chad to take control of the country. In their turn, some of the imams and other Muslim leaders pushed their followers to prepare an attack against Christians and other believers of the South. Those most often targeted were some Sara tribes who thus far had resisted Muslim influence (Nolutshungu, 1996, pp. 106–107).

On February 12, 1979, Habré launched his attack in N'Djaména. Very quickly the civil war spread to many villages and towns in Chad. Nigeria attempted to stop the fighting and brought the opposition leaders together that same year in a first conference at Kano, March 10–14. Representatives of FAN (Forces Amrées du Nord), CNSM, FROLINAT, and the Third Army led by Aboubakar Abderamane met to talk. As a result of the conference, Maloum withdrew from the post of president, and Habré stepped down from the post of prime minister. Maloum went into exile in Nigeria (Nolutshungu, 1996, pp. 124–125). It was after three more peace conferences (Kano II, Lagos I, and Lagos II) that the African Unity Organization (OUA) found a way to reach peace among the factions of rebels. The OUA shifted the meeting out of Chad altogether, to Dougia, Cameroon. It took about two months before OUA reconciled the leaders of rebels.

On March 23, 1979, Goukouni Weddeye was appointed president of Chad. Kamougué Abdelkader was named vice president. Mahamat Acyl became foreign minister. Hissène Habré became minister of defense. The military forces of the various ethnic and tribal groups were not unified, and it was Habré's responsibility to bring those forces together into an army for the government of Chad (Nolutshungu, 1996, p. 133).

Struggles Among the GUNT Leadership

The transitional government was known as the National Union Chadian Government (Gouverment d'Union Nationale de Transition), or GUNT. Unfortunately, Goukouni continued close relationships with Libya and brought Libyan military personnel into the capital to support his power. Despite his influential position in the government, Habré was not able to dissuade Goukouni from seeking "fusion" with Libya. Hissène Habré launched another attack against Goukouni. He had the help of Idriss Déby and Gouara Lassou (and probably Western countries). Goukouni, Kamougué, and Acyl riposted to this attack by Defense Minister Habré, and Habré was forced to flee to Cameroon and then continued to Darfur, Sudan, with Sub-lieutenant Déby and Captain Lassou (Henderson, 1984, pp. 48–74).

Less than two years later, Hissène Habré, Idriss Déby, Idriss Miskine, and Gouara Lassou returned from Darfur, Sudan, with a great force to overthrow GUNT. President Goukouni lost his international support when his intention of combining Chad with Libya became known (Nolutshungu, 1996, pp. 159, 184). France, the United States, and the African Unity Organization (Organisation de l'Unité Africaine, OUA, now known as the African Union, AU) did not salute that idea. They all supported Habré. On June 7, 1982, Hissène Habré seized N'Djaména, and by September he was in control of the entire country and proclaimed himself the president of the Third Republic of Chad (Dumas, 2005).

Idriss Déby was commander-in-chief of Habré's military forces. Only seven years later, this apostle of Habré's returned to Darfur, Sudan, the country of his ancestors, to reorganize and strengthen forces loyal to himself. With the blessing of General Omar al-Bashir, president of Sudan, Déby gathered Sudanese mercenaries, ethnic Zaghawas, and Chadian refugees behind him to return to Chad. In effect, he returned to overthrow a dictatorial regime of which he himself had been one of the pillars.

Al-Bashir of Sudan

Who was this president of Sudan? General Omar Hassan al-Bashir has claimed the presidency of Sudan since June 30, 1989. Al-Bashir received his military training in Egypt and then returned to Sudan, where he was one of the key figures in the government's military assault on black southerners led by John Garang. In 1989, al-Bashir led fellow officers in a military coup d'état against Prime Minister Sadiq al-Mahdi. Not four months after he became president of Sudan, al-Bashir extended his influence beyond Sudan by providing Déby with the mercenaries, Libyan supplies, and logistics he needed to attack Habré's troops that October. (See a biased but insightful description of al-Bashir in *New Internationalist* magazine, 2001). Habré at first laughed at Déby's attacks as mere pirate raids and was able to capture Déby's elder brother and another rebel leader, Hassan Djamous. Habré soon discovered, however, that Déby and al-Bashir were preparing a serious assault. On November 10, 1990, Darfur Sudanese mercenaries and Chadian rebels launched a three-week series of attacks so successful that Habré fled to Senegal via Cameroon and left the country to Déby. Habré is reported to have said, "If Déby wants the power, I leave him the power" (Brody, 2001).

After one year in power, Déby used his Chadian army, including the Sudano-Chadian Darfur forces of his rebel movement, to help al-Bashir fight the Sudanese rebels of John Garang known as the Sudan People's Liberation Army (SPLA) (Aubert, Brana, & Blum 1998).

A young man named Madina, who had served in the Green Commandos (CODOs) in the 1983 civil war in Chad and later served in the Chadian army under Déby, reported to this author in 1994 that two years earlier he and other government troops were ordered to attack the SPLA. He said that the Sudanese army and Chadian forces gathered in Sudanese territory and launched a huge offensive against the rebels. He added that they seized many towns and villages controlled by SPLA in the southern areas of Sudan (now South Sudan) and killed hundreds of civilians. Madina estimated that thousands of residents of southern Sudan ran away, presumably becoming refugees in neighboring countries like the Central African Republic, the Democratic Republic of Congo, Ethiopia, and Uganda.

Déby's Troubled Relationship with al-Bashir

While Déby sent Chadian forces to help al-Bashir fight against John Garang and the SPLA of south Sudan, the other Zaghawas were killing the people of Chad, destroying their towns, and taking their goods to Darfur. These were tragic days for the people of Chad, because there was no rest, no peace, and no justice for them. Déby maintained a strong relationship with Sudan for more than ten years before distancing himself personally in 2001. The political break did not occur until 2004 (Madina, 1994).

Why did Déby turn his back on al-Bashir, the man who had helped him achieve influence, wealth, and political power? Was it because the Janjawiid attacked Chad, and Déby sought to defend his people? There is little evidence for this argument.

Did Déby suddenly turn against al-Bashir because Déby had established a business relationship with Ibn Oumar Acheik Yusuf, a wealthy Sudanese deputy from western Sudan? That relationship is likely to have rankled al-Bashir. The businessman was interested in developing Chad's oil fields and building refineries in Chad. This project would perhaps devalue Sudanese oil, upset al-Bashir's patron-client relationship with Déby, and change the balance of political power in the heart of Africa.

Most likely, the Zaghawa fighters in Deby's own troops forced him to take direct action in Darfur. The leader of the February 2003 Darfur rebellion against Sudan was a Chadian Zaghawa named Abbaka; both before and after his death in 2004 there had been disagreement among the Chadian and Sudanese Zaghawas about whether to support the rebellion, and Déby initially helped out his friends in Sudan by seeming to quash the insurgency. When the Zaghawas in the Chadian National Army revolted in May 2005, Deby had to fill top military positions with Zaghawas known to support the cause Abbaka had initiated in Darfur (Prunier, March 5, 2008).

These changes led to Chad's switching allegiance and supporting the rebels in Darfur, which provoked a reaction from Khartoum in late 2005. Although it is not clear what issue or event caused the rift between al-Bashir and Déby in 2001— after more than ten years of strong and warm relationships between the two men — the repercussions have been staggering. One outcome has been the war in Darfur.

CHAPTER 9

A Leader in Deception and Corruption

How bad is Déby's government? According to opposition leaders quoted in Daoud (2008), this is a "régime génocidaire, dictatorial et mafieux"—a genocidal, dictatorial, and Mafia-esque regime. *La revue AfriquEducation* refers to Idriss Déby this way: "*C'est connu, excelle beaucoup dans le faux*" (It is known, he excels in many forms of deception) (AfriquEducation, 2006). Xavier Verschave, a critic of continued French control of former French colonies in Africa, calls him "Déby, le mal choisi," the evil chosen [by France] (Verschave, 2000, p. 153).

Because of the poverty of its people, Chad is not well known in the world despite its rich resources, but those who knew the country in former days respected it well. At the time of its liberation from direct French colonial rule, Chadians had a reputation for honest dealings with others. Social life in the country is characterized by generosity, kindness, and respect for neighbors, be they Christian, Muslim, or Animist. The people of the South are agricultural and therefore would seem to need peace as a prerequisite for making a living. In the 1980s, the army of Chad was listed as the 20th most powerful military force in the world. This was when the United States supplied Hissène Habré with Stinger missiles to drive Muammar Khadafi of Libya from the mineral-rich Aouzou region of northern Chad, France supplied MILAN anti-tank guided missiles, and the Chadian army picked up the modern equipment left behind by fleeing Libyan troops (Reuters, 1987). Today, unfortunately, Chad is famous — that is, notorious — for corruption, as documented by a letter to Secretary of State Condoleeza Rice by Senators Feingold, Russell, Landrieu, Lieberman, Leahy, and Dodd (Feingold et al., 2008).

Despite these incidents and others like them, France and many international institutions and organizations continued to favor Déby and his regime. What they did not realize then was that these crimes of Déby's — not only counterfeiting but drug deals and military involvement in neighboring countries — would shape the politics of the region and cause a human rights crisis across several national borders (AfriquEducation, 2006).

Harsh criticism of President Déby was offered by François-Xavier Verschave, an expert on Franco-African relations who passed away in 2005. In his book *Silence Noir (Black Silence)*, he accused Idriss Déby (Chad), Sasou Nguesso (Republic of Congo), and Oumar Bongo (Gabon) of torture, murder, drug crimes, and national and international financial crimes. He made these three men the main characters of his book and thereby informed the international community and especially the people of France of the heinous criminals kept in power not by the will of their peoples but by French military forces.

Despite the honors shown to President Déby at the Komé oil field ceremonies, within a few months of his taking power, Déby was known to be an embezzler and the leader of a corrupt regime, a ruthless dictator, a counterfeiter of national and international currencies, a seller of drugs, and a destabilizing intriguer in the heart of Africa. Vershave (2000), who makes this claim, cites newspapers in Chad, the *N'Djaména Hebdo* (August 27, 1998); in Niger, *Le Citoyen (Niamey)* (September 22, 1998); as well as across France, *La Lettre du Continent* (September 247, 1998), *Le Parisien* (September 30, 1998), and *Le Monde* (June 28, 1999). Despite certain knowledge of all Déby's "qualifications," the international institutions, oil companies, and foreign presidents supported his policies. Maybe they had hope that the regime of Déby would one day change, if guided by the international community and the World Bank. Unfortunately, to date there is no sign of positive change or reform. Perhaps this is because Déby surrounds himself with yes-men: in Chad only the members of the uneducated Zaghawa tribe and their allies hold positions in the administration or rank in the Chadian military (Kebzabo, 2005).

Election Fraud

According to informants both in and out of Chad, there have been numerous irregularities in all recent Chadian elections. According to a critical International Crisis Group report, "The 1996 and 1997 elections were marred by fraud; those of 2001 and 2002 were farcical" (June 1,

2006). Human rights activists, opposition leaders, and religious leaders have been arrested and tortured or killed because they have refused to support these irregularities (Bangui-Rombaye, 1999; Afrique Express, 2001; ARDHD, 2001; Yorongar, 2006).

The 1996 Elections in Chad. In 1996, two top members of the Independent National Electoral Commission resigned from their posts in frustration. Archbishop Mathias Ngartéri and prime minister and former vice president of the National Sovereign Conference, Youssouf Saleh Abbas, both members of Commission électorale nationale indépendante (CENI), left the Commission because of fraud, they said. It was their opinion that the election had been manipulated by Jérôme Grand d'Esnon, a French specialist with expertise in fraudulent elections in Africa, and other supporters of Déby's party, the MPS (Billets D'Afrique, 1996; Bangui-Rombaye, 1999; Yorongar, 2006). Ngartéri was then arrested by Déby's regime and tortured in October 1997. Abbas was lucky enough to escape arrest and reach France (Yorongar, 2006).

Antoine Bangui-Rombaye (1999) described in *Tchad: Élections Sous Contrôle* how French officials, Elf Oil Corporation, and Déby manipulated the 1996 and 1997 elections (PressAfrique, 1990–2004; Amnesty International, 1997). According to Bangui-Rombaye, France sent special agents to Chad to manipulate the elections. Documentation is provided by a letter written by French agents at the French embassy in Chad on behalf of the European Union to get more power and to use all means possible to give victories to Déby in 1996 and 1997.

The 1996 Election Outside the Country. African elections in foreign countries turn in favor of those in power. It was in 1996 that Chad, for the first time after 35 years of civil war, organized a general referendum and held legislative and presidential elections. Hopes were high.

In Nigeria, where I resided at that time, the Chadian census and presidential election were organized by a Commission Électorale Nationale Independante, also known as the Independent National Election Commission (INEC). Among the individuals selected to serve on INEC, the most educated had high school degrees, and half of the group had not finished elementary school. Of the students and other educated individuals who presented their résumés to represent the INEC in Nigeria, only one of them was selected, probably because he was a member of the president's political party.

In March 1996, the sub-group of INEC and representatives of political parties started registering Chadians living in Nigeria. I was a teenager, the only person representing the opposition on behalf of the Federalist coalition parties. Colonels Hamdan and Moussa, attached to the Chad embassy in

Nigeria, represented the presidential coalition on behalf of the Patriotic Movement of Salvation (Mouvement Patriotic du Salut, or MPS), Déby's party.

The registration period was to last one month. During the first week of the job, Hamdan argued that any person who spoke one of Chad's dialects could be registered to vote if one or two people vouched that he or she was Chadian. I argued that we could not change the rules of the constitution and INEC by ourselves in Lagos, lest we register more people than the entire population of Chad. Hamdan eventually agreed and next suggested that if this were the case, we could restrict acceptable dialects to Sara and local Arabic. But, he added, any Chadian that was not able to speak one of the two main languages but spoke Haousa because he was born in Nigeria should be registered too. Otherwise, we would leave out many people. In the presence of voters and INEC's representatives, I explained again the importance of following the rules of the constitution and INEC.

Moussa was the security guard and representative of MPS in Lagos. He received a portion of the money that his party sent for the campaign in Nigeria and used those funds to bribe potential voters or pay for the transportation of Chadians or anybody from neighboring countries like Nigeria, Niger, or Cameroon who wanted to vote for Déby. The first week was tough for Hamdan, Moussa, and me, because I opposed their strategy of finding foreign people to vote for their party.

As the representatives of MPS were thus thwarted from registering foreigners as Chadians, Hamdan started wearing his pistol on his hip on the fourth day of registration, perhaps to intimidate me. A few days later, two representatives of political parties for the West Africa region came to Lagos to meet with the representatives of political parties that were helping voters to register for the election. Because in Chad more than 95 percent of political parties are opposition leaders during the day and MPS at night, the two representatives were present only to support MPS during the election of 1996. Hamdan met with them, and then they came out with a quickly crafted local rule that the first-position representative of each political party would not receive the daily 5,000 CFA franc allowance, about $10 USD. The other party representatives would qualify for the daily allowance. Because I was the only representative for the Federalists, this was just a way to eliminate any payment to me, but I chose to remain in my position even without pay.

Hamdan was furious, but there was nothing else the party representatives could do. Hamdan and I worked together like dog and cat until we finished the voter registration drive in Lagos. But for other regions in

Nigeria, representatives of MPS registered however they liked and probably without much resistance.

When the day of the presidential election came, I was ashamed to see the way the election was held in Lagos. Moussa and Youssouf exchanged CFA francs for naira, the official currency of Nigeria, not far from the polling place. Besides Youssouf and Moussa, there were other MPS members who stood at the gate of the Chadian embassy to instruct voters to vote for Déby's logo. The instruction was that any voter who put Déby's logo in the urn and came out with the symbols of the other fourteen candidates to present to Youssouf and Moussa would be rewarded with 100 to 200 nairas, about $1 to $2 USD. The strategy worked for MPS despite its illegality according to the constitution and the rules of INEC. I complained to the authorities of the embassy and INEC representatives, but no one wanted to listen to me on election day.

Mr. Ngak, a Chadian from the region of Kassiré Coumakoï then residing in Lagos, and El-hadj, a Kanembou from the region of Lol Mahamat Choua, helped me by providing a small amount of naira to take a taxi and find television journalists to document these irregularities. Unfortunately we were not successful. We were told that we had to inform them at least 24 hours before the election if we wanted journalists to cover the event.

At the end of voting, I refused to approve the election, because it did not conform to the texts of Chad's constitution or INEC rules. When pressured to sign, I escaped from the embassy. Ambassador Tahir, when informed that I refused to approve the election, was also frustrated. He was from Ouaddaï and may have been afraid that his comrades of the MPS would accuse him of colluding with me because of the crimes against humanity that Déby had committed there in 1994. He really needed my signature on those documents before leaving for N'Djaména with the election results.

I searched for a business center in my neighborhood of Lagos to send a copy of my report to the Federalist opposition in Chad so they could take the matter to INEC's headquarters. Unfortunately, the fax was not able to go through because of faltering electric service. At that time there was no cellular telephone service in Chad to communicate with people. Finally, I sent a letter that I hoped the opposition would receive before the election results were announced in three days. Tahir sent five men to take me to the Chadian embassy that night to approve the election.

One of the men had a general idea of where I lived through some of my close friends, and they were able to locate my home in Nigeria. Unfortunately for them, my neighbors did not know me by my real name. Emmanuel and others described me, but none of my neighbors knew me as a

Chadian. Finally the emissaries of Tahir had the idea of asking the address of my friend Jackson Koumandoh. I was indeed at Jackson's house. His house was about 1.5 kilometers from where I lived. It was hot that day and we were outside taking the fresh air. When the emissaries were about 100 meters from Jackson's house, they parked their embassy car and walked toward us. Before Emmanuel and others reached us, Jackson's wife recognized the men by the light of a nearby bar and quickly hid me. The ambassador traveled back to N'Djaména without my signature on the election documents. Someone else probably signed them in my place, but I was clear in my conscience. I also knew that irregularities like those at our polling place gave Déby's party a huge victory in 1996.

The 2001 Election in Chad. Four years later, in the election of 2001, many fraudulent actions were again reported. Children and people who were not registered were allowed to vote in support of Déby. There was no limit on the number of times supporters could vote. Leaders of the MPS, Déby's party, distributed extra voting cards to children, Sudanese, Cameroonians, and many other unqualified persons. Election observers who confronted party leaders were punched by government officers and then beaten by police. The beatings were serious enough that some election observers were hospitalized (ARDHD, 2001).

Judé Nadoumngar's experience in the 2001 elections is illustrative of the treatment of opposition representatives and election observers in Chad. Judé was a representative of the URD political party (Union pour le Renouveau et la Démocratie) as an election observer. It was difficult for opposition leaders of some areas of Chad to send their party representatives to the North because of violence and insecurity. At that time, URD was supported by the majority of the population of Chad. Judé chose to observe elections in a large town in north-central Chad. According to Judé, on election day suddenly representatives of the ruling MPS party insisted that anyone even under the age of 18 could vote, with or without any documentation that they were Chadians or eligible to vote. Judé refused to permit this violation of the constitution and election rules and was threatened for opposing the MPS directives (Afrique Express, 2001).

That evening after the election, the election observers shared a ride to N'Djaména to present their observations to their parties and to the Independent National Electoral Commission. The MPS representatives ordered the driver to stop on the desert road and demanded that all the representatives sign a revised statement in favor of Idriss Déby for their town and the surrounding area. Judé refused. He was thrown out of the vehicle and walked through the wind and cold that night to reach N'Djaména. Later, soldiers came to Judé's house, arrested him, and took him to a jail in N'Djaména, then to Massaget Prison. Were it not for strenuous efforts made by Judé's relatives and his party, human rights organizations would not have learned of his plight and arranged for his release (Nadoumngar, 2009).

Despite all the irregularities against opposition candidates, Yorongar Ngarlejy was reported the winner in the 2001 election. However, he was not permitted to take office. Chadian women who went to the French embassy to protest unfairness against Yorongar were beaten. Grenades were thrown at them by Chadian soldiers. Yorongar and five other candidates were arrested by soldiers and taken to different jails. Under international pressure, Déby released his opponents. According to Yorongar, he was beaten in prison with steel rods. This information was confirmed by a physician in Paris. Many supporters of the opposition candidates were wounded, tortured, or even killed (Afrique Express, 2001).

After the 1996/1997 elections, people said they would not vote next time for Déby. Why should they vote in 2001 for a man who would kill them or give them worthless money and leave them hungry? Unfortunately, in the 2001 presidential election, Déby claimed that he had won the presidency for the second time, and by a wide margin. According to the opposition, Déby had come in at sixth place with less than 10 percent of the vote (Yorongar, 2003; Verschave, 2000, p. 174). Nevertheless, Déby imposed himself and his administration on the people of Chad. The opposition did not have the power to oppose him. When opposition leaders challenged his "victory," Déby had them kidnapped and beaten.

The 2006 Elections in Chad. The most recent presidential elections in Chad, in 2006, were especially problematic. First, Déby had changed the constitution during his previous term so that he could be elected president for life. All potential political leaders, civil societies, senior leaders of Déby's party, and even his relatives had rejected the idea of changing the constitution, but Déby maintained his decision. As a consequence, many Chadians revolted against his regime, and today there are more than 15 rebel groups opposing Déby's rule (Mas, April 16, 2006).

CHAPTER 10

A Skeptical Look at "the Usual Suspects"

The Darfur conflict needs to be analyzed from multiple perspectives — economic, economic, religious, and political — to explain so much suffering. Julie Flint and Alex de Waal in their more recent book on Darfur (subtitled "A New History of a Long War," 2008) brilliantly trace economic, religious, and especially political sources of the conflict but focus almost exclusively on Sudan and its government and travails. Because Darfur is a territory of Chad as well as Sudan, the larger sub-region needs to be considered in any analysis of the Darfur crisis. Millions of people now pay the price for disasters created not only by Omar al-Bashir of Sudan but also by Idriss Déby of Chad. We cannot attempt to solve the problem of Darfur without the courage to find the larger cause of the problem. Our explanation must be founded not on what we see happening right now in the desert sands of Darfur but rather on the firm ground of causation miles away.

Today Déby and al-Bashir face serious social and military problems arising from the multiple conflicts of the region, many of which conflicts they themselves created. By their actions in the central sub-region of Africa, Déby and al-Bashir now involve all the world in their problems. The usual economic, religious, and political explanations for the Darfur crisis need a skeptical review here.

Economic Sources of Trouble in Darfur

The rebels of Darfur themselves have claimed economic reasons for the timing of the Zaghawa rebellion. The rebels claimed they sought the attention of Sudan's government to ameliorate their economic plight. This may be so. Indeed, the entire region is far from the oil wells of the White Nile that quench China's thirst for petroleum and enrich the government of Khartoum. Nor does the Darfur region contain the vast mineral wealth and other natural resources of the forests of southern Chad and Sudan. Darfur was poor and under-developed for many years before Déby started sending mercenaries to the region. Now there are plenty of jobs for young men who know how to fight.

The rebels claim that their motivation is economic justice. If the Darfur rebels were truly motivated by pure ideology and shared vision, would they not have taken action earlier, during the time that the rebel SPLA of John Garang was fighting the rulers of Sudan for that same cause? Some rebel groups did seek secession from the Khartoum government to create a separate government in southern, resource-rich Sudan, while others wanted a new government with representation and shared power for all ethnic groups. The inhabitants of Darfur, however, were not involved in these rebel conflicts. Or, rather, they participated in John Garang's rebellion by fighting not with the rebels but with the regime in Khartoum. If the Zaghawa rebels truly sought reform of the Sudanese government, it is odd that they did not align themselves with rebels like John Garang in the civil war fought for more than 20 years to bring justice to the dispossessed in Sudan. One suspects that something or someone else motivated the rebels of Darfur to attack al-Bashir's regime when and where they did.

Religious Sources of Conflict in Darfur

One cause of the current war in the Darfur area of Chad and Sudan is said to be religion, but terms must be defined carefully. The conflict in Darfur has been reported as a massacre of Animists by Muslim Janjawiid supported by the Islamic regime of Sudan. It is an error to misconstrue the religious conflict of Darfur in this way. Journalists with more understanding of the region see that 95 percent of the fighters on both sides of the conflict are Muslim. There is religious conflict in Darfur, but the conflict is not between Islam and Animism but between African Arabs in power and other African tribes out of power; all of them are Muslim (Prunier, February 19, 2008).

As journalist Steve Bloomfield explained in 2007, this is actually a war among people of different cultures within one religion:

> Darfur's four-year-long conflict ... has claimed the lives of at least 200,000 people and forced nearly three million from their homes. What began as a

rebellion by three non–Arab tribes against perceived marginalisation by the Arab-dominated Khartoum government has escalated into a complex multi-layered conflict.... There are Arabs fighting alongside the rebels and Africans siding with the government. Arab tribes are fighting other Arab tribes — some are even fighting themselves. Desertification has increased tensions, between everybody, as tribes fight to gain control over precious water points. If it was ever as simple to describe the conflict as a "genocide" of black Africans by an Arab government — and few analysts in Sudan believe it was — it certainly is not now. Sudan's government is arming any group that is prepared to attack anyone connected with the rebels, be they African or Arab. In some cases they have even armed both sides of the same mini-conflict. It is less about ethnic cleansing and more about power [Bloomfield, 2007, p. 1].

Political Sources of the Darfur Conflict

One wonders why the Arab rulers of Sudan, when they sought to establish an Islamic regime in Chad, failed to help the white Arabs of that country to control the country and instead always supported black Africans in their bid for power. Sudan most strongly backed first Ahmed Hassan Musa, then Hissène Habré, Idriss Déby Itno, and Mahamat Nour, and now al-Bashir's favor has fallen on Mahamat Nouri to lead Chad to Islam. All of these men proclaim the Muslim faith but are black Africans rather than white Arabs (Tchadactuel, 2007).

One reason the leaders of Libya and Sudan have not been successful in placing Arabs in Chad's Presidential Palace may be that the white Arab population of Chad is quite small. Unlike the masses of Arab peoples in Libya, the smaller population of ethnic Arabs in northern Chad is too small to constitute a power bloc.

A second reason for Sudan's support of black Africans in Chad may be Sudan's expectation that an African, once in power in Chad, will remain under the control of his superiors in Sudan. A black African could open the door to Islamification of Chad, to be undertaken under the religious and political leadership of white Arabs (Mayadi, 1996).

A third reason for Sudan and Libya to support black Africans as political leaders in Chad is to conceal somewhat their intentions for turning Chad into an Islamic country. Umbrage might be taken by other world forces to see the large southern, Christian region of Chad oppressed and besieged by Arabs in the north. A black African might conceivably achieve rapprochement between native Africa and Arab doctrine. Of course, such harmony has not been achieved as yet. So far, the men Sudan has supported have been unable to erase completely the Christian and other non–Muslim cultures of Chad (see Survie-France.org; Mayadi, 1996).

Religious, Economic and Political Sources Interwoven

There is a remarkable confluence of religious and political explanations for the genocide in Darfur and the decades of civil war in Sudan. Why, though, did the regime of Sudan bring Déby to power in Chad in the first place? Déby's promise to transform Chad into an Islamic country, spanning the gap between Libya, Sudan, and Nigeria with a strong bridge of support (Mayadi, 1996), has already been explained. Now it remains to understand the political aspects of the question.

The government in Sudan has been struggling for many decades to break through the colonialist wall separating the regions of Africa dominated by Islam (along the Mediterranean coast) from the regions dominated by Christians and Animists (in the middle and south of the continent). Because Chad's territory constitutes that barrier, Sudan with its allies tried to put in power people who could promise to increase Islam's power in Africa. Unfortunately, Sudan has always chosen unwisely. From Ahmed Hassan Musa (founder of the FLT rebellion in Chad) to Mahamat Nour (leader of the ADL rebellion in Chad and now defense minister in Déby's administration), and Mahamat Nouri (former defense minister and ambassador to Saudi Arabia), without forgetting Hissène Habré and Idriss Déby Itno themselves, Sudan has not yet found the right leader to create an Islamic empire over all of Africa, though it has sought the help of Iran, Pakistan, and other fundamentalist regimes (Mayadi, 1996).

Besides the desire to establish an Islamic regime in N'Djaména and foster the development of Arab interests in Chad, al-Bashir apparently wanted to "grow" his new political and financial power by having a protégé in the presidential palace in N'Djaména. In fact, shortly after ascent to power in Chad, Déby seems to have returned the favor by helping al-Bashir against the SPLA rebels of John Garang in southern Sudan. In the process, Déby learned the political strategems he needed to expand his own power beyond Chad: development of oil resources, investment of resulting funds in the military, support of insurrection in neighboring countries, and so on. In the complex political puzzle of Darfur, Déby is now accusing al-Bashir's regime in Sudan of trying to overthrow his government through Darfur rebels, even though al-Bashir's regime brought Déby to power in Chad. Both parties now seem embarrassed to have shared their former patron-client relationship: al-Bashir is sorry to have fostered Déby, and Déby rankles under al-Bashir's aegis (Aubert, Brana, & Blum, 1998; Mayadi, 1996).

Shall we borrow an analysis of the situation provided by William Foltz, professor emeritus of African studies at Yale University–Khartoum? He recognizes the complexities of the current situation. Although it is clear that Déby came to power in the 1990s by means of al-Bashir's military force, "now it's not clear who's backing whom, or when, and under what circumstances" (Voice of America, 2009).

Tribal politics are always as much of a consideration as military strength. President Idriss Déby took the additional name Itno — "an important Zaghawa name [— for the purpose of] emphasizing his Zaghawaness. But here the blood ties come to play, so that you have Sudanese Zaghawa rebelling against the Sudanese government and bringing in their brothers and cousins from Chad to help them out in their battle" (Voice of America, 2009, para. 8). And from what section of Sudan has the struggle been launched? Darfur.

Earlier in this chapter it was explained that the conflict in Darfur is not primarily religious or economic. Nearly all the participants — rebels and rulers on both sides — are Muslim. We must not ignore the fact, however, that this conflict takes place within the larger context of Arab hostility to other religions in Chad and Sudan. When he was prime minister of Chad, before his army captured the presidency, Hissène Habré did attempt to wipe out non–Muslims — especially Christians — in Chad. He used naïve Chadian Muslims to start the attack on his own citizens in N'Djaména on February 12, 1979 (Nolutshungu, 1996, p. 106). That religious war spread over all of Chad and became a civil war between the Muslim North and the Christian South. From then until even after Habré became president in 1982, that war took the lives of at least 100,000 innocents and caused many other losses and griefs as well. (For more details, see Toïngar, 2006).

Hissène Habré and Idriss Déby killed many Christians, primarily intellectuals from the South, but Habré was not able to establish an Islamic regime in Chad before he was replaced in power by Déby. Déby had a strong willingness to accomplish tasks assigned by Sudan. As evidence of his intentions and commitment, when Déby took power as president, he installed in his administration many Muslims from different Arab countries, including even Pakistan and Iran. It seems apparent that these imported ministers were trying to shift Chad's power system from secular to religious and its laws from laic to Sharia. According to Robert Buijtenhuijs, during the National Sovereign Conference, the Imam of N'Djaména wanted Chad to use Sharia in the place of other juridical laws (Mayadi, 1996).

Among the Islamists that Déby put in administrative posts, at least 50 were or are members of the National Islamic Front of Sudan. The names and functions in the government of Chad are listed below for some of these men:

- Adouma Ali (assassinated in 2004 by Idriss Déby) was special advisor to Déby in the area of general investigation. He later became an executive director for the National Society of Road Maintenance (Société Nationale des Entretiens Routiers; SNER).
- Colonel Hassan Hissein is imam of the largest mosque in N'Djaména. His role was to promote Islam in Chad through a variety of means, such as encouraging Chadian Muslims to move from other areas of the country into towns and villages in the South and build mosques and preach the word of Islam. (These men are greatly resented in the South; as armed merchants and traders, they despoil women and girls and force them to prostitute themselves.) By contrast, Colonel Hissein does not allow Christians from the South to go to the northern or eastern sections of the country and promote Christianity.
- Tahir Gassi was special advisor to Déby in the area of political investigation.
- Dr. Ibrahim Mahamat was a special advisor to Déby.
- Engineer Saleh Abdallah Ahmed was special advisor and also executive director of the Advanced Financial Corporation in Chad (Société AFCORP-Tchad).
- Mahamoud Bechir Djama was a member of the Ouma Party and former Sudanese minister of Sadeck Al-Mahdi's irrigation project (Allazam, 2006; Madonet, 2004; Yorongar, 2003, p. 121).

Today with the guidance and support of the Islamists named above, the Muslims in Chad are allowed to install themselves in different towns and villages in the known Christian and Animist areas. These Muslims impose themselves on every aspect of society. People in Christian areas are deprived of their rights. Mosques have been built everywhere, in any place the intruders claimed for them, regardless of previous rights of ownership. Churches as well as the homes of Christians have been burned to the ground (Amnesty International, October 16, 2001). All goods and property of southerners can be taken away from them at any time without any reason. Today many people in the South of Chad are compelled to become Muslims in order to get jobs, food, or any advantage in Déby's political system. Worse yet, not only military personnel but even most of the civilian Muslims carry weapons and terrify the *kirdi* ("filthy ones") who live in the South (Nako, 2003).

In contrast, Christians have no such religious rights. Until recently any Christian who tried to go to the North to preach would be brutally attacked by Muslims. Because Déby is the source of all power in Chad, no authorities in the North would intervene. When a Christian congregation attempted to go en masse to evangelize one town or region in the North for one day, the Muslims refused, apparently with support from the government. Now that Déby is in conflict with his former supporter, Omar al-Bashir, he accuses him of wanting to bring radical Islamic groups into Chad to indoctrinate people. So long as Protestants were forbidden to proselytize in northern Chad, it was difficult for Déby to enlist their support against al-Bashir, so once again Protestants are quietly allowed to send missionaries into some regions of northern Chad for one week per year, and an official amnesty lets missionaries travel in the region for the prescribed time without threat of harm. Missionaries who attempt to visit northern Chad at other times of the year may "disappear." Although such matters are talked of by the people, it is difficult to find reliable sources documenting these events.

Why can Muslims go to the South and impose their religion on everyone but Christians are not allowed to participate in similar activities in the North or even in some central regions of the country? Why is a Zaghawa or any Muslim from the North permitted to kill someone from another tribe—especially a *kirdi*—without punishment? Why is a *kirdi* who accidentally hurts someone with a bicycle or kills someone with a motorcycle ferociously punished with all his family by the Débian legal system? Religious tensions seem to be behind some of the North-South conflicts in Chad but seldom are reported in the press.

The problem of Darfur is thus not only political or economic or religious but a combination of the three. One needs also to look at how they play out in power, justice, and spirit. It is not only the problem of Arab Muslims against African Muslims in the Darfur region of Sudan, but the tragedy of the region may also be the consequence of greed and hatred and ignorance of ordinary people in Darfur, too. Were they wrong to accept goods stolen from Chad and the Central African Republic without asking the source of so many things? Were they misguided to follow blindly and without question the orders of men like Déby? It is hard to argue that either the residents of Darfur or the power regimes of Chad and Sudan can claim virtue and exoneration from blame for so much torture and killing.

Since the war started in Darfur, Déby and al-Bashir have used diplomatic means to accuse each other of causing the commotion. But they have never spoken openly about the pact they signed before al-Bashir escorted Déby to power with his mercenaries and his logistic help. Neither of them wanted to explain the real cause of the war in Darfur and eastern Chad.

Some pundits have reported in the news that the Darfur conflict broke out in 2003 between the Sudanese government and rebels demanding more political representation and a share of the nation's oil revenues, thus giving only political and economic reasons for the troubles. They say, "President Déby initially supported Khartoum against the rebels, even though many of them belonged to his own tribe" (*N'Djaména-Hebdo*, May 2003, p. 3). Those sources may be right, but it would be important for them to look more deeply into the background of President Idriss Déby before claiming only economic causes to the conflict.

Is Déby a man who has honored his word? Can his solemn declarations of non-involvement in Darfur be trusted? After all Déby has done to Pascal Lissouba (deposed president of the Congo Republic), Ange Felix Patassé (deposed president of the Central African Republic), and Omar al-Bashir (current president of Sudan), political observers might be accused of credulity if they trust Déby now. His betrayal of Yorongar le Moiban, Kamougué, Lol Mahamat Choua, Charles Kebzabo and others in Chad might make us doubt. Only if Déby is a truthful man should his assurances be believed that he was supporting al-Bashir during the first war in Darfur. Other evidence leads us to conclude that instead Déby instigated that war (N'Diékhor, March 31, 2003, p. 5).

It may be that Déby thought Sudan would be easy for him and his Sudano-Chadian forces to overthrow. After all, the destruction of the legitimate government of the Central African Republic took but a few weeks to accomplish. Unfortunately for Déby, the reaction of the Sudanese military forces to the Darfur rebellion was devastating. And then Sudan began to support the Chadian opposition leaders who menaced Déby's government. Now Déby claims himself to be the victim of external aggression by the very man who brought him to power (Madonet, 2004) and whose friendship he once greatly appreciated.

In the 1970s, the first president of Chad, François Ngarta Tombalbaye, created a system called "return to the source" or, in French, "*initiation*." This was an attempt to cast off the religions of outsiders, Christianity and Islam, and return to the traditions of the ancestors. In the Sara dialect of southern Chad, it is called "Yondo." Under Ngarta, the system was mandatory, at least for all southerners between the ages of 16 and 50. Those who because of religious conviction refused to mix their Christian or Muslim faith with traditional beliefs were tortured, and others were buried alive. Yorongar le Moiban and General Kamougué Abdel Kader initiated a successful coup d'état on Ngarta in 1975 in part to end this spiritual oppression (Collins, 2007, pp. 54, 58, 60–65).

In the 1980s, the entire region of the South paid the consequences for the actions of Yondo leaders who tortured Christians and even other

Animists. Hissène Habré sent the two brothers, Idriss Déby Itno and Ibrahim Itno of the Zaghawa tribe, accompanied by neighboring Hadjraï to burn the houses, loot the goods, and kill the people of the South. (For more information, see Toïngar, 2006).

Late in the 1980s, members of the Hadjiraï, Zaghawa, and Gorane tribes that Habré had sent to the South to loot and kill paid the price for their inhuman actions in a different way. The goods of southerners that Hadjiraï fighters took home to their region or sold in other regions created negative consequences for them and their families. When Habré next turned his power against his former allies, the Hadjiraï people, it was their houses that were burned and their cattle that were looted by Zaghawa and Gorane fighters. Poor innocents were hunted down and killed, just as they had earlier hunted the Sara people during the years of Black Septembers in Chad (Amnesty International, October 16, 2001; Nolutshungu, 1996, pp. 234, 236).

After the Hadjiraï, it was the Zaghawas' turn to suffer. Idriss Déby Itno's family had attempted a military coup d'état against Hissène Habré. Idriss Déby was lucky enough to escape, but Ibrahim Itno was arrested and tortured for many months before he was killed. When Habré was eventually defeated by Déby's rebels and had to leave Chad, he finally had Ibrahim put to death, and most likely he murdered Hassan Djamous at the same time. Djamous was a famous commander-in-chief of Chadian troops who defeated Libyan forces in 1986. In the last weeks before Déby's military took power from Habré, many Zaghawa were tortured and killed by Habré's followers.

Some Chadians and Sudanese have communicated to the author that they believe in the need for humility now. They believe that it is now necessary to bow down before God and ask forgiveness for evil actions done to all others. Not only is it necessary, they say, to repent of hostility toward their enemies but also, and especially, to repent of evil deeds done to the innocent people of Chad. Through belief that true repentance brings forgiveness, these individuals hope to free their consciences and bring prosperity back into their lives, now blighted by hatred as well as suffering.

Those who have experienced a lifetime of murder and mayhem in Chad now anticipate a bloodbath if Chad continues on its present path. From the reality of what is going on now in Darfur and the sub-region of Central Africa, they now find it obvious that war and hate will not bring peace. No one is perfect in this world, it is argued, so some Chadians hope that one day the regime of al-Bashir will ask forgiveness for having helped Déby to destroy his own country and indeed the entire sub-region of Africa. Sudan helped Déby with logistics, military intelligence, and mercenary fighters to overthrow the government of Hissène Habré. By helping Déby, those Sudanese helped themselves too. They killed hundreds of Chadians and toted their looted goods into Darfur, Sudan (Human Rights Watch, 2007).

The spiritual and moral dimension of events in the sub-region, then, would seem to compel Déby to ask Chadians to forgive him. To bring balance and make some kind of atonement, Déby needs to ask forgiveness for bringing Sudanese into Chad to kill Chadians and plunder their goods. Even more importantly, a repentant Déby would acknowledge the thousands of deaths he himself directed and ordered (Toïngar, 2006; Yorongar, 2003).

Déby appropriated Chadian embassies and public buildings, sold them, and pocketed the money. Déby was chastened when the villas he had built in Darfur from this dirty money were destroyed later by Sudanese forces, but he has not yet achieved humility. For the benefit of Chadians and of Déby himself, Déby would seem to need the forgiveness of the peoples of other countries, as well — including the people of the Congo Republic, the Congo Democratic Republic, and the Central Africa Republic — for ordering his Sudano-Chadian troops and mercenaries into these regions. If Deputy Yorongar, former CAR president Ange Felix Patassé, and former president Pascal Lissouba of the Congo Republic can be believed, many blood-drenched goods were taken from these people to enrich Zaghawas in Darfur and Chad.

CHAPTER 11

Birth of the Janjawiid (Militiamen with Horses)

The eastern region of Chad and western region of Sudan are historically, culturally, socially, and economically tied. People from both sides of the border are linked by marriage, language, and tradition. It is only the longtime natives of the area who can distinguish between the Fur of Chad and the Fur of Sudan — one people divided by the international border. With this problem of conflict between Chad and Sudan, the situation becomes confusing for outsiders trying to differentiate among the different nationalities and tribes living on the international border of Chad, Central African Republic, Libya, and Sudan (Larché, 2007; Dika, 2005). (For a more detailed description of the history of this region and its tribes, see Flint & de Waal, 2003, 2008.)

Many of the Arab tribes in the north of Chad were as victimized by atrocities as the other tribes. During the rule of Hissène Habré, Déby and his fighters looted and killed not only Sara and Hadjiraï people (primarily Christians and Animists who had been forced to convert to Islam) (Nolutshungu, 1996; Toïngar, 2006), but also Arabs in central-eastern Chad, too. Their cattle and livestock were rustled by Zaghawas and Zaghawa allies during the rule of Hissène when Déby was commander-in-chief. Some Arabs were killed by the Zaghawas.

To save their lives, many of the victims of Déby's atrocities ran away from Chad to Sudan Darfur, where there were other Arabs. Déby, who had weakened many other tribes one by one, now wanted to overthrow his boss, Habré. Unfortunately, his coup d'état against Hissène was not successful, and Déby himself had to run away. When he was granted exile in Sudan, he went to Darfur to appease his former victims and negotiate with them. Perhaps naïvely, some of those Arabs, Hadjiraï, and Sara accepted his apologies and agreed to join him to launch attacks on Habré. After an initial military setback, Déby and his Chadian allies and Sudanese mercenaries were successful in their attacks. His army walked into N'Djaména within a month of starting the insurrection.

Déby Creates the Janjawiid

After just ten months in power, Déby reinstituted his divide-and-conquer system of fighting one tribe at a time (the Hadjiraï, then the Sara, followed by the Ouaddaï, and so on) to consolidate his power and eliminate all rivals, including intellectuals, nationalists, potential rebels, and potential soldiers (International Crisis Group, 2009; Nolutshungu, 1996, pp. 250–254; Verschave, 2000, pp. 151–153).

The Arab people in Chad, as Déby's temporary allies, had a chance to enjoy a few years' respite from Déby's raids and to profit from raiding other Chadians on Déby's behalf. These years in the 1990s, when Déby used Chadian Arabs as his personal army, he was crafting them into the Janjawiid, though they were not known by that name until al-Bashir of Sudan started arming them to attack his own victims in Sudan. But then Déby turned against them. This time their cattle and livestock were stolen not only by Chadian Zaghawas but also by Sudanese Zaghawas who were serving Déby in Chad. Many Arab victims of those atrocities — including Younous Ibedou, Mahamat Garfa, Ahmat Mahamat, and Acheik Ibn — escaped to Sudan and other countries.

Besides those Chadian Arabs, there were many other tribes that ran to Sudan's Darfur as refugees of war or political refugees. The government of Sudan, which at that time had a good relationship with Déby, did not allow these political refugees to gather armies against him but instead let them settle in Sudan so long as they kept the peace. Then in December 2002, Déby and his mercenaries of Sudan created a rebel group in Darfur named the Sudanese Liberation Army (SLA) and in early 2003 attacked the airport of El Fashir, in northern Darfur (Madonet, 2004).

Surprised by the rebellion and attacks clearly instigated by their "friend" Déby, the government of Sudan sent a delegation led by the interior minister of Sudan to meet with Chadian authorities, including the interior minister of Chad. Apparently, they received an unreliable agreement from Chad to deal sternly with the militants in Darfur (who by this time were safely back in Chad). Déby may not have thought through the consequences of playing games with al-Bashir of Sudan as he had with Mobutu of Zaire, Laurent Kabila of the Democratic Republic of Congo, Pascal Yusuba of Congo Brazaville, and Ange Felix Patassé of the Central African Republic (N'Diékhor, April 16, 2003b, p. 5).

The Arabs who had been evicted by Déby's Zaghawas from their Chadian rangeland and homes had been waiting for an opportunity to take revenge. They seized al-Bashir's offer, in 2004, to be given arms and horses to attack both Chadian and Sudanese Zaghawas. Those militias were eventually called *Janjawiid*, which literally means "armed militia with horses." They rounded up cattle and other stock from the men who had stolen from them. Anyone who tried to stop them would be killed. Those evicted nomad Arabs may have taken such devastating revenge for many reasons. They took revenge for their stolen cattle and livestock but especially for their loved ones murdered in the attacks by Sudano-Chadian Zaghawas. Helpless against violence before, now the Janjawiid were well armed.

Al-Bashir armed other groups of Chadian rebels too, and activated them against his former friend Déby. Some of the exiles from Chad had been ministers in Déby's government. For example, Abdallah Soubiane had served as interior minister and ambassador to the United States. Ibedou Younous served as education minister, and Mahamat Nouri had been defense minister and ambassador to Saudi Arabia. They now sought revenge against Déby for his treatment of their people. Between the Janjawiid (created initially by Déby to destroy his enemies in Chad) and Déby's new militants, the lives of many innocents in Sudan, the Central African Republic, and Chad have been made truly miserable (Human Rights Watch, 2007). If the Janjawiid were conceived in Sudan, then they were born in Chad.

Yorongar's letters to Prime Minister Moussa Faki (Yorongar, August 19, 2004; November 18, 2004) explain that the inner circle of advisors and ministers around Déby — dominated by Sudanese — had developed a pseudo-history of Chad. They said that the peoples of southern Chad were not in fact genuine aborigines of Chad, the true inhabitants of the land, but that they were immigrants from the Central African Republic and Cameroon. It was the French government, these advisors said, that brought the inhabitants of southern Chad into the country to cultivate the cotton fields for France's benefit and profit. Déby and his inner circle said those immigrants of the Central African Republic and Cameroon could be forced back to the lands of their ancestors through repression, mayhem, or military action. Clearing the South of its native tribes would make the land available for Arabs from the North. (Obviously this "history" of Chad is at variance with more authoritative histories. The northern tribes are the relatively recent occupants of Chad.)

As reported by Nguiffo and Breitkopf (2001), Déby ordered national troops to massacre hundreds of civilians in the Doba region in 1997 and 1998 "for the sake of 'pacifying' the region to make way for oil development. These massacres have never been investigated. The situation worsened again shortly before the [Chad-Cameroon oil pipeline] project was approved, when government officials went to harass, intimidate, arrest and torture inhabitants of the Doba region" (p. 9).

Informed of Déby's plan to destroy the peoples of the South, Yorongar (a senator from southern Chad) exposed it in the two letters written in 2004 to Moussa Faki, Prime Minister of Chad. He revealed Déby's plan to weaken and destroy the people of southern Chad and to transform Chad into an Islamic country. (It was explained in an earlier chapter of this book that both Déby and al-Bashir sought the goal of an Islamic Chad.) The international committees searching for the source of trouble in Darfur believe they have found it in Sudan.

Déby and al-Bashir have lately accused each other of trying to destabilize their respective countries, and they have had some harsh words about each other, yet they have never betrayed their plan to massacre the peoples of southern Chad and Sudan for the purpose of expanding Islam. Chad has operated as a bottleneck that militant Islamists have wanted to break through. Soon, when southern Chad is sufficiently weakened and no longer serves as a barrier of Christian and Animist peoples, they will finally be able to break through to the rest of Africa (Mayadi, 1996).

Déby and his advisors created the Janjawiid in Chad to make that dream successful. Before Déby gained power, many Muslim militias were fighting against each other, some for Hissène Habré and some for Idriss Déby. Immediately after Déby seized power, however, the Islamic forces merged to work together. Whereas earlier the South had been terrorized by Déby's Sudano-Chadian fighters, when he seized power in December 1990, he armed civilians from his tribe and then the nomadic herders (*éleveurs nomads*), who became powerful and untouchable. They seem to have been hired by Déby's inner circle of advisors. The local authorities from the North, such as brigade commanders and commanders of sub-prefects and regions, were used as links between the Janjawiid and their bosses in N'Djaména. (The source of this last information is a March 21, 2004, newsletter from ADES, the Association pour le Dévelopement Économique et Social de Yemi, a Chadian group headquartered in N'Djaména, formed in the late 1990s to slow loss of social and economic development in the country.)

The nomadic herders were armed with semi-automatic weapons and worked in communication and coordination with the local authorities of their areas. As the regime of Déby instructed, they would employ a variety of strategies to remove the southerners from Chad. One approach was to make the life of the farmers very miserable. Chad, with its economy and culture based 80 percent on agriculture, faced serious problems with the regime of Idriss Déby. The Janjawiid brought their cattle to graze in the millet fields of the poor peasants during the rainy season (when the crops were beginning to grow) and again during the harvest season. This destroyed that year's crop almost completely and also the seed for the following year's fields (Madjirangar, 1991; JeuneAfrique, 1994; Konto, 2004; N'Djibo, 2004; Yorongar, December 3, 2004).

Any villager who tried to take action to protect his crop would be shot by arrow or semi-automatic rifle. As the villagers did not know the connection between the Janjawiid and authorities, when someone from a village went to inform the local authorities to come and help them, the request was turned against them (according to ADES, 2004; Konto, 2004; N'Djibo, 2004; Yorongar, December 3, 2004). The authorities would ask the peasant if there had been any fighting between the villagers and Janjawiid. If the peasant said he had not fought anyone and it was only the cattle that were destroying his field, the authorities would demand a high fee to reimburse them for the cost of gasoline they had used to come to his field to investigate. The assumption seemed to be that it was normal and reasonable for the cattle of the Janjawiid to eat the peasants' fields of millet, as young plants or ripe crops. If the peasant reported that there had been fighting, the authorities would inquire further to know if there had been any injured or killed during the dispute. In the case of an injury, the authorities would come but then would charge a high investigation fee against the village or villages. Déby's Janjawiid were not fined.

In the case of a death on either side of the dispute, the entire village or several villages would pay a very high fee for the laborious investigation — and following that would be another attack by the Janjawiid, sometimes with military assistance. If there was even a single death on the Janjawiid side, the villages around would soon be under attack by the Janjawiid and their allies who were fighters from the north (ADES, 2004; Konto, 2004; N'Djibo, 2004; Yorongar, December 3, 2004).

A typical example of this conflict was an event in the village of the author's grandmother documented by the Association pour le Development et l'Action Sociale dela Sous Prefecture de Bédio (ADASS). Now a subprefecture, Bédio was at the time a village led by a chief named Kodadingar, better known as Camou, a well-educated man seeking to provide good governance for his people. One day his men caught an ox that had been stolen from Janjawiid herders and notified the herders of its recapture. Though Camou explained that the thief had not been from his village, the herders said they suspected someone from Bédio of the crime, and that individual might be the same man who murdered their brother sometime earlier, a trumped-up charge. Two days later, they ambushed and beat a villager in "retribution" for their brother's death.

Chief Camou summoned the chief of the Janjawiid herders in that area to bring the herders to the village for judgment, because they had badly injured a native of Bédio for no reason. When the herders met with the village and showed no remorse, the beaten man's elder brother attacked the herders with his fists. Camou stopped the fight and sent the herders back to their mobile village, informing the local brigade commander and the prefect of Bodo about the situation. As it happened, some of the cattle belonged to the commander.

Some days later, the brigade commander and the prefect of Bodo came — the top authorities of the region — and announced that people of Bédio had beaten one of the herders so badly that the man had died from his wounds, another trumped-up charge, according to an ADASS investigation. They ordered Bédio to pay a fine of 5 million FCFA within a few weeks and ordered CotonTchad to make the payment for the villagers' harvested cotton not to the villagers but to the brigade commander's office.

Camou understood the intentions of the authorities and called for help from people of Bédio who had employment in town. If they did not help contribute the amount needed for the fine, the entire sub-prefecture would pay the consequences. It was known that the brigade commander's men and a large group of herders were planning an attack to loot the sub-prefecture if the blood fine were not paid. When the news reached Bédio's people in N'Djaména, they delegated ADASS to plead the case of the people of Bédio to the authorities in the capital. At the same time, ADASS sent its delegation to meet the authorities of Doba and continue to Bédio for the investigation.

The delegation of ADASS met with the authorities and pleaded for their intervention. A man named Joel, one of the officers at Doba who was a native of Bédio, was appointed by his commander to take some soldiers and resolve the dispute in Bédio.

Joel and the ADASS delegation discovered that no murder had been committed and that the commander had schemed to take both the CotonTchad payments and the villagers' cattle. The brigade commander and prefect of Bodo seem to have received messages from their superiors in Doba and N'Djaména to act very carefully, because some diplomats in

N'Djaména had already been informed. The planned attack was called off, and the cotton funds were saved because of Camou's quick action and intervention by Joel and ADASS.

However, Joel would indirectly pay a price for his diplomacy. A few months later, Joel was arrested and brutalized for no apparent reason, and his bodyguards were beaten. When he recovered, Joel was sent to N'Djaména and then to Ouaddaï on military service, probably to face the rebels in eastern Chad. This was another signal to people in the region that under the current regime in Chad only injustice could reign.

For the previous few hundreds of years, the nomadic herders had lived peacefully with the millet farmers, grazing their cattle in the bush. They would arrive in the South after the rainy season as the bush grew rich for grazing. Four herders usually controlled about 50 cattle — one in front to guide them to the grazing, two flanking the sides to keep the strays in order, and one in back to urge on the stragglers. They set up their temporary dwellings two to five kilometers away from any village to protect their cattle from smugglers and also to keep them from doing harm to the fields. From time to time they came to the village to barter milk and cream for the villagers' millet. After the millet harvest, they were often invited to graze their cattle on the harvested fields to clear off the remaining stubble, till the soil with their hooves, and fertilize the fields with their droppings. Just before the rains came from the south, the nomadic herders would move north, grazing their cattle as they traveled to areas of the north where they would not have to endure the rain.

These new Déby-fostered Janjawiid, however, did not return north during the rainy season as the nomadic herders had done during peacetime (i.e., before the 1980s). The Janjawiid built their huts in the peripheral fields surrounding the villages in the South. They destroyed the millet fields of the villagers through complicity with Déby's government, as described by N'Diékhor (September 21, 2003). The people of those villages were always hungry because they could not grow and harvest their crops as they used to.

Some farmers could no longer resist during the rainy season because of starvation. The Janjawiid proposed a deal: the farmers' children would be employed by the Janjawiid to take care of their cattle, and in return the boys' parents would receive something to eat or a small amount of money to buy something to eat so the family could survive until the dry season (ADES, 2004). Villagers who took the risk to give up their children for few months to the Janjawiid to get in return the equivalent of $10 to $15 during the rainy season never saw their young sons or daughters again. Either the Janjawiid moved with the children to a different area, or they simply refused to let the children return to their parents. The parents did not have power to pursue the Janjawiid, who are untouchable because they are protected by Déby's regime (Nako, 2003). Human rights organizations are currently investigating these kidnappings and abductions.

The children were used as slaves in different ways. For domestic work they were responsible for brewing tea, grinding grain, fetching water, looking for dry wood to make fires, and washing clothes and dishes. The young boys and girls were also used to tend the cattle. They were instructed to take the cattle to the millet fields of the village of their parents or neighboring villages. Those Janjawiid — the very ones who had deceived the children's parents — were eager to discover whether the children would deceive them or properly execute their orders (Nako, 2003).

The herdmasters would check the droppings of their cattle. If during the rainy season they discovered only millet leaves in the droppings, the children were fine. They had indeed obeyed orders to destroy a villager's crops. During the dry season if the herdmaster saw only millet seeds in the stools, the children had obeyed orders. If, however, they found other plants or seeds, the poor children were severely punished.

The sufferings of the villagers in southern Chad did not end with the loss of their farm fields or their children. To make the lives of the peasants even more miserable, the Janjawiid, with the complicity of their employers in power in N'Djaména, stole the peasants' ox teams that served as their tractors to plow and cultivate the millet fields. Usually the Janjawiid terrorized the village children who grazed these oxen in the periphery of the village and stole their cattle. Sometimes the children survived the attack and ran quickly home to alert the village. When peasants tried to pursue the Janjawiid to retrieve their cattle, the Janjawiid opened fire on them. Judging from the swift organization of these operations, the Janjawiid were acting in coordination with the military and mercenaries. If the villagers tried to resist, other nomadic herders in the neighboring villages would come to support their comrades. And if the Janjawiid rushed to the place where there were fighters, they got reinforcements from them, too (Yorongar, August 19, 2004).

Sometimes the herders launched an attack on a village or several villages at a prearranged time. They killed some unlucky villagers. (Other villagers were able to escape in time to avoid death.) That gave the Janjawiid an opportunity to run away with all the cattle of the village (ADES, 2004; Konto, 2004; N'Djibo, 2004; Yorongar, December 3, 2004).

The Janjawiid and their protectors created an entire international economy based on cattle stolen from the villages of southern Chad. The first group of Janjawiid took the cattle to the second group, usually fighters in the employ of the government's forces. These fighters crossed the border from Chad into the Central African Republic. The cattle might be sold there or herded all the way to Congo Brazaville, where they could be sold at an even higher price. Written documentation is lacking, but these facts can be supported by interviewing the troops involved and their leader, Abdoulaye Miskine, also known as General Koumtamadji. President Patassé himself of the Central African Republic could corroborate. The practice continues, as mentioned in *Revue de la Presse Internationale*'s report on human rights to the United Nations (Gagnon, March 19, 2008). Some Chadians said one of the coordinators of these actions was a former defense minister of Déby. The former regime of Ange Felix Patassé in the Central African Republic (deposed by Déby's forces in March 2003) would be in a good position to comment on these actions because, during the years 2001 and 2002, his army many times exchanged gunfire with the Janjawiid of Chad. Most of them were armed men on horseback who tried to cross his country illegally to sell their stolen cattle or take them through to the Congo Republic.

Déby Strengthens the Janjawiid in Chad

According to Ngarelnan Ndolé, canton chief of Yomi in Moyen Chari in southern Chad, his canton has been victimized by Janjawiid attacks since the 1990s. He stated to officials that not only were his villages and their millet fields devastated by the cattle of the Janjawiid, but Janjawiid stole their ox teams, too. There was no way to face the marauders because they were armed with automatic weapons. He and his villagers complained about their sufferings, but the local authorities refused to help them (ADES, 2004; Konto, 2004; N'Djibo, 2004; Yorongar, December 3, 2004).

The victimization continues in Moyen Chari, in the section now known as Mandoul. On March 21, 2004, more than 100 Janjawiid living not far from the village of Maïbogo launched a deadly attack on that village at around five o'clock in the morning. According to ADES, it was a deadly attack made by Janjawiid fighters. At least 21 villagers were left dead, many were wounded, and 147 oxen and 181 sheep were stolen (ADES, 2004; Konto, 2004; N'Djibo, 2004; Yorongar, December 3, 2004).

The assailants attacked the village with both light and heavy automatic weapons like A-52s. After this horrendous attack, representatives of ADES were brought from N'Djaména to investigate. Villagers accused the brigade commander of Bebo Pen of training the assailants how to attack the villagers with heavy guns. The commander's offense was too glaring to be overlooked, though the authorities who were behind that attack tried to cover up the problem. At least 24 who had participated in the attack were arrested and their guns taken by the authorities. One of the assailants, before turning in his weapon, addressed himself to the people who had gathered from neighboring villages: "This is nothing. We have more automatic weapons elsewhere that we can use" (ADES, 2004).

In the neighboring prefecture of Oriental Logone, similar attacks occurred. In the early 2000s, the villages of Békôdô I and its neighbors were attacked by Déby's Janjawiid. A man named Sangar was killed and his leg cut off and taken away by the raiders. Two teams of plowing cattle belonging to his relatives were among the village cattle stolen by the Janjawiid. The military brigade of Bodo is located about four miles from the villages. The authorities were obviously implicated in the Janjawiids' actions, because although the brigade had been informed of the murders and thefts, no action was taken and the cattle were taken away without reprisal at the time or later (based on personal communication from a Chadian who wishes to remain anonymous).

When men are armed to oppress another people, how quickly a trivial incident can become a war. In late 2002, during the weekly market of the sub-prefecture of Bodo (in the prefecture of Oriental Logone), there was a deadly attack. It started with a simple question of whether a young boy of Bodo had bumped into an older boy from the North. A man from a nearby village tried to quash the scuffle between the locals and the northerners selling their goods in the market, when suddenly a northerner pulled a knife from his sleeve and attacked the villager. When he defended himself, other northern merchants pulled out the guns hidden under their display cases and started shooting in the air and even into the people in the market of Bodo. One or two people were killed, including the man who had tried to keep the peace. Many were wounded (according to personal correspondence between the author and a member of the Association of Bodo).

The attack was well prepared. The sub-prefect of Bodo joined the looters and burned the houses of Bodo. He ordered the vehicles in Doba to come to Bodo. Once the vehicles arrived, the sub-prefect of Bodo and his followers emptied the food stocks of the people of Bodo. Many other items of property were burned, destroyed, or taken to Doba. In this way, the sub-prefect made himself rich with the goods of the people of Bodo. When the victims complained to relatives in N'Djaména and Doba about this treatment, their relatives demanded that the sub-prefect prepare a report of the incident. He refused and at the same time resigned from office. (With his plentiful ill-gotten gains, he did not really need the government job.)

Déby's militants who attacked Bodo, the sub-prefect who refused to investigate the incident, and the military brigade of Bodo have never been taken to court. All of them report to Déby, according to personal correspondence between the author and a member of the Association of Bodo.

According to letters from the opposition leader Yorongar to the prime minister of Chad (Yorongar, August 19 & November 18, 2004), between the years of 2003 and 2004 Adoum Salet played an important role as liaison between the local authorities in Oriental Logone and the Janjawiid in that region. The man resided between Komé and Mikou in the canton of Beboudja to direct his cattle rustling and armed robbery operation against the natives of that region. With the help of the brigade commander of Beboudja, Adoum Salet and his assistant Adoum Zougoulou directed operations. Day and night they took the people of that region hostage. Most of their night operations involved the brigade commander of Beboudja and his military police. During those operations they "collected" money from the villagers. The operations did not stop at stealing money, but the cattle of the villagers — the source of their food and future wealth — were stolen, too. Yorongar named Léon Ndeidoum and Robert Bessané as but two of Salet's victims (December 3, 2004).

Early in the second week of August 2004, one of the Janjawiid living in the area of Moundouli (then considered part of Oriental Logone), a village neighboring Mbikou, killed a native of the village. When the murderer tried to run back to his base, he was cut off by the relatives of the dead man and killed. Adoum Salet and some of his comrades immediately gathered the Janjawiid living in the areas of Mbikou and Bao. On August 13, 2004, many Janjawiid launched an attack on those two villages with automatic weapons. The houses were burned, many cattle were stolen, and other goods were looted and taken to the Janjawiids' huts (Yorongar, December 3, 2004).

Among the dead from that attack were Edouard Allahbarem, Alfred Djépatamia, and Ferdinand Dillah. Their beheaded bodies were found and given burial. There were some lucky people who had been wounded but were still alive to testify about this horrible attack. Adoum Salet is said to have gloated after the attack, saying, "So long as Idriss Déby remains in power, I will be untouchable" (Yorongar, December 3, 2004).

As we have seen, the inner circle of Déby had decided to use all systems possible either to eliminate the population of the South or to force the people out of the South and over the borders into the Central African Republic and Cameroon. Not only has Déby armed the nomad herders known as Janjawiid and the civilians of the North living in the South, but he has made a concerted effort to destroy the economy of the resource-rich South as well. Farmers who tried to tend their millet fields were attacked by the Janjawiid. Southern traders and storekeepers have been persecuted by northern traders, storekeepers, and local authorities.

As an example, on October 27, 2004, Djimlelngar, a native of Beboudja, was selling his empty sacks at a price of 150 FCFA. (Farmers purchase the sacks for their millet harvest.) A non-native from the North who was a trader in Beboudja sold his sacks at a price of 300 FCFA. He stopped Djimlelngar in the market and demanded to know who had authorized him to sell his sacks at a low price. When Djimlelngar tried to explain himself, the angry non-native punched him in the face. Djimlelngar reacted to this affrontery by punching back (Yorongar, December 3, 2004).

Fortunately, the prosecuting attorney of Doba, Mr. Pazeu, arrived at the moment the fight started. He risked his own life to separate the two fighters. As he knew the perspective and prejudices of the non-natives against the southerners, he did not trust the brigade commander of Beboudja to settle the matter. Instead, he telephoned the military police of Doba to come more than 20 miles to Beboudja to stabilize the situation. The military police of Doba arrived quickly and stayed there for two days. As soon as they left Beboudja, however, the northerners — with the very active complicity of the brigade commander of Beboudja, launched another attack (Yorongar, December 3, 2004).

Djimlelngar returned to the ancestral marketplace on October 30, 2004, three days after he was attacked. The man who had fought him on the earlier occasion suddenly attacked Djimlelngar again — this time with a knife. Luckily, Djimlelngar was able to dodge the blade, grab the knife from his attacker, and wound the man. At this, the non-natives in the market pulled out their hidden guns and were joined by the local military police. Apparently they had been hoping for just such an opportunity to finish off the village and take their goods. Mahamat Ali, Hissein, and Akim Alyo were the main instigators of this deadly attack and were well prepared. They ordered three vehicles to bring the Janjawiid living in Doumbogo and other vehicles to quickly gather the northerners living in Moundou and Doba to come reinforce their numbers. The people of Beboudja were shot and killed by this amalgam of non-natives, military officers under Déby, and Janjawiid. The houses of the village were burned, cattle were stolen, and the food in the granaries and huts was taken away. None of the murderers and thieves has ever been taken into custody (Yorongar, December 3, 2004).

One indication of Déby's complicity in this sustained pattern of violence is what happened to the prefect of Sarh. Grabé Ndoh, horrified by the carnage in Sarh, ordered his military authorities to collect weapons from the Janjawiid. Soon afterward he was arrested and imprisoned (Yorongar, December 3, 2004).

U.S. ambassador Herman J. Cohen (2006) warned the world about the danger Idriss Déby Itno poses: "As long as President Déby remains in power with the support of his tiny minority ethnic group, which is starting to split apart, Chad will continue to suffer from instability and bouts of violence. The majority southerners of Chad are essentially observers as they watch the northern groups tear themselves apart and steal all of the oil money." Unfortunately, the peoples of Chad's South are experiencing Déby's violence more intimately than as mere observers, but Cohen makes a good point about Déby's desperately strong hold on power, emphasizing that Chad under Déby has destabilized the entire region of Africa.

What has Déby's factional, tribal policy of control brought to the region? "We're seeing a regional war against civilians, with armed groups on both sides of the border actively supported or tolerated by the Sudanese and Chadian governments," said Peter Takirambudde, Africa director of Human Rights Watch (Takirambudde, 2007). Indeed, Déby has exported his war beyond the borders of Chad.

As former SLA leader Minni Arkou Minnawi said to President George W. Bush in 2005, so long as Idriss Déby Itno rules over Chad, people should forget about peace; there will be no peace in the region (Doumnandé, 2006).

Chapter 12

The Voiceless Children

For more than four decades, the young people of Chad have been at particular risk. The loss of the current generation of young people in the heart of Africa will forever endanger Chad and its neighbor countries, if not the rest of the world. This is a strong statement requiring solid evidence and cogent support.

Child Soldiers

At least 15 groups of rebels, hostile to Déby, enroll children in their rebellions, by force or coercion. To counter these rebels, some of whom are Déby's former military officers and relatives, Déby enrolls children by force into his army. It may be that because of constant fighting, too many of his soldiers have died or defected. The author was once a child soldier in Chad (Toïngar, 2006) and escaped many times from forced enrollment into Déby's army. The official president of Chad at the time was Hissène Habré, but since Idriss Déby controlled Habré's military forces, he was de facto strongman and thus ran the country. The people of southern Chad suffered greatly under the regime of Habré. But now the situation becomes even more desperate for children in Chad (Takirambudde, 2007).

Déby argues that he enrolls soldiers and that the rebels hire mercenaries (Ngarmbassa, 2008). In fact, Déby has used up his Sudanese "advisors," Zaghawa tribesmen, and northern tribes that used to make up his fiercest fighting forces. Now he must rely on children. According to the Coalition to Stop the Use of Child Soldiers (2008), in Chad, "Despite an agreement by the government to facilitate the demobilization of child soldiers, an estimated

7,000 to 10,000 children remained in armed forces and groups in September 2007" (para. 1). This was before the rebel attacks of early 2008, so the situation may be even worse now.

Are these children trained to serve Déby in the military? Most of them are between 12 and 18 in age. Their training consists of little more than learning how to put their fingers on the trigger. They are ordered to fire their weapons on anybody without reason when they are in areas they even suspect of being sympathetic to rebels. Before battles they are drugged with cocaine, marijuana, and local whiskey. In battle, they fight without any skill and fall down under the bullets of their "enemies" like ripe fruit from trees. If they begin to come to their senses — when the drugs and alcohol wear off— and realize the danger they are in, they cannot retreat from battle. Déby's special soldiers are there to block their escape to the bush or the desert. Thus when helpless children are taken away from their parents, they are marched off to almost certain death (Toïngar, 2006).

The rebels apply a similar strategy. Some children are enrolled in the rebellion because of the atrocities caused by Déby's regime. They join the rebels because their parents were tortured or killed by Déby and his disciples of sorrow. All of their family's goods may have been destroyed or taken away by Déby's troops, and they can best protect themselves and their families by leaving the rubble of their village and joining the rebel groups. Unfortunately, some children are forced against their will or the will of their parents to join the rebels. These children are drugged and fear nothing. Indoctrinated in the belief that they cannot be harmed in battle so long as they have faith and fear not, they fight unafraid. Even if they survive and return to their parents, an ongoing concern is that the children have become remorseless killers (Tran, 2007; Waging Peace, 2008).

Early in 2007, the UN urged both Déby's regime and the leaders of rebellions against him not to engage children in their warfare (Human Rights Watch, July 16, 2007). Both groups acknowledged their error in breaking international rules of war and claimed that they renounced the enrollment of children in their troops (Hancock, 2007). With the deadly battles that Déby's fighters faced in late November and early December 2007, however, both sides enrolled children into their ranks by force, as usual (Takirambudde, 2007).

According to the president of Chad's human rights organization and the representative of the International Red Cross in Chad, people of the capital city of N'Djaména and many other towns live in total fear. Many children and men were arrested in different towns in Chad to be sent to the northeast to face the rebellion.

Chadians are dying of internal war, hunger, and sickness. Despite all this chaos, some families have tried to produce children to replenish their people. Some of these children are now orphans because of Déby and the rebel groups that so savagely fight against him. Worse yet, the rebels of Movement for Justice and Equality (Darfur rebels) are allowed by the regime of Chad to force these Chadian children to fight in Darfur (Waging Peace, 2008).

Slavery

Slavery is not a "cultural tradition" of Chad. It is a violation of Article 20 of the constitution of Chad, as Chadian political leader Ngarlejy Yorongar notes on his website (Yorongar, December 3, 2004). Children in Chad are victims of slavery because of socioeconomic and ethnic problems imposed by Déby's regime for almost two decades. The economic problems caused by disorder, violence, and interrupted farming and commerce in Chad mean that most families are poor, but many are destitute and starving. As mentioned earlier in this volume, it is ethnicity that determines social standing in Chad, and now determines even survival. It seems to many Chadians that the real mission of Déby has been to eliminate all the educated people of Chad who are not from his tribe, and especially to target educated people from southern Chad who live there or have migrated elsewhere in the country, including the capital city and its environs.

After having applied his divide-and-conquer strategy, Déby extended his mission to poor villagers in Chad by arming the nomads, through his high military authorities, to destroy the millet fields of the villagers, killing them and then using their children as slaves (Konto, 2004; N'djibo, 2004; Yorongar, August 19, 2004; Madj-kida, September 18–21, 2003; Nako, June 29, 2003a).

These practices have been applied in all the southern regions of Chad. One suspects this kind of enslavement occurs also in other regions of Chad when children are kidnapped by nomads and Zaghawa fighters. One survivor's story in the region of Oriental Logone has already been told in a memoir of survival (Toïngar, 2006). Another region in Chad, Mandoul, has been chosen here as but one example of many. Enslavement of children in Mandoul has not been extensively researched, but sources are available to document the existence and extent of the problem there. No doubt the stories of Mandoul that follow may be applied to many other regions in the country. Mandoul is the new name for a region in south-central Chad. About ten years ago, Déby's regime reorganized the prefectures of Chad, giving his home territory in the north more divisions (and thus more representatives to government councils) and combining prefectures in southern Chad to reduce their political power.

According to Madj-kida (September 18–21, 2003), after eliminating the educated people of Mandoul by poison, torture, starvation, or assassination in the towns, Déby armed his nomad tribesmen and ordered them to kill the rural villagers. The remaining population was terrorized and had to submit to any demand made by a representative of Déby's regime or anybody from Déby's tribe, however unlawful the claim. To give up one's child to such monsters is a horror. To refuse means death for the parents, and the children must still be taken into slavery. Today in that region of Mandoul, many villages are attacked by nomads with military weapons. Where could those nomads obtain military-issue weapons and ammunition? Only Déby and his fighters can answer that question (Madj-kida, September 18–21, 2003; Nako, June 29, 2003a).

The villagers of Mandoul were caught in the pincers: Déby's troops, unpaid by his regime for weeks at a time, needed to take the villagers' goods and food so that their own relatives might survive, but at the same time the nomads were taking the villagers' cattle and pasturing their own cattle on the villagers' crops. How could the villagers survive? Some families had to hand their children to the nomads or local representatives of Déby's regime in Mandoul to get perhaps the equivalent of $50 to $200 a year and thus save the lives of the rest of their family (Madj-kida, September 18–21, 2003; Nako, June 29, 2003a).

Some of those starving children joined the nomad shepherds and fighters just to get milk to drink or food to eat, and then they served their pretended masters. Others had been rented by their parents for a period of one year or more with the hope of getting at least $50 or an ox to help the rest of the family survive. When a Zaghawa authority said he needed a villager's child to serve as a shepherd or domestic, there was no choice for parents even if they suspected their child would be taken away to fight. They had to accept the tribesman's "offer" in order to avoid worse options (Nako, June 29, 2003a).

These children are treated cruelly in a kind of slavery that has become genocide. Early in the morning, those 8 to 16-year-old children fetch water from a deep well and carry the buckets on their heads to the bush where their masters have their base. They prepare tea as breakfast for their masters and their families. After breakfast they wash the dishes and then take care of the cattle. They are specifically instructed to take the cattle to the millet fields of their own people to pasture them. If they hesitate to thus destroy their family's crops, they will be wickedly beaten by their employers. On their way back to the base with the cattle, the slaves have to look for dry wood to build a fire and cook for their employers, grinding millet or rice in the mortars and helping to fix other food (Madj-kida, September 18–21, 2003; Nako, June 29, 2003a).

Enslaved children who try to run away are pursued by their masters on horseback. They are captured and tortured. Children "employed" by Zaghawa authorities in the South or sent to serve the Zaghawa families back home in the North receive the same treatment (Yorongar, December 3, 2004; Nako, June 29, 2003a). There are hundreds of such cases, but in this chapter only a few names of child slaves, their sellers, and their buyers are given. Human rights organizations or individuals who want to investigate allegations of child slavery are thus able to locate the victims identified here and find eyewitnesses to confirm these allegations.

In the Mandoul village of Kahi, Moukoïgué was in service to Mahamat Zène with the complicity of the head of the village, Paul Noïngar (Nako, 2003a).

Djassam Thomas Woulingar was unwillingly rented out annually by his father, Woulingar, to a former sub-prefect of Koumra, Hassan Aguid, with the complicity of Brahim Hemchi (the brigade commander of Koumra) and Hassan Nigué (first compagnie gendarmerie of Koumra). Thomas was immediately sent to Dar Tama, near Darfur, to serve there as a shepherd (Nako, 2003a).

Nosso Albaye, the son of Ngarmadje and Gillé Rosalie in the Dilnda I quarter of Koumra, was unwillingly taken by Mahamat Hamit to serve his family as domestic slave in Abéché, in northeastern Chad. Hamit is originally from Fada and was born in 1948. Nosso was taken with the complicity of the canton chief of Koumra (Nako, 2003a).

Many other unbelievable examples were presented by Yorongar and Nako, too many to write down in this chapter, but these three cases seem to be typical. Because Chad signed the human rights declaration of the United Nations guaranteeing protection of the rights of children, Chad's co-signers must protect the country's children from those who would enslave, torture, and kill them.

According to Yorongar's letter to President Déby, the prime minister, justice minister, internal minister, and defense minister to stop slavery in Chad, Déby's parents-in-law and other relatives own many slaves from different regions of Chad and also from other countries, including Niger (Yorongar, December 3, 2004, see Tome I, Articles 19–20). Yorongar warned the regime of Chad many times about the slavery issue but never received a reply from Chadian authorities.

One of Déby's uncles-in-law, "General" Mahamat Salet Brahim, had many slaves in his village, Batadjana (Yorongar, December 3, 2004). In a letter to the high authorities of Chad by Yorongar, a human rights activist in Chad, at least 40 Chadians and one boy from the Niger Republic were named as slaves of "General" Brahim (Yorongar, December 3, 2004). One of the boys, from Moundou, was ripped from his mother's arms and taken to Batadjana as a slave in the 1990s. The boy was given the name of his master, Mahamat Salet Brahim, and called Ousman. His job was to take care of the cattle of Fadoul Salet Brahim on land between Chad and Darfur. This Fadoul is a brother of Brahim. While young Ousman was serving as cattle herder, Mahamat added his (Ousman's) name to the list of government forces in the region. It was Mahamat's wife who received Ousman's salary while he served in the National Nomad Guard.

A boy from Bosso named Abaye was also taken to Mahamat's village as a slave. To prevent Abaye from running away, "General" Brahim had the boy's Achilles tendon cut. Today Abaye is far from his own village, enslaved to serve the native tribespeople of Batadjana, in the North, near the home village of "General" Brahim and of Idriss Déby (Yorongar, December 3, 2004).

A child from Guéra was forcibly taken from his mother and transported to Batadjana. The boy was tortured by his master, Abderaman, who is chief of the district (canton) and a father in-law to Déby. Today the boy from Guéra is still a slave in Batadjana. His name is unknown. Yorongar was not able to get information from him. The boy is now deaf from the torture he received (Yorongar, December 3, 2004).

A boy from the Niger Republic was taken away from his parents into slavery. In 2004, the boy was serving the eldest son of Abderaman, a man named Abakar Abderaman. The slave has been nicknamed "Niger." Niger's main job was to fetch water for the people of Batadjana. Niger escaped one day and headed west, toward his native country. Unfortunately, he was seized by someone from a neighboring village and taken back to Batadjana. Poor Niger was probably tortured after he was returned to his master (Yorongar, December 3, 2004).

Another boy, named Issa, was stolen from his family in the South and taken to Dagdagou. The boy was owned by "Colonel" Abakar Choua, commander of the Military Training Center of Moussoro. Issa was serving as a herder (Yorongar, December 3, 2004). These are just five of the children known to be enslaved by a few of Déby's relatives.

Besides the children who have been taken from their parents and used as slaves by authorities of Chad and their relatives, there are many other victims. Cattle, camels, goats, and sheep of many people in different regions of Chad were stolen by those who were in power or had their relatives in power. As an example, not only did "General" Mahamat Brahim steal cattle, goats, camels, and sheep from the people of Chari-baguirmi, Lac, Batha, and Kanem, but he also seized their owners and took them to Batadjana as his slaves to serve the people of his canton. At least 40 of those herders escaped from the hands of their master in Batadjana (Yorongar, 2003, pp. 137–141; Yorongar, December 3, 2004).

Not just children and young men, but young women, too, have been enslaved during the current regime in Chad. Yorongar tells the stories of several women in his 2003 book and in the letter that he addressed to Chadian authorities in N'Djaména (Yorongar, December 3, 2004). Mrs. Mariam Daoud was inhumanely treated and tortured by a director in Déby's cabinet. That man put pepper and a pistol into Mrs. Daoud's body. A woman of Abéché was accused of being a girlfriend of someone from the opposition party. Her bottom lip was slashed by a fighter who was close to Déby (Yorongar, 2003, p. 9). In February 1992, Augustine Yogueadé was assassinated in Walia, Ndjaména. Her daughter, Irène Rémadji, was wounded by the men who had killed her mother and was left there to die. The fighters who committed those crimes would not allow Rémadji to be taken to the hospital. It took more than half a day before the police arrived, lifted her from the body of her mother, and took her away. Instead of taking Rémadji to the hospital, though, they took her to jail, where she spent a night in a cell with male prisoners (Yorongar, 2003, pp. 9–10, 252, 303–319).

Not all children taken by the Zaghawa are reported to authorities or civil rights organizations, because their parents understandably fear reprisals. Nevertheless, this is a list of slaves reportedly used by Déby's relatives in the region of Fada, listed by name, as reported by Yorongar:

1. Hacky Mahamat Hissène
2. Youssouf Mahamat
3. Chidi Choua Abakar
4. Issa Hassan Moussa
5. Mahamat Alhadj Eliza
6. Moussa Mahamat Nour
7. Mahamat Saleh War
8. Abderaman Adoum Ali
9. Hacki Mahamat Saleh
10. Mahamat Hassane Saleh
11. Hassan Abakar Oumar
12. Abderaman Moussa Outocdr
13. Abderaman Mahamat Issa
14. Adoum Djibrine Mbodou
15. Moussa Mahamat Issa
16. Adoum Hassane Taher
17. Brahim Taher Abderaman
18. Kella Akouna Adoum
19. Bechir Djosbo Abderhaman
20. Galmai Draya Barka
21. Youssouf Hardne Hassan
22. Minaï Mahamat Souleyman
23. Alhadj Youssouf Moussa Adoum
24. Moussa Saleh Dasse
25. Abderaman Hamit Yusuf
26. Saleh Taher Allatcha
27. Youssouf Adoum Soukouni

28. Hassan Mahamat Abdoulaye
29. Moussa Mahamat Hassan Hagar
30. Mahamat Adoum Armine
31. Youssouf Dary Koromi
32. Mahamat Nour Mahamat Zene
33. Haky Tchaï Djibrine
34. Bokor Tchaï Djibrine
35. Issa Tchaï Djibrine
36. Hassan Abdallah Issa
37. Mahamat Zoundi Kerima
38. Mahamat Nour Souleyman
39. Mahamat Ali Koussoumi
40. Youssouf Bara Brahim
41. Toura Abdoulaye Souleyman Soumaïne

Although we cannot be sure that all 41 listed here are children, it is known that only vigorous young people are taken as slaves (Yorongar, December 3, 2004).

CHAPTER 13

They Called Each Other "Younger Brother, Older Brother"

In 1993 Ange Felix Patassé became the democratically elected president of the Central African Republic (CAR). Shortly thereafter, Chadian president Idris Déby Itno initiated a friendship with Patassé based on their respective national interests. Déby's agenda was probably to eliminate CODOs (the rebels against his power in Chad), control the region of Central Africa, and extend his empire into Sudan. Déby was referred to as "younger brother," and Patassé was referred to as "older brother," as a sign of Deby's respect and admiration for Patassé. The professed brotherhood manifested itself in a number of ways, including allowing Patassé to occasionally travel on Déby's presidential airplane.

Mutual Favors

Déby needed to secure the border between the CAR and Chad, which at the time was menaced by rebel leader Kétté Nodji Moïse and his commandos (CODOs). In 1994 Déby made even friendlier overtures (and offers of his pilot and jet) to Patassé when Bardé Laoukeïn returned to the *maquis* to lead another group of rebels against Déby. This turn of events necessitated close friendship with Patassé, to urge his agreement to prevent rebels from setting up bases for men and materiel in the Central African Republic. With the southern border secured, Déby could turn his attention to the rebels of the North, the MDD, and another movement a few years later, the MDJT.

In 1993, Kétté's second in command, Bardé Laoukeïn, journeyed to Chad's capital to represent the CODOs at the National Conference, an assembly of opposition leaders and government officials, to negotiate a new constitution. Kétté and his rebels had agreed to stay in a temporary green zone in the town of Goré, to wait for word about the new constitution. Under international pressure, Déby had agreed to a cease-fire, the creation of no-attack green zones, and safe conduct for representatives. While Laoukeïn was at the meeting, Déby betrayed the cease-fire and sent troops to the South in a surprise attack on the CODO base. The rebels, having anticipated trouble, were divided into two groups. When Déby's soldiers arrived, the group under Kétté faded back into the forest and Laoukeïn's group stayed out of reach in Moundou. Upon hearing of the double cross, Laoukeïn left the conference and returned to the South, pretending he opposed Kétté's actions (to avoid being attacked by Déby's soldiers). Once Laoukeïn felt safe back in Moundou, he and his rebels rejoined Kétté's group (according to personal correspondence with Captain Doumro, a young southern rebel, recently deceased).

In CAR, Patassé, who trusted his "younger brother" Déby, threatened Kétté Nodji not to attempt to use the CAR as an escape route from Déby's reprisals. Yet both Patassé and Kétté Nodji share tribal relationship in the Central African Republic and Chad. These family entanglements are similar to the relationships Déby has with some of the Zaghawa rebels of Darfur. Patassé had to make a choice between his friendship with Déby and his family relationship with Kétté Nodji. Patassé chose the former and rejected Kétté. Kétté Nodji, now rejected by the country of his mother, lost the opportunity to establish a strong rebel base in the CAR. This made it more difficult for Kétté to get enough materials (weapons and supplies) to challenge Déby's army. As a result, Kétté decided to negotiate with Déby under the supervision of an international committee. Patassé saluted Kétté's decision, which seemed to him a victory he had won for his "younger brother" Déby (according to Captain Doumro).

Because Kétté had agreed to negotiate with Déby, Patassé invited Kétté and his group to come to Bangui (the political capital of CAR) to prepare the key points of the CODO proposal to the Chadian government and to meet with the International Committee. All the senior leaders of the rebellion met in Bangui to create the foundation of the new political party, the Comité de Sursaut National Pour le Developement (CSNPD). With the help of the International Committee, CSNPD and the Chadian government met in the Hotel La Tchadienne in N'Djaména, where they discussed many issues and agreed on most of those proposed by the leaders of the newly formed party (from correspondence with Captain Doumro).

By the end of August 1994, the negotiation between the CSNPD and Déby's regime represented the strongest and most solid relationship his government had formed with any rebel group since Déby had assumed the presidency in 1990. Unfortunately, the agreement would not last long.

The rebels of CSNPD came out of the bush and stayed in the southern regions of Chad, the Oriental and Occidental Logones, awaiting their time to be inducted into the Chadian army. Laoukeïn, however, decided to keep his forces together and wait to see how the negotiation would turn out between Kétté and Déby. Laoukeïn could well remember Déby's past deceptions and the betrayal in 1983-84 when, as commander-in-chief for President Hissène Habré, Déby ordered his forces to kill the CODOs when they mustered to join the regular army, following peace and reconciliation negotiations with the government (Yorongar, 2003; Madonet, 2004). Laoukeïn could also recall what Déby tried to do to Pierre Tokinon's rebels: in September of 1984, the CODOs were armed and waiting to be mixed with government forces, but Déby planned to kill them. The CODOs intercepted that message and pulled back into the bush. In more recent memory, Laoukeïn knew what had happened the previous year, during the National Conference of 1993 (Toïngar, 2006).

After the second negotiation, Laoukeïn definitively separated his CODOs from Kétté's CODOs and gave his troops the name "Forces Armée de la Republique Fédérale" (FARF). Déby sent his former minister Youssouf Togoïmi to negotiate with Laoukeïn. The negotiation was successful. Laoukeïin came out with his rebels and was waiting for the next step. Unfortunately, Déby reverted to his habitual method of operation. Many innocents as well as CODOs were killed during a surprise attack. Togoïmi was disgusted. He described Déby's action as criminal and resigned from the government. One year later Togoïmi founded his own rebellion against Déby and named it the Mouvement pour la Democratie et la Justice au Tchad (MDJT) (Aubert, Brana, & Blum, 1998).

Patassé Seeks Security Forces

At that time Patassé did not have a national army in the Central African Republic. The existing army was dominated by the people of the southern part of his country, especially the tribe of the former president and general André Kolingba. When Patassé felt that his power was about to be threatened by the southern forces and that he would be unable to get young men of his own tribe trained quickly enough to serve as a protective force, he started recruiting some of the CODOs of southern Chad, who had abandoned the rebellion of Kétté and Laoukeïn and — rather than join the military forces of Chad and be pressed into service in the North to fight a futile desert war — preferred to seek safety at a refugee camp in northern CAR.

Déby would surely not have been happy that his "older brother" was trying to protect his power using ex-rebels who had fought against Déby, but he kept quiet and waited for an opportune time to deal with the matter. Many such Chadians did join the CAR military. This special presidential unit protected Patassé and saved his power many times during the insurgency in Bangui by the national army of CAR. Patassé also relied on mercenaries of the Mission to Monitor the Implementation of the Bangui Agreements (MISAB) for protection, among whom were fighters sent from the North by his devoted friend Déby (United Nations Security Council, 1997).

During the genocide in Rwanda in 1994, Chadian soldiers were called to help restore peace. In 1995, under the guise of helping CAR president Patassé defend himself against military insurgents, Idriss Déby sent troops to the capital of the Central African Republic. More than half of the 750-plus soldiers sent to keep peace in the CAR were Chadians (Verschave, 2000, p. 229). These soldiers were predominantly from Déby's tribe, the Zagawha.

Déby Profits from Mercenaries

According to a Chadian soldier named Nadjita Moussa (1996), who served as a lieutenant's bodyguard on the Mission d'Intervention et de Surveillance des Accords de Bangui (MISAB) to the Central African Republic, this "peacekeeping" move served Déby in three ways. First, it created an opportunity to kill Sara tribespeople — whether civilians or soldiers — from the southern regions of Chad who were living in the CAR and might be supporting Déby's hated rival, Kétté Nodji Moïse. Second, sending soldiers to the capital, Bangui, ostensibly to protect President Patassé, in fact gave the men an opportunity to identify who had goods and money. As soon as the area was destabilized, they could loot the shops and homes and hasten the goods to Déby and their tribal relatives. Third, Déby's troops in CAR made it possible to scout out and monitor the flow of diamonds in that country.

Thus it is not surprising that soldiers from Mali, Senegal, and other

African countries did not fight the CAR insurgents as tenaciously as did the Chadians, who knew which shops sold diamonds and could be looted for quick gain. The fighters from Chad had been directed to kill for goods, and they killed with a fury (Moussa, 1996), while those conscripted from Mali, Burkina Faso, and Senegal seem to have taken to heart their mission as MISAB peacekeepers (Verschave, 2000, pp. 229, 236–237). On January 6, 1997, Alain Richard, defense minister of France, said that this was the first successful mission in Africa. He was pleased that the MISAB forces had done so well. They had proven themselves capable of handling African affairs and facing crises on their continent. He praised the way MISAB soldiers had boldly gone into the insurgents' territory. There was no word of regret from Richard that troops had targeted primarily defenseless civilians (Verschave, 2000, pp. 229, 236–237).

Much of the fighting in Bangui was between the insurgents of southern CAR and "Patassé's defenders"— mercenaries sent by Déby. These were bloody scenes. On occasion, Chadian soldiers who were distracted from defense duties by the charm of precious goods to be looted in rebel strongholds were later found dead, chopped into pieces. Their bodies were literally butchered: the rebels first chopped off the soldiers' hands and then their arms, their feet, and their legs, so that they died in pain and horror. When their bodies were found and identified, they were sent back to Chad (Moussa, 1996).

At that time Déby seems to have become aware of the enormous amount of money to be gained in the sub-region of Africa. One source of funds turned out to be found in mercenary soldiers' pay. In 1996, President Mobutu of Zaire requested that mercenaries be sent from Chad to help defend his government against rebel forces led by Laurent Desiré Kabila. Payment for services to be rendered by the mercenaries was given to Déby to distribute to his forces. Unfortunately, there is no evidence that the troops received payment. In fact, the 30 or so soldiers who survived and returned to N'Djaména complained to their leaders about not having been paid their salary for eight months. In response to their request, the president invited them to the palace — where the Presidential Guards surrounded them and opened fire. Some were only wounded; the others died (Verschave, 2000, p. 338).

Besides payment for the services of mercenary soldiers, Idriss Déby found another source of money in Central Africa: death payments for his soldiers. When a number of the troops were ambushed by Kabila and killed in defense of Mobutu's government, Mobutu paid Déby a fee in honor of their service (Ali, 1999).

Later, when Desiré Kabila had successfully overthrown Mobutu; cast off Mobutu's name for the country, Zaire; and installed himself as president of the renamed Democratic Republic of Congo (DRC), Kabila, too, requested Chadian mercenaries to protect him from the rebel forces of Jean-Pierre Bémba (Prunier, 1999; Simpson, 1999). Déby apparently held no grudge against Kabila in spite of the earlier massacre of his troops, nor did he scorn the payment he would receive for these troops in turn. By the spring of 1999, rebels against Kabila were struggling to capture Mbuji-Mayi, the diamond center of the Democratic Republic of Congo (Simpson, 1999), and it was likely that whoever controlled that territory would control the diamond mines, which had produced as much as $1 billion per year in valuable stones (Talbot, 1999). Diamonds and gold, then, were another motivating force for Déby to get involved in affairs of Central Africa (Madonet, 2004). As Doyle (2003) quipped, "Diamonds are a warlord's best friend."

Déby sent 2,227 troops to Kabila in September 1998, of whom more than 100 are reported to have died in the fighting before the force was withdrawn following a peace agreement brokered by Libyan leader Muammar Khadafi (Ali-Dinar, 1999). There is evidence that these troops were ordered by Déby's administration to plunder the countries they served and bring back diamonds and other valuable goods for Déby's own profit. An impassioned diatribe against the pillaging conducted by these mercenaries of the region's diamonds and gold appears on the Congoline.com forum (Musualuendu, n.d.).

Among the troops sent to the Democratic Republic of Congo to bolster Kabila against his rebels were CODOs, the Chadian commando forces formerly fighting against Déby who had been "reconciled" to his regime (Verschave, 2000). Neutralized by the capture and assassination of their leader Laoukeïn Bardé, these members of the group had accepted the offer to make peace with Déby's regime.

Despite the dangers to his soldiers and the CODOs, then, Déby found this business of providing mercenary "peacekeepers" to be profitable (Talbot, 1999). Déby continued to sustain a reputation outside the country as a generous man, willing to help his friends, even while within his own country he was considered a criminal and was attacked by rebels on all sides. Through these missions — to Rwanda, the Central African Republic, then three different campaigns in Zaire/Democratic Republic of Congo — it was the Zaghawa tribes of Sudan and Chad who profited along with Déby. A few other soldiers from different tribes might benefit from excursions into Zaire, depending on their technical skills (Verschave, 2000, pp. 336–337).

Déby "Discovers" Diamonds

From the Zaire campaign in the late 1990s, Déby acquired even more diamonds than he had procured in the Central African Republic. By this time, "blood diamonds" were risky to trade (GAO, June 2002; Partnership Africa Canada, January 10, 2003). Déby arranged a business deal with a French jeweler to turn the diamonds into cash. Déby took the cash but unfortunately delivered fewer diamonds than had been agreed upon. The French jeweler was swindled (Yorongar, 2003).

According to Chérif Ahmat (2006), "the Chadian," Déby sent some diamond experts into the Democratic Republic of Congo with the Chadian forces to assure that the diamonds were removed in optimal condition and brought to him. Fortunately for Déby, his looters managed to obtain some diamonds while in the DRC. Unfortunately for him, however, regulation of the international diamond trade was undergoing reform at that time. Now only countries producing diamonds could sell diamonds (GAO, June 2002). The only way for Déby to sell diamonds obtained illegally from another country was to work through someone authorized to sell diamonds, that is, someone in a diamond-producing country. As Chad produces no diamonds, Déby turned to Patassé, president of the Central African Republic, whose country was classified as a diamond producer. Déby's "elder brother," Patassé, agreed to sell the diamonds for Déby, for a certain commission (Chérif, 2006).

The story of what happened next makes one wonder if perhaps Yorongar, the radical opposition leader in Chad, was correct in saying that Idriss Déby is a man of vengeance (Madonet, 2004). Indeed, spiteful revenge is one explanation for Déby's actions against Patassé. Libya had been financially supporting the Chadian forces sent by Déby to bolster Desiré Kabila and prop up his regime in the DRC against Bémba's rebels in 1998 (Talbot, 1999; Prunier, 1999). Libya's Muammar Khadafi had plans to annex Chad as the first step to creating an "Arab belt" across the Sahel region and thus gaining control of Central Africa (Flint & De Waal, 2008, p. 22). Instead of sending Libyan troops, Khadafi may have hoped to expand Libya's influence and ultimately become leader of the United States of Africa by quietly supporting certain foreign forces.

Regardless of the reason for Libyan support, Chadian troops supplied with Libyan military equipment traveled south through the CAR to its border with the Democratic Republic of Congo, to establish a base there at Bangui. Locating the command in the CAR was useful in case the Chadian troops encountered too much resistance from Bémba's roving bands of rebels and needed to retreat over the border. Some of the payment from

Khadafi was to be used for salaries for Chadian soldiers. The rest of the funds were to be passed on from Déby to compensate Patassé for use of his country's territory for the retreat base. Authorities from Libya gave the money to Déby. For some reason Déby failed to give Patassé, his "elder brother," his share. Perhaps because Déby and Patassé relied on each other, and Patassé enjoyed the special privileges Déby provided, he did not press Déby on the matter of these funds (Chérif, 2006).

When Déby later asked Patassé to sell some diamonds for him in early 2000, Patassé welcomed the opportunity to be of service to his "younger brother" and agreed to help. Instead of giving Déby money for the diamonds, though, Patassé applied the diamond sales to the debt owed for having hosted the Chadian military base at Bangui. Now Déby was in a bind. He had intended to sell the diamonds, not give them away. For the time being, however, he had to keep quiet because he had his own problems, including international detection of his counterfeiting operation and continued complaints from the French jeweler who several years before had paid for more diamonds than he had received. In addition, the diamonds Déby was trying to sell were in fact stolen from mines in the DRC. For these reasons he had to swallow his anger at Patassé and be obliging (Chérif, 2006).

Déby Prepares Revenge on Patassé

Nevertheless, Déby sought revenge and looked for an opportunity to remove Patassé from power. Déby would exploit the close working relationship that existed between then-Colonel Daoud Soumaïne, leader of the Chadian mercenaries Déby had sent to protect Patassé, and General Bozizé, who was at that time commandant-in-chief of the military forces of the Central African Republic (Mandolet, 2004). As it happened, Bozizé was a cousin-in-law to Patassé. Soumaïne had developed a strong friendship with Bozizé during the time Déby was using Patassé to weaken the rebellion in the southern regions of Chad. In fact, Daoud Soumaïne was one of the leaders of the Chadian forces sent to Bangui in the 1990s for the MISAB (Mission d'Intervention et de Surveillance des Accords de Bangui). At that time, it was the Chadian forces who saved the Patassé government, at least twice, and those forces worked closely with Central African Republic forces led by General Bozizé (Verschave, 2000, pp. 229, 336).

In 2002, Patassé suspected that Bozizé was working to overthrow his regime. His suspicions were in fact correct, and when Patassé had Bozizé summoned to the court to answer some questions, Bozizé first ignored requests and orders to appear and then, on a third attempt to serve him with a summons, opened fire on the military police and escaped from Bangui to Sarh, in Chad, with approximately 20 of his bodyguards (Madonet, 2004). Déby seized that opportunity to use Daoud Soumaïne, his military chief of staff, to recruit young Chadians to provide military support for Bozizé from the region of Guéra and in the villages and towns that share a border with the CAR. He recruited these young men, most between the ages of 16 and 35, to help Bozizé return to Bangui, by force if necessary. By the end of 2002 and early 2003, Déby and Daoud made sure those young men were trained to destabilize the democratic regime of the CAR. Déby would not need to repay his debts to Patassé if Patassé were no longer in power.

When Patassé took power in the Central African Republic in 1993, his military forces were dominated by people from the southern part of the country. (People from the north had supported the previous president.) Now that Patassé saw his power base weakened by rebels in southern CAR, he needed to expand the military forces available to him and looked to the refugee camps in the northern part of his country. (This perspective is provided from personal correspondence with Captain Madjiri, a member of the forces recruited by Patassé.) Meanwhile Déby was besieged in N'Djaména by more than 15 rebel groups, the most ferocious of which were based in the northern regions of Chad. It would benefit him to eliminate all threat to his rule from southern Chad and wipe out all rebel forces in that region so that he could concentrate on the war in northern Chad. Déby therefore forewarned Patassé that to build up his army with rebels from southern Chad would not be a good idea. Patassé, wanting to keep peace with Déby, stopped recruiting in northern CAR. As we will see, however, shortly thereafter the "younger brother," Déby, would start a fire in the country of his neighbor and "elder brother," Patassé, and then overthrow his government (Mas, April 16, 2006).

In order to maintain control of his regime, Déby had to totally destroy the rebellion in southern Chad both by direct military action against his citizens in the South and by flanking action from south of Chad, that is, from the CAR. To put a puppet ruler in Bangui, the capital of CAR, he needed to remove Patassé from power and enlarge his own power there (Moussa, 1996). Although on the surface relations between the two leaders were amicable, there had been three issues of contention.

The first involved oil. Patassé had known since 1974 that his country, like Chad, lay over rich petroleum deposits. Conoco surveyors conducting a search in Chad had accidentally drilled in the Central African Republic and discovered reserves. Realizing their mistake, the surveyors stopped and pulled the team out to go to Miandoum, a village near the town of Doba, in the Oriental Logone prefecture of southern Chad (Madonet, 2004). When Patassé became president of the Central African Republic in 1993, he expressed a desire to drill into the oil basin underlying the border between Chad and the Central African Republic (Kahn, 2003). Patassé may have assumed that he and his "younger brother," Déby, could share the pipeline which would be constructed with World Bank funds and would pass from Chad through the Central African Republic on its way to the Republic of Congo and the coast. However, Déby resisted sharing the wealth of their mutual natural resources with his neighbor (Madonet, 2004).

A second disagreement emerged when Déby flew to Malabo, Equatorial Guinea, for a meeting of leaders of the Central African region in 2002. Déby had picked up Patassé in Bangui (capital of the Central African Republic) en route. At the meeting, in front of the other presidents of the region, Déby suddenly started accusing his "elder brother" of not being a true friend because he was providing safe haven in his country for Déby's enemies, men like the physician Dr. Nahor, the veterinarian Dr. N'djébété, and others, who posed a threat to his regime (Madonet, 2004). Patassé was reportedly surprised by Déby's accusation; he had not known that these individuals were in his country. Wanting to oblige Déby, he telephoned from Guinea and ordered his police officers to find any Chadian opposition leaders who were living in the CAR. Apparently no Chadian opposition leaders were found in his country, and the other presidents at the meeting probably knew that Déby's allegations were not true (Madonet, 2004).

The third argument against Patassé was also based on a false accusation. After the regional meeting in 2002, Déby accused the CAR military forces of trying to attack Chadian forces in southern Chad, Moyen Chari. In reprisal for this imaginary incursion, Chadian forces entered the Central African Republic and made surprise attacks on the CAR troops. These attacks killed and wounded many CAR soldiers and took many prisoners (Couvé, 2002).

A fourth disagreement developed later. This issue revolved around a brave soldier in Patassé's army named Martin Koumtamadji Nadingar, whose nickname was Abdoulaye Miskine (meaning "simple man"). Early in 2002, Déby accused Patassé of hiring a Chadian rebel officer who happened to have the same name, Abdoulaye Miskine. On August 7, 2002, Déby accused Abdoulaye Miskine of not only attacking the rebels of Bozizé (Patassé's enemies) but also trying to attack Déby's army in Chad. In fact, Patassé had sent his fiercely loyal officer, Abdoulaye Miskine, to northern

CAR to protect people of the region from cattle thieves on raids from Chad who instead of paying the toll for crossing the CAR were using weapons provided by Déby's regime to loot and steal as they made their way to the Republic of Congo. Patassé, who did not know the real intention of his "younger brother," used all his diplomatic skills to explain that his Abdoulaye Miskine (Koumtamadji) had a mother from the CAR and a father from Maro, in a region of southern Chad. Furthermore, the Abdoulaye Miskine that Patassé had in his army was not a second lieutenant like the Abdoulaye Miskine of the Chadian National Army Forces (African Union, January 14, 2003).

Déby said that if Abdoulaye Miskine did not leave the Central African Republic, he would take action to protect his regime in Chad. In the face of this demand, the presidents of the states in the region — that is, of the six-country organization, the Economic and Monetary Community of Central Africa (CEMAC); the Community of Sahel and Saharan States (CEN-SAD); and the African Union — urged Déby and Patassé to send both Bozizé and Koumtamadji (Abdoulaye Miskine) into exile (African Union, January 14, 2003). The rationale was that Patassé would not have to worry about Bozizé and his rebels in the north of CAR and Déby would also be assured that Abdoulaye was no longer in the Central African Republic to disturb his regime.

Apparently Patassé was satisfied with the decision of the three international organizations. Patassé first sent Abdoulaye to Togo. A few weeks later (in February 2003), during their Franco-African meeting in Paris, Patassé made an arrangement with the president of Algeria, Abdelaziz Bouteflika, to allow Bozizé to be in his country as a political refugee. Once Bouteflika approved the idea, Patassé went to Idriss Déby and informed him that he had talked to the president of Algeria who had agreed to provide asylum for Bozizé. Déby informed his "older brother" that he had arranged for France to provide asylum for Bozizé. Then Déby added that Patassé should not allow the rebels of Jean Pierre Bémba near the oil of Doba (in southern Chad) or allow them to harm in any way the Chadians in the CAR; otherwise Chad would have to take action (Boisbouvier, 2004).

The last but not the least of the arguments Déby trumped up against Patassé was the presence of Libyans who came through CEN-SAD to protect the democratic government of the CAR when it was seriously menaced by at least six different insurgencies and averted at least eight coups d'état. Déby, whose regime belonged to that organization (CEN-SAD), accepted the deployment of Libyan forces to CAR in December 2001 (International Crisis Group, December 13, 2007). Later, in 2002, he denounced the presence of those forces by saying the Libyans, who were in southern Chad, constituted a danger to his regime (Soudan, 2002). (In 2008, Déby would do something similar with the United Nations forces. First he called for their involvement on the border between Chad and Sudan and then, when the United Nations agreed to send multi-national forces, Déby changed his mind. Apparently Déby would have preferred French soldiers to a multi-national force.)

Based on these five fraudulent grievances, Déby began his assault on the CAR. Patassé, like other presidents in the region, had underestimated Déby. At first, Patassé tried to find a way to reestablish peace between the two countries. However, other Chadian politicians like Yorongar, Lol Mahamat Choua, and Charles Kebzabo, as well as journalists who knew Déby well, were acquainted with how deceptive Déby could be.

To avoid a war between the two countries of the region that formed the Communauté des États Monétaires de l'Afrique Centrale (CEMAC), the presidents of the Republic of Congo, Gabon, Equatorial Guinea, and Cameroon worked out a solution to the dispute pertaining to the Libyan forces. They created a committee in 2002 to investigate the accusations of both CAR and Chad. CAR accused Chad of supporting the rebels of General Bozizé (in the former CAR), and Chad accused the CAR of trying to control a part of Chad (International Crisis Group, 2007). That committee went to the border between the two countries and then returned to Bangui, declaring that the rebels they met were not Chadians but Central Africans. Furthermore, they added that among the rebels there was one of Bozizé's sons, Francis. This evidence seemed to support Déby's claims (African Union, January 14, 2003).

It is likely that Patassé now finally sensed Déby's intention to remove him from power (International Crisis Group, 2007). A few weeks later Déby conceived another way to do just that. Déby said he did not want to see the Libyans or the rebels of DRC in the CAR (defending Patassé's regime) because Chad had had problems with them in the past. Although members of CEMAC, CEN-SAD, and AU could not exactly understand Déby's rationale, Patassé acceded to Déby's demand. The Libyans were sent home, along with the rebels of the DRC (Soudan, 2002).

Chapter 14

The Fall of Bangui

The fall of Bangui was something that politically astute Chadians had predicted many years before, when Déby and Patassé began their friendship. Judging from personal correspondence with residents of N'Djaména in 1993, a cynical perspective was that Déby finds people who need help, uses them for his own purposes, and then disposes of them. Patassé did not know it at the time, but he was doomed.

As has been noted, Patassé's people were kin to peoples of southern Chad. Once Patassé had helped Déby to finish off the rebellion in southern Chad in 1998, Patassé became expendable. Déby could ensure the downfall of Patassé's regime and install someone whom he could control more easily (Mas, 2006).

Déby seems to have fomented a rebellion in northern Central African Republic (Debos, 2008). How could Déby have incited rebellion in another country, across the southern border of Chad? Is it true that Chadian military forces and Sudanese mercenaries were able to overthrow the democratically elected president of the Central African Republic? The story of the fall of Bangui involves mercenary groups in several countries of the region and a complex network of international intrigue, just as in Darfur (International Crisis Group, 2007). Although Déby was only one African leader with chess pieces on the board at the time, the argument will be made here that Patassé would not have fallen from power in March 2003 had Déby not engineered it.

As noted above, when General Bozizé of the Central African Republic escaped arrest for an attempted coup against Patassé, he found refuge in Sarh, in southern Chad. This was the area of Chad where Déby's regime had recruited and armed many young fighters to help Bozizé capture Bangui, the CAR capital. At that time the central government of the Democratic Republic of Congo (DRC), just to the south of CAR, was menaced by the rebels of the Movement for the Liberation of Congo (MLC), led by Jean-Pierre Bémba. Bémba and his rebel forces used the Central African Republic as their trading base to receive war materiel and also to export precious stones and minerals from the zone of the DRC which they controlled (Ouango, 2006a, 2006b).

Unhappy about the assistance and patronage that Patassé's regime seemed to be providing to Bémba, the DRC government of Joseph Kabila, son of Desiré Kabila, sought to break up that relationship. The Democratic Republic of Congo gave Déby weapons, ammunition, and billions of FCFA to recruit Chadian mercenaries from schools and universities and train them in an effort to support Bozizé in overthrowing Patassé. For an explanation of this complex effort by the DRC to overthrow the CAR by getting the president of Chad to send a CAR rebel against its president, see France Afrique's interview with Ngarlejy Yorongar entitled "Idriss Déby, nouveau patron de l'Afrique Centrale?" (Madonet, 2004).

According to Yorongar (Madonet, 2004), Colonel Daoud Souleïman, from the region of Guéra, was sent by Déby to his homeland to recruit the mercenaries. Instead of telling them honestly what their assignment would be — supporting Bozizé in an attempt to overthrow the president of the Central African Republic — he told them that ExxonMobil was in need of young people to secure its oil fields in Doba, Oriental Logone, in southern Chad. He added that the recruits would gather at the military training camp of Pazangué in southern Chad to receive appropriate training by Americans before being taken to the oil fields.

Daoud was very successful on this recruiting trip. His ability to recruit young people so easily was due, in no small part, to the fact that only 3 percent of Chadians have a regular income. Most of those who can count on being paid regularly for their teaching or government service are members of President Déby's inner circle. That inner circle, as mentioned before, consists primarily of relatives who, not incidentally, have become extremely rich (Debos, 2008).

In desperation and naïveté, then, many young men and teenagers of Guéra trusted Daoud without knowing the truth of the instructions he had received from Déby. In this amazing process of international intrigue and politico-commercial connections, young soldiers from southeast Chad and western Sudan (Darfur) would help Bozizé to return to Bangui as victorious general and then self-proclaimed president of CAR. The struggle to Bangui, however, would be a long one.

Training for the Chadians was quick (and of course did not involve the promised American trainers from ExxonMobil), and soon the young soldiers were sent to war against Patassé's regime, which was already weakened by various insurrections. There the young mercenaries were often defeated by the CAR forces because of the inadequacy of their training and lack of experience on the battlefield. Déby grew increasingly frustrated with the ineptitude of Bozizé's rebels and his Chadian mercenaries. For his part, Patassé was lucky that he was able to get assistance from Bémba's rebel troops and also Khadafi's Libyan air force through CEN-SAD. (See Verschave's *Noir Silence*, pp. 336–338, and International Crisis Group, 2007, for the French connection in all of this.)

The first time the young fighters from Guéra entered Bangui, they were pushed back by the Libyan forces who had come to help Patassé (at the urging of France, according to Yorongar [Verschave, 2000]). At this time, Patassé also summoned Bémba's Congolese rebels to help defend Bangui. All these forces—Patassé's army, Libyan air and ground forces, and Congolese rebels—combined to push the young fighters from Chad back to northern CAR. Unfortunately for Patassé and the popularity of his government, however, when the young Chadian fighters had been pushed out of the way, his friends the Congolese rebels turned to raping and looting in Bangui. Before long, the Chadian fighters reentered Bangui. Again, the Libyan forces and Congolese rebels repelled them. At this point, Déby was irate over the lack of results and sent experienced forces from his Zaghawa tribesmen to bolster the young trainees. These men, too, needed the job and the money (Kahn, 2003; Priest [Abbé] Yambassa, 2003).

Even these mercenaries were repeatedly defeated by Patassé's allies. Apparently these veteran Sudano-Chadian forces recalled their unfortunate adventure in the Democratic Republic of Congo and did not want to face Bémba's rebels again. In their 1999 campaign to assist Joseph Kabila against the Congolese rebels, Chadian mercenaries were captured and either killed or disfigured by having their noses, tongues, feet, or hands chopped off, and were allowed to cross back over the Ubangi River into the Central African Republic (Verschave, 2000, p. 337). As the news kept coming into Chad in 2003 about the repeated defeat of the mercenaries, people joked about Déby's mercenaries who always pulled back when they heard that Bémba's rebels were moving in their direction.

Because the military solution in the CAR was proving to be more challenging to achieve than Déby had planned, he needed to trump up new charges against Patassé. Déby expressed a concern about Libya to his peers in the six-country Economic and Monetary Community of Central Africa (CEMAC). From his previous experience with Libya, Déby did not think it advisable that Libyan troops be permitted anywhere near Chadian oil fields. He suggested to the CEMAC leaders that they help Patassé find more appropriate allies in the sub-region, someone more appropriate than the Libyans (Soudan, 2002).

This, then, was Déby's diplomatic approach. Claiming a desire for peace, Déby sought help from CEMAC. CEMAC arranged for Déby and Patassé to meet. Déby's conditions included removal of Libyan forces, removal of Bémba's Congolese rebels, and removal of Abdoulaye Miskine from the Central African Republic. Of course, Déby had no quarrel with Patassé himself, he said, but his "elder brother" had involved himself with inappropriate friends (Miskine, 2002).

Patassé seems to have realized at last that to concede to these terms would render him too vulnerable, so he asked CEMAC for help in negotiating a reasonable deal with Déby. As a result, CEMAC agreed to send a coalition of troops to replace the Conoglese and Libyans and support Patassé from rebel threats. The troops arrived early in March. The CEN-SAD conference was set to convene a few days later. Patassé wanted to attend that conference despite the fact that he had been warned by Ngarlejy Yorongar, an opposition party leader of Chad, that leaving his country at this time might result in a permanent vacation from Bangui. Despite the warning, Patassé decided to attend the conference to be reconciled with his "younger brother" through Muammar Khadafi (Madonet, 2004).

In Patassé's absence, the young Chadian forces entered the capital for a third time. This time they were not alone. They were joined by 5,000 of Déby's own fighters (Madonet, 2004). Moreover, this time they had the blessing of France (Oulatar, 2003; Mas, 2006; International Crisis Group, 2007) and would be successful.

Members of CEMAC (Gabon, Congo Republic, and Equatorial Guinea) began training their forces and sent them to Bangui as peacekeepers to replace Bémba's rebels and Khadafi's forces. As mentioned, at that time the 22 members of the Sahel and Saharan Community (CEN-SAD) to which Chad, CAR, and Libya belong, were preparing their regional meeting in Niamey, Niger. Khadafi sought to seize that opportunity to reconcile the "younger brother" with his "senior brother," that is, to serve as regional peacemaker and to end overt and threatened conflict between Déby and Patassé. Apparently, both Déby and Patassé welcomed Khadafi's suggestion to find common ground, but with different calculations. For his part, Déby seized on Khadafi's move toward reconciliation with Patassé with great joy, because he knew that Patassé would leave Bangui to reconcile with him. Once Patassé left the capital to fly to Niamey, Déby would seize the opportunity to overthrow Patassé's government (Madonet, 2004). For his part,

Patassé most likely saw Khadafi's suggestion as the last chance to clear up whatever misunderstanding with Déby had caused the current predicament, now that he had satisfied all three of Déby's concerns by sending away Abdouaye Miskine to Togo, allowing Libyan forces to return home, and instructing Bémba's rebels to cross back over the Ubangi into the Democratic Republic of Congo. Patassé clearly overestimated Déby's desire for peace and reconciliation.

Though Déby had an opportunity to overthrow the government in Bangui while Patassé attended the CEN-SAD conference in Niger, he would need more help. Déby discreetly asked Bozizé to come to Chad from Paris. However, there was an official agreement with France that Bozizé would stay in Europe as a "political refugee" (so as not to seem to threaten Patassé). France either deliberately turned a blind eye so that Bozizé could return to Africa (Dédjébé, 2003) or gave more active support to his return (see International Crisis Group, 2007, especially note 75). To avoid detection by authorities in Cameroon and Chad, as well as by ordinary people in those two countries, Bozizé disguised himself and entered Chad via Nigeria and Cameroon (Maldong, 2003). When he arrived in Koussouri, the Cameroon town that shares a border with N'Djaména, he telephoned Déby (Madonet, 2004).

Déby sent Colonel Daoud Soumaïne to Koussouri to escort Bozizé to N'Djaména. Instead of publicly crossing the Ngueli Bridge that separates N'Djaména from Koussouri, he would take Bozizé across the Chari Baguirmi River by pirogue, to keep secret his presence in the country. The two men were poled across the Chari River, and when they landed at Douguia, a tourist area, they were driven to N'Djaména. They telephoned Déby again (Madonet, 2004).

While Bozizé was waiting in N'Djaména for the impending fall of Bangui, Déby ordered his fighters from different garrisons and especially those from N'Djaména, Mongo, Sarh, Amtiman, and Abéché to join other fighters of the Oriental and Occidental Logone regions in Goré. At least 5,000 fighters were mustered into Goré for an imminent surprise attack (Madonet, 2004).

Yorongar le Moïban, the Chadian Federalist deputy (that is, a senator from Chad's opposition party), was informed about the movement of thousands of Sudano-Chadian fighters toward Goré, a Chadian frontier town, not far from the northern border of the Central African Republic. Upon hearing the news, Yorongar telephoned Patassé's prime minister to inform Patassé of the danger and to persuade him not to leave Bangui even to attend the meeting at Niamey. If Patassé left the capital, Yorongar warned, he would never return to Bangui as president of CAR (Madonet, 2004).

According to Yorongar (Madonet, 2004), Patassé rejected his prime minister's advice, thinking that peace would be more likely if Khadafi could facilitate reconciliation between himself and Idriss Déby. Yorongar later said he found it ironic that at the moment when Déby and Patassé achieved their reconciliation and the two presidents embraced in Niamey, Zaghawa mercenaries were at the gates of Bangui (Madonet, 2004). However, the risk was not to CAR's capital alone.

At the end of the conference, Patassé and his delegation might have been arrested or even assassinated on his return to the International Airport of M'Poko, in Bangui, had he not traveled to the conference with his wife. They escaped catastrophe because Patassé's wife delayed their trip back home by more than two hours to go shopping at the Niamey market. The president and his delegation impatiently waited to depart for home. Had they traveled on the planned schedule, they would have arrived at the Bangui Airport just as the Zaghawas and other mercenaries were coming perilously close to the airport and had not yet been detected by airport security agents (Soudan, 2003).

Patassé—who probably boarded the plane in Niger filled with the hope of living in peace with his "younger brother" and eventually even attaining a pacific solution with Bozizé after so friendly a reconciliation with Déby in Niamey—only barely escaped assassination when he returned home. As his aircraft approached Bangui, his palace was already being looted by Déby's mercenaries. Patassé's salvation that day was a skilled pilot. When Déby's mercenaries shot at Patassé's plane on its landing approach to the airport, the Libyan pilot quickly diverted the plane away from Bangui (Soudan, 2003; Sangonet, 2003).

Patassé called President Oumar Bongo of Gabon to let him know about the situation in Bangui and request permission to land in Libreville, Gabon. Oumar Bongo advised him to land in Yaoundé, Cameroon, not far from Bangui, ostensibly to give Patassé hope of clarifying the situation in Bangui so he could return to the capital as president. (In *Noir Silence*, Xavier Verschave makes a strong case for Bongo's serving the interests of FranceAfrique with this advice, rather than the legitimate interest of Africa.) Patassé's hope probably disappeared once he reached Yaoundé in Cameroon (Soudan, 2002).

The troops sent by CEMAC countries to Bangui to replace the Libyan force and Bémba's rebels did not stand and fight when Bozizé's mercenaries attacked the airport and the city. They withdrew to their respective camps, which left Bangui undefended. The CEMAC force's chief of staff, Colonel Basile Sillou, was interviewed by the peace organization IRIN (Integrated Regional Information Networks) the next day, and he said, "Our mission was not to defend the presidential residence but the head of the state, and I think that we have not failed in our mission" (Kashagama, 2003).

Patassé was probably expecting Cameroon president Paul Biya to come to his airport hotel room and comfort him in his time of trial and betrayal and then to discuss with him and other leaders how they could help him return to power in Bangui. That is what had happened in the previous case, when President Tanja of Sierra Leone had been ousted from his country by a military coup. Unfortunately for Patassé, only Biya's general secretary and military chief of staff came to visit. Later, they returned and asked Patassé to look for another country in which to seek asylum. Patassé's eyes now were opened. He realized that he had been abandoned by his peers. Very soon, Patassé found a new home in Togo, the country of his wife Angele (Soudan, 2002).

A CAR source of information is available to corroborate the news articles published in Chad and Cameroon about the fall of Bangui. Zacharie Gounoumoundou, a scholar living in Bangui, wrote a documentary booklet on the history of Déby's coup of Bangui (*Histoire de la Democratie en République Centrafricaine: Origines du coup d'état du 15 Mars 2003*). In this booklet, Gounoumoundou documents the events leading up to the coup and the deaths and events resulting from it. The booklet has not been published in the United States or Europe and is therefore difficult to obtain.

The fall of Bangui on March 15, 2003, was a great disaster not only for elected president Patassé but also for his country, the Central African Republic. A careful balance of forces and interests was thrown off. Indeed, in late 2002 when Patassé was menaced by Sudano-Chadians mercenaries engaged by Idriss Déby, he begged for help from the regional states of the Sahel (CEN-SAD) and even from the Movement for the Liberation of Congo (the MLC, led by Congo rebel leader Jean-Pierre Bémba). CEN-SAD agreed to help and was represented by Libyan, Sudanese, and Djiboutian forces (Agence France-Presse, 2002).

The rebels of Bémba also were eager to protect the regime of Patassé and thereby to protect their own interests. Those rebels knew that Déby's military forces had propped up the regime of Kabila (the father) in Congo during the previous year. Bangui in the Central African Republic served as an escape base for these rebels, just over the border and out of reach of Kabila's Congo forces. Kabila had given Déby money to pay mercenaries to help overthrow Bangui and wipe out Bémba's rebels (Madonet, 2004; Partnership Africa Canada, 2003). The worst-case scenario for Bémba and his followers would occur if Déby's Sudano-Chadians were able to take over Bangui while Congo troops patrolled the border, in which case they would be taken in a pincers movement.

On the one hand, Bémba's rebels were very helpful to President Patassé, because they had saved his regime many times. Mercenaries from Chad and Sudan had threatened Bangui in the past, and Bémba's rebels protected their base and Patassé's government by pushing out the mercenaries at Bangui's door. On the other hand, of course, Bémba's rebels constituted a real danger for the population of Bangui. Homes and businesses were looted, and women and girls were raped by these rebels. In fact, the actions of these rebels, by their association with Patassé, had destroyed the president's popularity in that area (Grignon, 2008).

Patassé's government was threatened by many outside enemies and internal insurgents. It was menaced by the insurgents from the tribe of the former president, André Kolingba, who sought to return to power. Then it was threatened by Bozizé, who is an ethnic Baya, that is, a member of one of the largest ethnic groups. Having suffered much, the population needed change that led to peace, not endless warfare.

It has been mentioned that in early 2003 the leaders of CEMAC, lobbied hard by Déby, convinced Patassé to replace CEN-SAD's forces (Libyan, Sudanese, and Djiboutian troops) and the rebels of Bémba with CEMAC's forces (African Union, 2003). Even before Bémba's rebels had left the Central African Republic and crossed the Ubangi River, Déby's forces were already in control of the International Airport of Bangui. On the 15th of March, when Déby cast Patassé out of leadership of CAR, was it CEMAC that betrayed Patassé? Or rather was it Déby who betrayed CEMAC and the African movement toward peace and democracy?

As described earlier, Déby's mercenaries had failed at least twice before to take Bangui, because it had been defended by Bémba's rebels and the Libyan troops. As soon as Déby was quite sure that those forces had been replaced by CEMAC's troops and also that Patassé would be in Niamey for the CEN-SAD conference, Déby quickly sent about 5,000 mercenaries to Bangui, including even regular Chadian Forces in addition to the mercenaries (Madonet, 2004).

The 5,000 fighters sent into the Central African Republic were divided into many units and occupied the towns from the north all the way to the south where the capital, Bangui, is located. The fighters were not sure whether they would enter into Bangui or would be pushed back by CAR forces. Only some of the units tested the strength of the defenders in the first assault. Some units were stationed at the door of Bangui in the quarter called PK12.

If the people of Bangui had sought change, it arrived on that day, Saturday, March 15, 2003. The public welcomed Bozizé's mercenaries with great rejoicing. Some spread out cloth on the ground for the rebel vehicles to drive over, welcoming the rebels as liberators. They had no way of knowing if the Sudano-Chadian mercenaries brought them the kind of peace that they had hoped for (Debos, 2008).

When the Chadian fighters first arrived in Bangui, the supporters of Bozizé called them "our liberators." Twenty-four hours later, the population of Bangui started seeing those "liberators" as criminals and thieves of the highest level. At that point the situation became worse than it had been when Patassé was trying to deal with corruption from the Democratic Republic of Congo rebels, particularly the partisans of Jean-Pierre Bémba (Debos, 2008).

The first of the Chadian units to loot Bangui stole vehicles and looted shops. These actions led to many civilian injuries and even deaths. Thus most of those mercenaries immediately got out of town with their booty and fled to Chad, and probably to Darfur as well (N'Diékhor, March 31, 2003; International Crisis Group, 2007). The following unit entered and violently helped itself to the town's goods the same way. However, the next units were not so lucky in their attempts to loot stores and steal cars. They were too late and started looking for other possibilities. Some of those later units looted the goods in government offices and houses. Those materials also flowed to Chad directly and to Sudan via Chad. Half a day later, the Bangui people who had danced and welcomed the rebels now cried out for their goods and wept for their loved ones now deceased (N'Diékhor, March 31, 2003).

In Bossangoa, the city north of Bangui in the center of the Central African Republic, when mercenaries there heard about what had happened in Bangui, they started looting their town, too. In Bossangoa, most institutions were looted, including cotton manufacturing companies, shops, and of course most of the homes. By the time the rebels were finished, the main cotton manufacturing business in Bossangoa was empty. The mercenaries hauled off all the vehicles, office machines, and doors. They looted other businesses and institutions, taking schools and administrative offices, as well. They even removed the big ginning machines installed at the cotton factory and took those machines to Chad (International Crisis Group, 2007). When they drove the machines up to Chad, they offered to sell them to CotonTchad, the cotton manufacturing firm. CotonTchad refused to buy the machines from the mercenaries, knowing the cotton industry was so regulated that the machines could eventually be traced from the Central African Republic to Chad (N'diékhor, April 16, 2003a & 2003b).

Furthermore, CotonTchad had no need for the machines, in part because president Déby had destroyed their business by paying them in counterfeit money. The cotton ginning machines eventually had to be driven all the way back to the Central African Republic, when Déby ordered all non–Zaghawa mercenaries to return their stolen goods to that country.

In addition to the rebel looters, there were some people from Bangui who seized the opportunity to steal whatever remained from their fellow citizens during this period of upheaval. A young man of the Central African Republic whom we will call Edgar provided information about these events in Bangui at the request of the author. According to Edgar, CEMAC's forces knew the Sudano-Chadian mercenaries were uneducated and ruthless. To save their own skins, then, CEMAC decided not to help the population of Bangui, despite the severity of looting and human carnage. Apparently CEMAC pleaded to leaders in their respective countries to persuade Déby to curb his mercenaries and save the honor of CEMAC's forces. Déby responded positively to the request from the CEMAC leaders because it enabled him to remain in Bangui and to increase the number of his troops there (N'Djaména Hebdo, March 24, 2003; Agence France-Presse, March 24, 2003).

The new units, sent within a day or two by French Transall C-160 transport, went to Bangui under the guise of curbing Déby's rebel forces who were already there. To add insult to injury, some of the new forces functioned under the label of CEMAC. Once they arrived, they worked fast. After two days the new arrivals themselves joined in the looting. According to N'Diékhor, even high-ranking government officials and dignitaries were not spared the humiliation and cruelty inflicted by the looters, whom they termed "animals" (N'diékhor, April 16, 2003a & 2003b). The new troops were quite clever in giving the impression of curbing the earlier rebel groups and providing order in the city. One technique they used was to establish themselves in strategic areas, such as a major crossroads. They controlled the flow of activity in and out of certain sectors, allowing Déby's rebels easy access and relieving Bangui looters of newly procured riches. Of course those who initially refused to relinquish their stolen goods were threatened and even physically harmed (according to Edgar, the informant from Bangui).

According to one CAR looter, the Chadian fighters positioned themselves at junctions of roads and in official and institutional buildings to stop the looters. They played a double game. The fighters allowed the local looters to steal the goods in the shops, institutions, and official buildings. The informant reported, "If the fighters saw you with those goods and liked them, they would take them away from you. Sometimes they would give you the chance to go back and try your luck again. If you found another interesting bit of goods, they would take that, too. If you had something of no value to them, you could take it away and benefit from your enterprise."

The young looter who provided this information continued with his commentary by saying that those fighters were always ready to kill. When they demanded the looted goods and someone tried to resist or ignore them, they would kill. He said the best way to survive was to bring one's loot directly to them and "let them sort through and select what they wanted, leaving the rest for you."

The Chadians became more and more rapacious over time. In spring 2004, one year later, Bozizé decided to try to get rid of them, lest they hurt his chances in the impending election in the Central African Republic. He paid those liberator-thieves their indemnity and asked his friend Déby to take them back. He did not want to offend Déby, however, and reassured his "good friend and benefactor" that he had not forgotten his promise to help Déby reclaim the money from the diamonds Patassé had sold.

Bozizé's decision to return the young men of Guéra and other fighters to Chad was a hard equation for Déby to process. Déby did not want the Guéra fighters in his Chadian army, for two reasons. First, these young men were not Zaghawa, of Déby's tribe. Secondly, Déby rarely paid his own soldiers, with the exception of Zaghawas, and he did not want to expend any money on the Guéra fighters when he no longer needed them. Finally, Déby thought of a solution. He would offer them to Khamis Abdallah, the leader of the Liberation Movement of Sudan (MLS), in Darfur (Chérif, 2006).

Déby and Khamis concluded that it would be a logical transition for the young men of Guéra to fight in Darfur because most of them were from the tribe of Dadjo Sil-lah, in Sudan. The Dadjos are a black African tribe who live in southwest Sudan and in Guéra, in the region of Goz Beïda and Gadjira near to Mongo in Chad (Chérif, 2006).

Once the ex-liberators got their pay, the airplane took them directly from the Bangui airport in the Central African Republic to André, a Chadian town near Darfur where the rebels of Khamis (MLS) had their base. It has been reported that most of these ex-liberators had to share some of their pay with Déby before they were sent to Darfur (Chérif, 2006). The leaders of the Guéra mercenaries, who had very little schooling, had expected to be welcomed into Déby's troops in N'Djaména and were somewhat affronted to have been shunted aside to Darfur after their many sacrifices on Déby's behalf in the Central African Republic. At this point, they decided they would refuse to fight against another country without any reason. So they contacted the Chadian rebels of the Alliance des

Démocrates Résistants (ADR) based in Darfur. That group was led by former Chadian police commissioner (precinct captain) Néné Ehemir and former engineer Hisseine Ahmat, who in turn was under the coordination of Dr. Younous Ibedou (who was living in the United States at that time). They became rebels against Déby (Chérif, 2006).

Once these ex-liberators joined the ADR, together they fused with another group in Darfur called the United Front for Change and Democracy (FUCD). Together, they launched an attack in March 2006 at the very door of the capital in N'Djaména. Without the help of France, Déby would have been removed from the Presidential Palace by this rebel force. Because French troops shot at them from military helicopters and fighter jets, however, their coup was unsuccessful. Most of these troops, along with their new allies, were arrested in N'Djaména and presented to the Chadian public via television, as Sudanese mercenaries, not as the natives of Chad they indeed were. Then they were killed (Chérif, 2006).

Ironically, then, some of the men whom Déby sent as mercenaries to unseat Patassé and install Bozizé in CAR to ensure that a friend (in his debt) held the land south of the border were so disenchanted by their treatment that they refused to fight in Darfur and instead attempted to oust Déby himself. The actions Déby has taken to ensure his own security have not only destabilized the entire region (Darfur and CAR, especially) but also threatened his own rule. Without strong French support, Déby could not survive.

Chapter 15

Misperceptions

Early in February 2008, civil war caused great destruction in N'Djaména (Boisbouvier, 2008). To understand this war, Chadians and their friends around the world have to dig to the root of the conflict over the past 46 years in Chad. This chapter provides the broad outlines of the conflict and a quick review of previous chapters in this book.

From Religious Struggle to Family Squabble

As we have seen, troubles in Chad were first created by Sudan and then Libya a few years after the independence of Chad from France in 1960. Sudan, on the east, strove to promote Islam in Chad and even to transform Chad into an Islamic country (Nolutshungu, 1996, pp. 253, 258; Mayadi, 1996). On the north, Libya also wanted to promote Islam in Chad but intended to add Chad to its own territory (Nolutshungu, 1996, p. 146). In fact, in 1976 Libya had already annexed Aouzou, the northernmost strip of Chad's desert contiguous with its border with Libya.

Chad's neighbors — Libya to the north and Sudan to the east — could then have been expected to cherish Chad and its peoples in a spirit of brotherhood. Islamification of Chad might have meant that Libya and Sudan shared with Chad the message of love and peace espoused in the Qur'an. Instead, these two countries used Chad as an experimental lab for weapons and techniques of war, including widespread thievery, destruction of property and resources, and murder. Sudan and Libya continuously incited the people of northeast Chad, in Borkou-Ennedi-Tibesti (BET), to create rebellions throughout the country and take political, economic, and cultural control of the country (Prunier, 2007).

Thousands of Chadians have perished since 1963, in the 50 years of warfare caused by Chad's neighbor countries (Toïngar, 2006). It would be difficult to argue that such murderous warfare has been a blessing to Islam or has in any way benefited the Islamic faith. Instead, the fighting has benefited only the political leaders of Libya and Sudan, who use Islam as a way to manipulate others for their own private purposes.

It has been claimed by many in the media that the recent rebellion in Chad is one more instance of Sudan's attempt to take control of Chad. In part, this is true, because Omar al-Bashir of Sudan has taken advantage of Déby's political weakness to send Sudanese fighters to help those who rebel against him (Prunier, March 5, 2008; Yorongar, 2007). Some journalists claim instead that the current rebellion and the Darfur crisis are a religious conflict between Islamists in Sudan and non–Islamists in Darfur and Chad. In fact, though there are Islamists in Sudan with considerable influence over al-Bashir's regime, his support of the Janjawiid in Darfur and eastern Chad is not primarily religious. Omar al-Bashir's fighters are not theologians but pawns in his maneuvers for greater political power for himself and his inner circle against the other stakeholders in Sudan. The conflict has also been regional within Chad. Sudan trained rebels in Borkou-Ennedi-Tibesti in northern Chad, and Libya trained other rebels in the same region, to take control of the country and promote Islam. The media have also noted that conflict in Darfur and elsewhere in Chad can be attributed to tribal hatreds. To be sure, much of the conflict in Chad has indeed been the result of tribal warfare, especially between the Zaghawas and their longtime enemies. And today strife is growing within Déby's family and among the Zaghawas. Much of this fighting has gone on in the northern region of the country, often leaving corpses to rot in the sun, with horrendous consequences for the living inhabitants — human and animal. Into this hell have been thrown kidnapped youth, sent to fight Déby's enemies, raped and drugged and killed as cannon fodder on the front lines, so the tragedy there has consequences for other tribes and regions, as well. The entire country has paid the price in material goods, financial loss, and death to keep Déby's power secure (Lacey, 2006).

Beginning only three years after the independence of Chad, the first generation of the rebellion against the government involved deadly attacks that caused the death of thousands of Chadians, especially rebel and army forces, during the 1960s and 1970s. At the end of the 1970s, when Hissène Habré became prime minister of Chad (with the help of his friends in Sudan and with France's assistance), he brought war into the capital of Chad. That war, sprung on the South on February 12, 1979, was designed to eliminate intellectuals from the South and expand the power of the

North. Hissène Habré's war greatly damaged the country and of course decimated the South (Nolutshungu, 1996, pp. 92–115).

To maintain his control over the North, now threatened by Libya-backed rebels, Hissène Habré sprayed bullets to the north as well as the south. From 1979 to 1989, Hissène Habré and his allies — the tribes still ruling Chad today — at first killed most of the intellectuals, Christians, and non-believers who were not from the North. Then they attacked anyone with power or prestige who was not from the region of Borkou-Ennedi-Tibesti in northern Chad. Idriss Déby, Hissène Habré's commander-in-chief, even immolated some Christian congregations in their churches, claiming himself thereby a pro-Islamist Muslim and ingratiating himself with Sudan and Habré. In his role as commander-in-chief, Déby pushed his fighters to kill any Christians or non-believers in the South (Toïngar, 2006; Yorongar, 2003; Nolutshungu, 1996).

Once Habré and Déby had finished with the Christians and non-believers, they turned against some intellectuals and influential people of their own faith. They moved fighters into other regions, too, like Guéra in central-eastern Chad, to terrorize and kill. Finally Déby and Habré — both men from the region of Borkou-Ennedi-Tibesti in northern Chad and sharing the same religious heritage — ended by fighting each other. That war was known as a tribal conflict, Gourane against Zaghawa, by the people of BET. However, the war is more accurately seen by many other Chadians as a conflict between Chadian military forces on one side and on the other side a group of Chadian rebels and Sudanese mercenaries led by Idriss Déby under the aegis of France (Madonet, 2004).

When Déby finally ousted Habré from power, he undertook the same pattern of conflict and struggle as his former mentor, Habré. It was now Déby's role to weaken his enemies and expand the power of his own people. He reinstituted the same scenario of killing people from other regions, starting with the Hadjiraï and Sara peoples. Many intellectuals and influential people in the communities were assassinated — usually shot or poisoned. Christians and followers of other religions were assassinated. After the Sara and Hadjiraï were destroyed, it was the turn of the people of the Ouaddaï, Salamat, Biltine, and BET regions. To increase his own power, Déby needed to weaken all others (Madonet, 2004).

In 1993, the struggle shifted from a chastisement of enemy tribes in the same region to a conflict within the same tribe, the Zaghawas. The first conflict of this war was between Déby and his former military comrade and brother in-law, Abbas Koty, who was forced to flee for his life. With the complicity of Libya, Abbas agreed to sign a statement of peace and return to Chad. Within two weeks, Abbas Koty was assassinated in N'Djaména. After that there was another insurrection among the Tama (another sub-group of the Zaghawa), who challenged Déby's fighters and mercenaries. In addition to these first two insurrections against Déby's rule, there have been many other groups of rebels from that same region and from among the tribes of the BET that have plunged the country into mourning (Nolutshungu, 1996, pp. 250–253).

From 2004 to today, the war wages not only among people of the same region and among people of the same tribe; it is a war within one family. The struggle for power now rages between brothers-in-laws Mahamat Nouri and Idriss Déby and between nephew Timan Erdémi and his uncle Idriss Déby (Malitti, 2008).

Déby was used by the Islamic regime of Sudan for many decades. He killed thousands of Chadians to promote the political and religious agenda of Sudan. On the one hand, Déby promoted Islam in the towns and villages of Chad by giving Muslims higher status, preference in employment, and political advancement throughout the country, regardless of training or education (Mayadi, 1996).

Even today these practices are employed in Chad and especially preference one branch of Islam. Déby thereby makes himself not the president of Chad but the president of the Sebdo Muslims of Chad. At the same time, Déby tells the Western countries that he and his government are a bulwark of religious toleration against the Islamist regime of Sudan that seeks to install an Islamic regime in Chad.

All of this makes it difficult for outside observers to understand the truth about Déby's allegations against Sudan, his claim that al-Bashir has stirred up and armed mercenaries against his (Déby's) rightful government in Chad. Chadians and their friends in other countries who are closely watching the situation in Chad are beginning to understand the truth.

In fact, Déby was closely allied with Sudan for more than ten years. When he was Hissène Habré's commander-in-chief, Sudan helped Déby topple his president and take power for himself. Déby certainly did not complain at that time about Sudan's involvement in Chadian politics. It was only when Déby failed in his secret attempt to carve a Zaghawa kingdom in Darfur (Appendix F) out of the territories of Sudan and Chad — only when he failed to realize a dream that would have betrayed Sudan's former support for his regime — that he started accusing Sudan of trying to Islamize Chad (Madonet, 2004; HelBongo, 2008).

In theory, Chad is a secular country, not under the control of any particular religion. In practice, though, the country has been ruled by Islamic regimes for nearly three decades. Not surprisingly, Déby has not gained fame in Islamic circles for enlightened leadership or good governance. One wonders if any Islamic ruler in the world has so destroyed the reputation of his country in the world and at the same time committed multitudinous crimes against his own country as Déby has.

Yes, the majority of Chadians would agree with Déby that rebel groups from Sudan and Libya have been destroying Chad. Chadians know also that the recent rebels backed by Sudan would never bring democracy to the country even if they could successfully topple Déby from power. The people of Chad know that these rebels — Déby's own relatives and tribesmen — would bring only another round of murder and terror, just as the regimes of Hissène Habré and Idriss Déby did (International Crisis Group, 2006). The great majority of people in Chad are terrified of the rebels, who use the word "democracy" as their platform for eliminating Déby and taking power for themselves. This is because, as an old adage says, when you have been attacked by a serpent, you will be scared of a rope on the ground. So Chadians would of course be frightened now of any group of rebels coming from Sudan and Darfur. Prior experience with serpents Habré and Déby have taught the people of Chad to be wary of men from Sudan promising democracy (Amnesty International, 2001).

Déby claims that there is no civil war in Chad, and that, too, is correct. There is no well-organized Chadian party opposing Déby with force of arms, and no vast area of Chad has threatened to withdraw from the union. Déby is correct when he claims that Sudan wants to overthrow his regime with mercenaries and that only a few Chadians lead these Sudanese mercenaries. Déby also is accurate when he asserts that the government of Sudan wants to surround Chad with Islamists. Déby is right, but he does not tell the whole truth.

Déby does not tell the truth to the people of Chad and the world, the truth about the external attacks and internal problems that his regime has experienced. The Sudanese mercenaries that Déby claims Sudan is sending to overthrow his regime are of the same tribe as the mercenaries that Sudan gave to Déby to overthrow the regime of Hissène, and today these same mercenaries are in control of Chad and are murdering Chadians without pity or remorse (Yorongar, 2007).

Déby also neglects to mention that he has brought domestic and foreign pressure to bear on his regime both by massacres of Chadian citizens and by changing the constitution to bestow on himself the presidency for life. Finally, Déby neglects to acknowledge to the world that he himself created the rebellion in Darfur (Yorongar, 2007; HelBongo, 2008; Prunier, March 5, 2008).

If Déby were honest with himself and with the people of Chad, he would have spoken on television and radio after the rebels failed to oust him with their attacks on N'Djaména early in 2008. He would have apologized to the people of Chad and the world because his naïveté brought all these troubles to his country. He would apologize to relatives and parents of the hundreds of innocent people who were killed for nothing during and after these attacks against his regime. Déby would follow in the footsteps of the former president, Goukouni Weddeye, who accorded an interview to Radio France International (Boisbouvier, 2008) and offered his regrets for being so naïve as to be manipulated by others, resulting in the destruction of his country.

Goukouni added that the attacks in N'Djaména were "programmed" externally, by other countries. Although he did not name names, Goukouni was indirectly accusing Western countries, most particularly France. Goukouni's interview was well received by many Africans whose countries had been colonized by France, because those people well understand how FranceAfrique's politics have been damaging Africa and especially the region formerly ruled by France (Verschave, 2003).

Déby Destroys Chad, with France's Help

Probably Goukouni was correct in saying the attacks at the door of N'Djaména were pre-programmed. Those attacks were part of a three-player version of Stratego attempted by Sudan, Chad, and France. The big loser is Chad and the winners are Sudan and France — and of course Déby.

Chad is the big loser because the attacks in early 2008 damaged the country so greatly in so little time. The infrastructure that Chad had built up for decades was destroyed in only a few days. Artillery shells blew up public buildings, Central Market, and homes. These shells were fired by rebel groups as well as governmental forces and their mercenaries. The game was pre-arranged, Goukouni surmises, because certain parts of the city were spared. No shells fell on the airport. No bridges were destroyed. However, the parliamentary buildings were completely destroyed. The historical archives of the country exist no longer. Worse yet, many Chadians were killed, and the side effects of these attacks will affect many future generations of Chad (Boisbouvier, 2008).

Omar al-Bashir of Sudan can swagger now that he has won greatly in these attacks. He reprised his winning strategy of the 2006 confrontation. When the Sudanese rebel groups funded and armed by Déby took control of some areas in Darfur, Khartoum responded by generously arming and endowing Chadians — Chadian tribes rebelling against Déby's atrocities against them — and sending them directly against N'Djaména.

The trip took two to four days, giving Déby time to panic and order his Sudanese rebels to leave Darfur under minimal guard and come to the capital to save his regime. Weakly guarded Darfur was ripe for the plucking. Al-Bashir seized an opportunity to take back control of Sudan's territory from Déby's mercenaries in Darfur. To minimize loss of his own forces, instead of using the Sudanese army to face the rebels of Darfur, al-Bashir scrupulously employed Chadian rebels to harass the few forces holding Darfur and thus easily overran almost all of Darfur without harm to his own troops. Sudan won back almost the entire territory of Darfur, defeating Déby and the rebels of Darfur primarily by their absence from the field.

Another brilliant play of this 2008 game was that in employing Chadians to fight against Déby, Sudan's al-Bashir was able to minimize the effect of two peacekeeping forces sent to the region. EUFOR-Chad troops, primarily French, were setting up to patrol Chad's borders with Sudan and the Central African Republic on a mission to prevent alien forces from entering Chad. Just as in 2006, the forces entering Chad from Sudan were Chadians. The French leader of EUFOR-Chad troops on the border found the assignment a bit more "complicated" than anticipated. Instead of using his troops massed on the border to pressure Sudan, he found his troops massed on the border, neutralized. And UNAMID (United Nations–African Union Mission in Darfur) was thereby prevented from becoming operational (Prunier, March 5, 2008).

France may be the biggest winner of all in the 2008 rebel conflict because not a single French soldier was killed in the fighting in Chad, except one sergeant of EUFOR (European Union Forces) in a squabble in Darfur. France had complete capability to stop the Chadian rebels from crossing Sudan's border into Chad. Anywhere along the rebels' several days' drive from the border to N'Djaména, France could have halted their movement. The rebels could have been completely prevented from launching attacks against N'Djaména, thus sparing the capital and its people and buildings. Alternatively, France could have withheld its troops indefinitely and let the rebels take care of Déby so that the country could turn the page to a new chapter, to the harm or the benefit of Chad.

A cynical view is that France was playing a double game with the rebels and with Déby just to destroy Chad. Probably by doing that, France wrings everything from Déby — favors for diplomats, money for "advisors," and business for French interests. And Déby could not say no, because the rebels were at the door of his presidential palace.

The more charitable opinion is that France found itself in an untenable situation. Prunier (March 5, 2008) takes this view when he says that

France at first provided Déby with very little support to avoid criticism for propping up Déby's "dubious regime," but then took courage (when supported by the African Union and the United Nations) and said through Defense Minister Hervé Morin that France "would do what was necessary in the event of a renewed attack." Though the rebels begged France to adopt a neutral stance (Prunier, March 5, 2008), they were defeated not by Déby but by the arms, aerial surveillance, intelligence, and logistical support of France (Mas, April 14, 2006, among other sources).

If France really wanted to end the sufferings of Chadians and help the country and the sub-region to get peace, say the people of Chad, the last attack of February 2008 in N'Djaména would have been a good opportunity to bring the regime of Déby, the groups of rebel forces, and the democratic opposition leaders to the negotiating table. France could have exerted the pressure needed to end the war with its disastrous effects on all the sub-region. If the source of the trouble in the sub-region resides in Déby's palace, then France had its opportunity to liberate Chad.

Unfortunately, France chose a different strategy, one that damaged the capital of Chad and its environment, one that caused Déby to arrest Chad's democratic leaders and increase the tortures and crimes by his mercenaries in the country (Meynier, 2008). The level of assistance provided by France during the two-day attack against the regime of Déby by Timan and Nouri, Déby's nephew and brother in-law respectively, revealed to the world the nature of FranceAfrique politics and of their protégé, Déby.

Déby has won since 1990. His deceptions, however, have brought monstrous consequences to his own family, to the families of the people of Chad, and of course to the environment. Déby knows that after his presidency ends, he will either be jailed and charged with crimes against humanity, as Charles Taylor was, or tortured by fear of trial and reprisals. He has reason to fear leaders of the institutions he has damaged, family members of the people he has put to death, individuals whose reputations he has destroyed, and governments whose currencies he debased. So Déby clings to power like a squirrel chittering on the branch of a tree; if threatened, he hops to the next branch. The branches of Déby's support, the real powers behind his regime, are the petroleum resources of Chad which Déby has appropriated, the soldiers sent by France to keep his enemies at bay, and the rebels of Darfur, his mercenary troops.

Déby wins today but will lose tomorrow when those nations and international organizations wake up and discover the truth about this man. Changes in the political situation of Libya in 2011 make it less likely that France will need to prop up a regime in Chad to counter a new Khadafi. More and more, Déby becomes expendable. Experience teaches the truth of the adage that a liar will eventually be found out: in the heat of the day, a politician must eventually remove his cloak and reveal his lies. Déby has succeeded longer than most in cloaking the truth. Opposition parties within Chad, however, are not deceived about the nature of this man. A member of one opposition party says, "Despite our oil, our cotton, our rich farmland in the south, look at how poor this country is. We want some kind of change. We are not for the rebellion, but we are not for Déby either. The international community might say Déby is the lesser of two evils, but they are not living with him" (Polgreen, 2008).

Déby's ability to hang on to power after the second attack of rebels in N'Djaména in January and February 2008 was a gift from France. Unfortunately, keeping Déby in power further damages Chad and regresses the country by a century, moving it backward to a point before even the meager colonial development by France, before independence in 1960. It seems that Chad never had a chance to learn from other nations.

Nor has Chad learned from the bloodshed of the past 50 years. Déby's strategy when attacked was not to send his mercenaries out of the capital against the rebels but rather to arrest democratic leaders of opposition parties. He knows that these parties had nothing to do with the recent attacks. He knows that the attacks came from family and clan members whom he has betrayed (Tedga, 2008; Polgreen, 2008).

After the attack on N'Djaména, the rebels of Darfur who came to reinforce Déby's troops caused mayhem in the capital. While the world watched to see if Déby would be toppled from power, foreign logging companies and the "resources" company of Déby's older brother saw an opportunity to take advantage of the situation. While the world struggles to protect the environment, Déby and his pals are clear-cutting the trees all around N'Djaména out of fear that rebels might take cover among them (Rolley, 2008).

Many of the trees recently chopped down had been planted before the independence of Chad not only to beautify the city but also to protect the capital from bad weather. In fact, the trees lining the main street of the capital were centuries old (BBC News, March 4, 2008). They moderated the temperature, protecting people from the force of the sun and providing a kind of air conditioning for the entire city. In addition, the trees protected the city from violent windstorms and sandstorms that used to threaten N'Djaména's flimsy dwellings and government buildings. They created a kind of parkway of refreshment for all the people as well as an open-air market for the selling of many goods (Rolley, 2008). Many people in N'Djaména do not have money to take a taxi or to buy a bicycle to get to work. Itinerant workers walk, and sometimes they must walk in temperatures above 100 degrees Fahrenheit. Now the trees are gone, because

Déby fears attack by his nephew, and the city has been diminished and dehumanized (Herz, 2008).

Déby has not only cut down trees but has also razed houses and other buildings wherever the rebels passed through the city — or wherever future rebels might move secretly toward the palace. According to Human Rights Watch and Amnesty International, thousands of people were made homeless in early 2008 because of Déby's paranoia (Amnesty International, 2009). By mid-2008, thousands of people in N'Djaména were still living outside, without shelter. Even to get something to eat was a serious problem for them (Gagnon, April 2, 2008).

Because private citizens in Chad lack the means to rebuild elsewhere, destruction of their homes has seriously impinged on their survival. The typical Chadian has had to struggle for decades just to purchase land in the city, enough land for a small house. It would not be unusual for a family to sacrifice greatly, even going hungry for years, before building a single bedroom on the property. The reason for the destruction of so many homes seems to be Déby's interest in personal and national security. To protect the palace in recurring and recent fratricidal wars, he gave orders to his subordinates to destroy all the houses located in the areas where the rebels had launched their attacks against his regime in N'Djaména. Journalists have noted that Déby's claims to be a humanitarian are not supported by this kind of action. A soldier must respect the human rights of enemies, and a ruler has even greater responsibility with regard to the rights of his or her own people (Herz, 2008).

Has Déby found a way to offset this mass destruction of homes by providing funds so that former residents can take their children to their native villages? It is true that Déby has taken out some loans from Arab institutions and other countries, but to date he has not shared the resulting wealth with his nation's poor. Instead, he uses the money (and Chad's oil revenues) to hire mercenaries from different continents and purchase war materiel. While his people are suffering and starving, he pays $5,000 USD per flight to pilot mercenaries from Algeria and Ukraine. When one of these pilots reaches a target, he receives $10,000 (Tedga, 2008).

Satom, one of the biggest French companies in Chad, signed a contract with Déby for several billion CFA francs to dig a trench completely around the capital of Chad (Adoum, 2008). The trench was dug ten feet deep around the city (BBC News, March 4, 2008). N'Djaména is the only capital city surrounded by a moat.

The plan is probably to mine the roads into the city in case of future rebel attacks. This money could be used to help the people of Chad. It could be used for hospitals, schools, water plants, and buildings that have been destroyed by war. Does Déby really care about Chad? Do the countries that are supporting him realize that his continued hold on power means that millions of Chadians will continue to die and suffer for his greed? The World Bank recently canceled its deal to fund Déby's operations, recognizing the corruption of his regime and expressing sorrow that the monies intended to mitigate suffering in Chad have instead been used for private purposes (BBC News, September 10, 2008).

Nor is Déby's neglect of his people the worst of his crimes. The rebels of Darfur, secret agents of Déby, and the Presidential Guards have been deliberately making the lives of Chadians miserable. Some citizens have been arrested for no reason and then tortured or killed. Others have lost their property for no reason. Some women are victims of harassment, sexual abuse and worse because they belong to this or that tribe or are related to this or that man (Tedga, 2008).

Some countries had been protecting Déby by saying that Déby is a good leader. They see him as a president who is fighting for democracy in Chad (Tobner, 2006). The last attack of February 2008 and Déby's reaction to it, including the swift arrest and murder of his law-abiding political opponents, should clarify for us all that Déby is no democrat. After Déby, Chad will need many years and much assistance to dress the wounds that this man has created in Chad and in the world.

EUFOR Misguided

After the recent rebel attacks, European forces were deliberately sent not to N'Djaména but to the periphery of the country, to secure the borders from foreign aggression. These EUFOR troops are to protect refugees fleeing Sudan into Chad but also to keep enemy troops from infiltrating the "Sudanese" refugees. It is true that there are Sudanese refugees in Chad, but most of the refugees fleeing Darfur are in fact Chadians. Although EUFOR seeks the noble goal of keeping the peace, it is ignoring the many in the city for the few on the borders. Thousands more Chadians are refugees within their own capital city of N'Djaména (Yorongar, 2007).

As a demonstration of Déby's influence on media opinion, consider the example of the Darfur orphans. Déby tried to convince international organizations that there are a million Sudanese refugees and that he needed international assistance to protect them from the Janjawiid and hold back Sudanese forces. The United Nations created a camp and invited refugees to come for food and protection. What they did not realize was that most of the refugees were in fact Déby's Darfur mercenaries and rebels as well as Darfur villagers and Chadians. When Déby's political opponent Yorongar realized the situation, he warned international agencies that Déby was filling the camp not with true victims of Darfur but with people of his own region. This was demonstrated most dramatically when the French organization Zoe's Ark attempted to take to France what they thought were 103 "Sudanese orphans." It turned out that the children were not orphans at all, and at least 95 of the 103 were Chadians (Bétreau, 2008, p. 109). Déby finally had some difficulty convincing Europe that he had ever been overrun with Sudanese refugees.

Even today, most of the people whom EUFOR troops encounter in eastern Chad are Chadians rather than Sudanese refugees. Now that Déby's wrath and paranoia have turned him against the people of N'Djaména, the primary human rights abuses are found in the capital city. It would be useful if some of the EUFOR forces were deployed to help the thousands of Chadians now suffering in N'Djaména instead of in the zones where right now casualties are far fewer. EUFOR has the power right now to prevent the tragedies of tomorrow. EUFOR's primary purpose should be to stop the sufferings imposed on the people of Chad by their ruler, and particularly the residents of N'Djaména. EUFOR troops instead serve Déby, giving him a chance to stay in power.

Déby Expands His Power Through Deception

In 2001, when asked by a Radio France International journalist if he would step down after his second term, Déby responded that his job in his second term of office was to reinforce democracy in Chad. He would not change the constitution of the country even if 100 percent of the deputies in Parliament were of his party.

> *Je prends cet engagement publiquement: je ne serai pas candidat à l'élection présidentielle en 2006. Je ne modifierai pas la Constitution quand bien même j'aurais une majorité de 100%! Je le dis haut et fort: ce qui me reste à faire au cours de mon dernier mandat, c'est de préparer le Tchad à l'alternance au pouvoir, une alternance démocratique, pacifique, sans rupture. Je veux que ce pays passe d'une étape à une autre, en douceur, sans déchirure. Voilà la responsabilité qui sera la mienne. Je l'assumerai quoi qu'il arrive.*
>
> I publicly make this commitment: I will not be a candidate for the 2006 presidential election. I will not modify the Constitution even if I should have a majority of 100%! I loudly and strongly proclaim this: What remains for me to do during my last term as president is to prepare Chad for a power alternative, a democratic alternative, peaceful, without a breach. I want this country to move from one step to another, in peacefulness, without a split.

This is the responsibility which will be mine. Whatever happens, I will take this responsibility upon myself [Smith, 2001].

Nevertheless, in 2003 his party reviewed his eligibility for another term, and Déby was made president for life.

In 2003, Déby wanted to take control of the entire sub-region of Africa by overthrowing the government of Ange Félix Patassé of the Central African Republic. By March 15 of that year, he took over the country. His puppet now rules there.

In 2003, Déby formed the intention of creating the Great Kingdom of Zaghawa by merging 13 counties of this tribe in Sudan with four counties in Chad. He has nearly achieved that dream (Yorongar, 2007; HelBongo, 2008).

Déby shamed the World Bank in late 2001 (Useem, 2002). When Chadians told the World Bank that Déby was not the kind of president who would develop his country, Déby swore before the assembly that he would use his nation's oil revenues to bring wealth to Chad's people. The World Bank gave him the funds he needed to build pipelines. Today the World Bank is not in a good position to say that it helped Chad to fight poverty. The situation in Chad is worse than when there were no oil revenues. The country has more debt than before. The fund for the new generation has disappeared. All oil revenues are used to buy mercenaries and war goods to destroy the country.

When Déby was recently threatened by rebel attacks and called upon his friends in France to protect him, France convinced the United Nations to help by arguing that Chad is a democratic country. According to the three main rebel leaders of the 2008 assaults, Koulamallah, Timan Erdémi, and Mahamat Nouri, even before asking the UN's permission, France had ordered its troops to rescue Déby. Instead of justifying France's faith in his democratic principles and pursuing the rebels, it is believed that Déby arrested the democratic leaders of Chad who have nothing to do with the rebellions. The war is between members of Déby's tribe and family. It is not likely that outsiders would be involved by supporting the rebels (Tedga, 2008).

French president Sarkozy went to Chad to meet Déby in early 2008 (Agence France-Presse, 2008; Le Figero, 2008; Vincent, 2008). He was concerned about political leaders who had gone missing. (Déby denied that he had arrested his political opponents.) After assurances from Déby, Sarkozy announced to the world that an international commission would be established to clarify the situation to the satisfaction of all. Only a few weeks later, Déby announced that a *national* commission would be appointed, and foreign diplomats and human rights workers would be permitted to "observe" its functioning. Two years later, democracy and freedom have not yet come to Chad.

Chapter 16

The International Criminal Court

In 1998, the United Nations drafted the Rome Statute creating an international criminal court. The International Criminal Court (ICC) was empowered in 2002 to investigate and try crimes of genocide, crimes against humanity, war crimes, and the crime of aggression (although it cannot currently exercise jurisdiction over the crime of aggression until a definition of aggression has been agreed upon). According to the preamble to the Rome Statute, one impetus for creation of this permanent tribunal was the memory of the victims of war crimes, crimes against humanity, aggression, and genocide in the 20th century. Another was the UN's need to put an "end to impunity for the perpetrators of these crimes and thus to contribute to the prevention of such crimes" (United Nations, 1998). Human rights activists in Africa as elsewhere claimed the creation of the ICC as a victory for their tireless efforts. Opposition leaders who had suffered long under despotic regimes found the Court to be a useful means to end senseless wars imposed on Africa by external sources (AllAfrica, 2009).

However, some leaders in Africa have seen the creation of the ICC as yet one more form of neo-imperialism. Although France and other European powers granted independence to their African colonies decades ago, they still need to protect their Western interests and to deal with African leaders who long to create real economic development in their countries (Rwanda News Agency, 2010).

As Sudan's president Omar al-Bashir has said, "We [African leaders] think that the ICC is a tool to terrorize countries that the West thinks are disobedient (PBS, 2009).

President Paul Kagamé of Rwanda was one of these latter leaders in Africa. He was among those who refused to sign the statutes creating the ICC or to arrest Sudan's Omar al-Bashir for crimes against humanity.

> Not because I am opposed in principle to international justice, nor because Heads of State are above the law, nor because al-Bashir would *a priori* be innocent of the crimes he is accused of, but because I have no faith in the ICC. The International Criminal Court cannot render impartial and equitable international justice. The problem is not that up to now only Africans have been brought before this court. That is on the periphery. The problem is that, since the beginning, we have been able to see, feel and detect, in its very selective way of working, a mixture of political agenda and manipulation by the rich against the poor [AllAfrica, 2009].

Some leaders in Africa call the court's justice a system of "two weights, two measures," that is, a double standard (Chitour, 2009). Many presidents in Africa, including Abdoulaye Wade of Senegal, Muammar Khadafi of Libya, and the president of the African Union Commission, Jean Ping, have expressed similar sentiments. In fact, when Khadafi said the ICC represented a "new world terrorism" (AllAfrica, 2009; Agence France-Presse, 2009), few disagreed. More recently, Khadafi called the work of the ICC "neo-colonialism" (Teluu, 2011).

These criticisms of the ICC in some ways are deserved. So far, no friends of Western countries have been charged with crimes and taken to The Hague, although an attempt was made to chastise Israel for its treatment of residents in Gaza in 2008 (Slackman & Worth, 2009). And so far, everyone charged by the ICC since it began its work in 2002 has been African.

On the other hand, the International Criminal Court could also be blamed for not investigating enough crimes or indicting enough African leaders. So far, the ICC has charged more than 13 men (Adusei, 2009). Yes, each of these men has probably committed horrendous crimes against their fellow human beings. Nevertheless, Idriss Déby, president of Chad, has committed worse crimes, and he has not been charged. Consider the charges against the criminals currently in ICC custody or charged with crimes.

Germain Katanga and Mathieu Ngudjolo

Germain Katanga led the Patriotic Resistance Force in Ituri (FRPI), and Mathieu Ngudjolo Chui led the National Integrationist Front (FNI). They were arrested by Congolese authorities and sent to The Hague.

Katanga was arrested early in March 2005 and Ngudjolo on February 6, 2008, for the crimes that they committed in the Democratic Republic of Congo (Radio Nederland Wereldomroep, 2008).

The chamber of the ICC confirmed that the following war crimes were committed during an attack on Bogoro village in early 2003 by warlords Katanga and Chui:

• using children under the age of 15 to take active part in the hostilities;
• directing an attack against a civilian population as such or against individual civilians not taking direct part in hostilities;
• willful killings;
• destruction of property;
• pillaging;
• sexual slavery;
• rape; and
• murder [ICC, September 24, 2009].

Joseph Kony, Vincent Otti, Okot Odhiambo and Dominic Ongwen

Joseph Kony and his lieutenants Vincent Otti, Okot Odhiambo, Dominic Ongwen, and the late Raska Lukwiya have also been charged by the ICC. They have been accused of attacking and pillaging communities in Uganda and southern Sudan, killing thousands of men, women, boys, and girls from different communities, destroying villages and camps, and abducting thousands of individuals, especially children. After a full investigation, in July 2005 the ICC issued warrants of arrest for Joseph Kony and his lieutenants. The warrants of arrest referred to crimes against humanity and war crimes committed in Uganda since July 2002. The charges, more than 30, include murder, sexual enslavement, rape, and forced enlisting of children (AI Index, 2007).

Charles Taylor

President Charles Taylor of Liberia, when invited by U.S. president George Bush to step down, was guaranteed asylum in Nigeria in early 2006. On March 29, 2006, according to Nigerian government sources, he tried to leave Nigeria because of pressures that Nigeria was experiencing from Western countries to send him back to Liberia or to Sierra Leone to respond to charges against his acts when he was president.

From 2006 to 2013, Taylor was in the custody of the ICC where he faced 11 charges. Taylor was charged on the basis that he allegedly backed Revolutionary United Front (RUF) rebels fighting in Sierra Leone. Taylor was accused of having links with senior leaders in the RUF — such as Foday Sankoh, Sam Bockarie (aka Mosquito), Issa Sesay, and others (Reynolds, 2007). He was also accused of supporting the Armed Forces Revolutionary Council (AFRC) and is said to be responsible for Liberian forces fighting in support of the Sierra Leonean rebels (Reynolds, 2007; Open Society Justice Initiative, n.d.). He is said to have recruited children under 15 years of age and used them in hostilities (Coalition to Stop the Use of Child Soldiers, 2008). He will serve a 50-year prison term in Britain (BBC News, 2011). The specific counts against President Taylor are as follows:

- five counts of war crimes: terrorizing civilians, murder, outrages on personal dignity, cruel treatment, and looting;
- five counts of crimes against humanity: murder, rape, sexual slavery, mutilating and beating, and enslavement; and
- one count of other serious violations of international humanitarian law: recruiting and using child soldiers [Open Society Justic Initiative, n.d.].

Ahmed Haroun and Ali Kosheib

The ICC charged two Sudanese with crimes against humanity in April 2007. Ahmed Haroun was a minister in al-Bashir's government, and in 2003 and 2004 he was responsible for keeping the peace in Darfur. The Janjawiid he created, funded, and supplied to keep the peace in fact committed so many atrocities that Haroun is now charged with the crimes committed by his Arab militia. Janjawiid leader Ali Kosheib is accused by the ICC of ordering murder, mass rape, and torture of non-combatants in west Darfur (BBC News, 2007) as well as new crimes in 2013.

Jean-Pierre Bémba

Jean-Pierre Bémba Gombo, former vice president of the Democratic Republic of Congo, was arrested in Belgium for crimes committed by his forces in the Central African Republic. His rebels were in that country from October 2002 to March 2003 on demand of CEN-SAD (Communauté des Etats Sahélo-Sahariens), the organization of 22 Sahel and Saharan countries, to help protect the democratically elected government of Ange Felix Patassé. Patassé's power was at that time being menaced by the rebels of General Bozizé, who in turn was supported by Chadian armies sent by Idriss Déby.

Today, Bémba is in the custody of the ICC. He was initially charged with these crimes:

- seven counts of murder constituting a crime against humanity within the meaning of article 7(1)(a) of the statute;
- one count of rape constituting a crime against humanity within the meaning of article 7(1)(g) of the statute;
- six counts of murder constituting a war crime within the meaning of article 8(2)(c)(i) of the statute;
- two counts of rape constituting a war crime within the meaning of article 8(2)(e)(vi) of the statute; and
- eight counts of pillaging constituting a war crime within the meaning of article 8(2)(e)(v) of the statute [ICC, June 15, 2009].

Thomas Lubanga

Thomas Lubanga Dyilo of the Democratic Republic of Congo was a leader of the Union of Congolese Patriots (Union des Patriotes Congolais, UPC), a party in rebellion against the government of President Laurent Kabila. Lubanga was accused by the ICC of criminal responsibility for heinous crimes against humanity and war crimes from 2002 to 2003. In 2012, he was found guilty of war crimes consisting of enlisting and conscripting children under the age of 15 years and using them to participate actively in hostilities in the Democratic Republic of the Congo (ICC, July 14, 2009). As many as 30,000 children have fought in the Congo power struggles, and Lubanga is accused of having used children as young as 10 years old (Philp & Gibb, 2009).

Omar al-Bashir

On July 14, 2008, the ICC charged Omar al-Bashir of Sudan with war crimes and crimes against humanity in western Darfur during the period between 2003 and 2005. According to the ICC's prosecutor, there was evidence of a "criminal plan based on the mobilization of the whole [Sudanese] state apparatus, including the armed forces, the intelligence services, the diplomatic and public information bureaucracies, and the justice system" (Human Rights Watch, 2008). There was an earlier attempt to charge al-Bashir with three separate counts of genocide, but that accusation has been dropped, despite his implication in the deaths of 35,000 people (ABS-CBN News, 2009). The African Union has said it will not cooperate with the warrant and appealed to the United Nations to delay the case.

France Protects Déby from Prosecution

Although the charges against al-Bashir and others in the past seven years are probably justified by the crimes committed, there are others — guilty of crimes to the same or greater degree — who have not been charged. François Bozizé of the Central African Republic, Denis Sassou Nguesso of the Republic of Congo, and Idriss Déby of Chad have not had charges brought against them. Why is this?

French human rights activist François-Xavier Verschave charged in his book *Noir Silence* (2000) that the real problem is France. Verschave supported this contention with names, dates, and witnesses in 600 pages, indicting France not only for criminal activity in Africa but also for the deadly protection rackets serving the system of FranceAfrique. This "incestuous" protection system includes the African presidents in the zone of that network. (See especially pp. 15–69, 151–174, and 216–231). In *Noir Silence*, Verschave focused primarily on the administration of President Jacques Chirac, implicating Internal Minister Charles Pasqua and the leaders of French oil corporation Elf, French industrial group Bouygues, and French investment and industrial holding group Bolloré. According to Verschave, the president of France freely recruited mercenaries and controlled civil wars in Africa from the Elysée Palace.

Déby's Crimes Before the 2002 Adoption of the Rome Statute

Between 1990 and 2002, there was genocide in Chad, applying the definition of genocide found in the Rome Statute. During these early years of Déby's presidency, homes and churches of certain tribes in the South of Chad were burned to the ground. Other tribes (non-Zaghawas) were assassinated or butchered like animals everywhere in Chad. Leading Muslims and Christians and opposition leaders were assassinated in several regions of the country.

Hundreds of southerners were killed by Déby, including the Goré canton chief Gaston Mbainaïbey and all 15 of his village chiefs. Gaston had been invited to gather his villages' chiefs to meet with the regional sub-prefect, who was in collusion with a local military leader. The chiefs were surrounded, roped together, marched to the river, and shot by Chadian soldiers. Thousands of survivors in the region ran to Cameroon and the Central African Republic (Verschave, 2000, p. 151). Many Kanembous were killed in the region of Lake Chad. Hundreds of people of Ouaddaï were killed in the Abéché region and in N'Djaména. Many other regions had the same scenarios. Many people were tortured, and women were raped (Verschave, 2000, pp. 151–174; Amnesty International, 1997). There were no legal proceedings, no tribunals, and no trials.

In the North, in the region of Tibesti, the situation was inhuman during this period, while Déby conducted operations against the MDJT of Togoïmi. According to Yorongar Ngarlejy, Bichara Haggar, and Dobian Asngar, the Chadian army avoided attacking rebels and focused instead on burning houses, killing civilians, and shooting animals. Wells were poisoned by the government forces (CISR, 2000). These, too, are acts of genocide.

Between 1991 and 2008, Déby sent Chadian military forces to many countries in Africa as mercenaries, including the Central African Republic, Congo Republic, the Democratic Republic of Congo, and of course Sudan. Had the Rome Statute been in effect from 1991, all of these incursions would be considered war crimes worthy of a World Court tribunal.

For example, to support al-Bashir's soldiers, Chadian forces were sent as mercenaries into southern Sudan, where they burned houses and killed many civilians in the region controlled by John Guarang (Madina, 1994). Later, soldiers were sent to fight against al-Bashir; Chadian soldiers joined Sudanese rebels and have launched attacks in Sudan for the last 12 years.

Another example of war crimes conducted in a neighboring country occurred when about 350 Chadian forces were sent to the Central African Republic under cover of MISAB as "peacekeeping forces." They deployed into zones around the capital and killed more than 100 civilians; the rebels who had held the area had already retreated. The murdered civilians were of the same ethnic tribe as southerners in Chad, whom Déby considered his enemies (Verschave 2000, pp. 229, 335–337).

Farther to the east, more than 2,000 Chadian mercenaries were sent to the Democratic Republic of Congo between September 1998 and June 1999. These mercenaries committed war crimes and crimes against humanity, killing more than 300 civilians in Businga, a locality near the equator (Verschave 2000, p. 124).

In 1997, a large number of Chadian mercenaries were sent to the Congo Republic to eject the democratically elected president, Pascal Loussouba, from power. The Congolese defenders put up unexpected resistance, and French Transall C-160s and helicopters provided war materiel and reconnaissance information. There was widespread destruction in the Congo. Thousands of Congolese died; hundreds of buildings, roads, and railways were bombed from the air. Movable property was carried off by the mercenaries, who came from Chad and many other countries in Africa and even from Europe to oust Loussouba (Verschave 2000, p. 33).

Déby's Qualifications for ICC Indictment

Although Verschave and other human rights leaders may consider all of the above crimes worthy of prosecution in international court, they took place before international adoption of the Rome Statute in 2002. Since Chad signed the statute in 2002, has President Idriss Déby undertaken any actions that would constitute crimes against humanity, war crimes, or genocide? Would Déby's actions qualify him for the same kinds of charges (and the same kind of international trial) already found appropriate by the ICC for Omar al-Bashir, president of Sudan, and Charles Taylor, former president of Liberia? A number of actions ordered by Déby might provide evidence for serious violations of international humanitarian law:

• Terrorism, murder, outrages on personal dignity, cruel treatment, and looting (Lacey, 2006; Manga, 2006; Polgreen, 2008; Rolley, 2008; Tedga, 2008)

• Terrorizing, torturing, and assassinating political and civilian leaders (Polgreen, 2008; Rolley, 2008; Tedga, 2008)

• Murder, rape, sexual slavery, slavery, mutilating and beating, and enslavement (Konto, 2004; Madj-kida, 2003; Manga, 2006; Nako, 2003a; N'djibo, 2004; Yorongar, August 19, 2004; Yorongar, December 3, 2004)

• Recruiting and using men and child soldiers from Darfur, Sudan, to terrorize civilians, murder, conduct outrages on personal dignity, cruel treatment, and looting of people in Chad (Hancock, 2007; Human Rights Watch, July 16, 2007; Polgreen, 2008; Tedga, 2008)

- Recruiting and using child soldiers in Chad and outside of Chad (Hancock, 2007; Human Rights Watch, July 16, 2007; Polgreen, 2008; Takirambudde, 2007; Tedga, 2008). In addition, during the violent overthrow of Patassé's government in the Central African Republic in early 2003, more than 5,000 child solders were among the mercenaries, Darfuri, and Chadian forces that came from Chad and launched the assault that opened the palace to rebel leader Bozizé. That assault resulted in uncounted war crimes and crimes against humanity (Madonet, 2004)
- Children under the age of fifteen recruited to take active part in the hostilities (Madonet, 2004; Takirambudde, 2007)
- Terrorizing civilians, murder, outrages on personal dignity, cruel treatment, and looting (N'Diékhor, 2003a, 2003b; Lacey, 2006)
- Willful killings (Lacey, 2006)
- Pillaging (Kahn, 2003; Yambassa, 2003; N'diékhor, 2003a, 2003b)
- Rape and murder (N'Diékhor, 2003a, 2003b)

In summary, the ICC might well charge President Idriss Déby with the same kinds of crimes as those that Charles Taylor, Omar al-Bashir, and others have faced.

Will the ICC's Action Against al-Bashir End the Darfur Crisis?

Many people have accused al-Bashir, leader of Sudan, as the source of the atrocities in Darfur. Others blame Idriss Déby instead for causing the unrest, raids, gang warfare, and rebellions. Others accuse key individuals and policies in foreign countries in Europe and Asia, such as France and China, as the culprits of the crimes in Darfur and the sub-region. Since we have seen that all of these bear some blame for the Darfur problem, is there reason to accuse any one individual for troubles in the sub-region of Darfur, which includes Sudan, Chad, and the Central African Republic? There is hope that the International Criminal Court, by charging al-Bashir, will save lives in the sub-region and help establish peace and justice in Darfur, and even prevent genocide elsewhere in the world. Is this likely? These are important questions, worthy of the scrutiny of the many institutions, organizations, and individuals who consider the current situation in Darfur and want to help.

The International Criminal Court is an institution created to bring hope to victims of atrocity around the world. Theoretically, the ICC should intimidate dictators and despots and rein in their excesses. Unfortunately, many people have doubts about the credibility of the ICC and its ability to make wise judgments. For instance, Paul Kagamé, president of Rwanda, has made the case that the ICC is not truly impartial. Because it serves primarily Western powers, the Court cannot render impartial justice (Arieff, Margesson, & Browne, 2009; Arieff, Margesson, Browne, & Weed, 2011; Soudan, 2009).

Other leaders in Africa and the Middle East have joined Kagamé in his critique of the ICC, especially now that the Court has issued a warrant for the arrest of Omar al-Bashir. The Arab League and the African Union have both begged the United Nations to have the ICC drop the case against al-Bashir (JeuneAfrique, 2009). Those who by faith or race support Omar al-Bashir may suspect that the ICC has targeted him because Sudan is a Muslim country. Western powers have a long history of attacking Muslim lands. Another reason for their concern may be that African despots who hold their countries hostage worry that the Court, which has in the past indicted Charles Taylor, Jean-Pierre Bémba, and many others and now has come after al-Bashir, may next look at their actions. If they support the ICC's accusations against al-Bashir, are they in effect signing their own arrest warrant (Clottey, 2009)?

Other African leaders, including freedom fighters and even democratically elected presidents, might be forgiven for agreeing with Kagamé when he argues that the ICC is an institution created by rich and powerful countries against poor and powerless countries. They cannot fail to have noticed that African leaders who do not enrich the businesses of their former colonial rulers are in turn not supported by the privileged nations. Lending support to Kagamé's suspicions of the ICC is the fact that no African country formerly colonized by the French has so far been fingered by the ICC for crimes against humanity. Somehow the leaders of Francophone Africa are protected by the aegis of "FranceAfrique."

As an example, in 1997 the democratically elected president of Congo, Pascal Loussouba, was violently removed from power by Denis Sassou Nguesso with the military assistance of Chad, Angola, and other areas within "FranceAfrique." Thousands of people died during those tragic days in Congo, but still no action has been taken by the International Criminal Court against Nguesso or his strongman accomplices.

Ange Félix Patassé, another democratically elected president, was ejected from his palace in the Central African Republic in the same way, and by several of the same key players. Nevertheless, no action has been taken by the ICC against the protégés of FranceAfrique. Instead, the Court arrested Jean-Pierre Bémba, whose rebels came to save the legal government of the Central African Republic, in accord with Patassé and the league of sub–Saharan countries (CEN-SAD). Bémba's attorneys have made note of this injustice before the ICC.

And last but not least, Idriss Déby, the president of Chad, has so far not been accused of crimes by the ICC despite considerable evidence that he has been involved in crimes in his own country and in many other countries, including Sudan (Darfur), the Democratic Republic of Congo, the Republic of Congo, the Central African Republic, and Bahrain. He seems to have special blessing from FranceAfrique (Verschave, 2000).

On the other side of the argument, the International Criminal Court's arrest warrant for al-Bashir has been strongly supported by political leaders of some Western countries, Africans, and humanitarian organizations. They express hope that the ICC's action against al-Bashir may stop the ongoing war in Darfur and bring peace to the people in the sub-region of Darfur.

There is dispute, then, as to whether the ICC can end the war in Darfur. It is possible to analyze further the motivations on both sides, but the real problem today is not to judge the opinions of the two blocs but rather to solve the core problem of Darfur with fewer casualties and less suffering. Just as there is real danger from taking no action in Darfur and letting the atrocities continue, so there is also grave danger in taking rash action against al-Bashir.

Ideally, France and China could make common cause and end the war in Darfur. Their influence in the heart of Africa is tremendous. France has historical power in the region. China, by purchasing more than 65 percent of Sudan's oil (Prunier, *Sudan: Genocide in Darfur*, 2007), has bought political power in Sudan. Even though petroleum-rich South Sudan is now (as of summer 2011) an independent country, China still needs the pipeline through northern Sudan to get the oil to port, and Sudan needs the revenue.

In 2008 and 2009, while researching alternative solutions to the Darfur crisis, the author solicited opinions of two dozen Africans from this region of Africa. Their voices seem to represent the concerns and fears of those who seek justice yet fear that the ICC's current approach may not bring peace. The problem of Darfur, they say, can be solved only by diplomacy and not by the arrest of al-Bashir. Here is a brief summary of their concerns.

One young man of Chad claims that France is the main pillar of what is going on in Darfur — and in many other countries in Africa. Another young man, of the Central African Republic, says that France is behind all the troubles of the region, and it is only France that can end the troubles. A man from the Democratic Republic of Congo says that what Western people do not know is that France did horrible things during the colonial period and continues to oppress the region, but for some reason no country in the world talks about France's crimes. Of course, when something is happening in countries formerly colonized by England, Portugal, or Belgium, France seizes the opportunity to turn the eyes of the United Nations and European Union on the problem. This distracts everyone from what is going on in the zone of "FranceAfrique." Much of this, he says, is documented in the books *Noir Silence* by François-Xavier Verschave (2000) and *False Start in Africa* (1966).

Muslims from Niger and Chad say they are terrified of the consequences of the decision made by the ICC to arrest al-Bashir (ICC, March 4, 2009). They believe this will have more negative than positive consequences. It may cause disputes among Muslims and a serious division of opinion. Some may suspect that Europeans are hostile to Islam in the Middle East and Africa — that they are at war with the Muslim religion (Chitour, 2009). That is why yesterday it was Iraq that was attacked and today it is Sudan. Probably tomorrow many other Muslim countries will find themselves in the same situation, they fear. Muslims of the region who dread Western hostility can make many countries in Africa dangerous places for Europeans and other Westerners. Kidnapping of Europeans and Canadians has already spread from Algeria to Niger and Mali, because al-Qaida in North Africa easily finds recruits when it spreads fear of Western hatred of Islam.

Sudan is a black African country that not only has great influence on African Muslims but also has much money and many arms. It can cause great damage and death in the sub-region. Leaders of Sudan can motivate Muslims of other countries, such as Niger and Nigeria, to launch attacks against Christians and Animists in those countries. Experience has shown that when the United States attacked Iraq, many Muslims of Chad, northern Nigeria, and southern Niger called it a war between Christians and Muslims and sought to attack Christians in their own countries in retribution. Is it wise to seem to threaten yet another Muslim leader?

Most humanitarian organizations have supported the ICC's move against Sudan and al-Bashir, but several non-profit organizations — groups very knowledgeable about the situation in Darfur and Chad — believe a diplomatic solution is preferable to the ICC's approach (Katala & Wasiluadio, 2009). These organizations include Caring for Kaela (CFK), the International Committee for the Respect of the African Charter on Human and Peoples' Rights (ICRAC), Action Internationale Pour la Paix et le Development (AIPD), and 12 others. These groups believe France has the capability to end the war in Darfur, Chad, and the Central African Republic, as soon as it chooses to act.

Many leaders, organizations and ordinary people have come up with remarkably similar suggestions for bringing peace to Darfur. And based on their experiences as victims, soldiers, and rebels in the sub-region, many have expressed concern that the ICC's plan to arrest al-Bashir will be counter-productive to the peace process. It seems extremely dangerous to arrest al-Bashir without also dealing with other principal actors of the genocide in Darfur. It is not at all clear how al-Bashir could be arrested either in Sudan or outside Sudan without any consequences in the sub-region. No one can destroy a tree merely by cutting its branches; one also has to sever its roots. Al-Bashir of Sudan did not commit genocide alone. Idriss Déby, president of Chad, seems equally responsible for these calamities. If al-Bashir is arrested without rounding up the mercenaries of Chad and Sudan, his followers will likely arm thousands of Chadians and Sudanese and escalate rather than end the war. This advice is consistent with testimony by Senator Russell Feingold to U.S. Senate subcommittees (2007).

How is it possible to end this war in Darfur without spreading murder and chaos throughout the sub-region? The first suggestion is to use diplomacy to prevent French soldiers from propping up despots and arming Sudanese rebels, Chadian rebels, and Chadian forces. This advice is consistent with what Eric Bétreau urges in his book, *Arc de Zoé* (2008). Thus pressure should be put on both Déby and al-Bashir to force the rebels they send against each other to come to the negotiating table. Any rebel group that refuses to negotiate should not be allowed to keep its base.

If pressure on France is unsuccessful, then the ICC should deal not only with al-Bashir but also with Déby and the leaders of Sudanese and Chadian rebels. The world will know that the ICC seeks not vengeance against black Muslim Africans but rather justice in the problem of Darfur. According to Chadian opposition leader Yorongar, if people in the world truly want to end the suffering of the people of Darfur, Chad, Sudan, and the Central African Republic, they should take the ox by its horns and not by its tail. They should stop the deadly work of Déby and his former military supplier Omar al-Bashir (Madonet, 2004).

CHAPTER 17

Proposition for Peace in Darfur and the Sub-Region

Although human-rights organizations and institutions have been involved in the problem of Darfur and its sub-region since 2003, there still has been no positive change. Worse, the conflict is growing, spreading to other countries. It is very important that institutions and organizations try to get independent surveys from the region concerned. These would be assessments of local needs, current government and rebel services, and other issues. After these surveys, it will be very helpful if those institutions and organizations approached local and international human-rights organizations to seek an adequate map of the road to peace in that turmoil-troubled sub-region.

Many people suggest that economic sanctions be imposed on Sudan, while others think it would be better to remove from power altogether the regime of al-Bashir. In fact, neither of these suggestions would benefit the people of Darfur and its sub-region, which includes Chad and the Central African Republic. Why is it that these proposals are not likely to succeed? China and other countries have invested their resources in Sudanese petroleum. To get China's Security Council vote for strong sanctions against Sudan would be extremely difficult. The military option would likewise not be successful. Removing the regime of al-Bashir by force would bring more weapons and grief to the sub-region and indirectly to many other countries in Africa. This would also affect the credibility of the United Nations, because the problem of Darfur is not only a civil war, as is commonly supposed. It is more a conflict among multi-national companies, a kind of business war (De Waal, 2008).

One proposal for easing the crisis in that area may be a spiritual initiative. To resolve the horrendous conflicts among governments, rebels, and peoples of the sub-region will require "spiritual peace." So far, religious leaders have not taken an active role in condemning the atrocities on all sides of the conflict in Darfur, just as they remained silent during earlier conflicts. This is not to accuse religious leaders of having fomented these disputes. The religious differences among the tribes of the sub-region are not the primary cause of the troubles. Nevertheless, the peace negotiations so far have struggled with political power-sharing deals and economic wealth-sharing deals.

An ecumenical peace process involving Christians, Muslims, and Jews of Africa does no disrespect to any of the three religions. Even the non-religious and Animists of Central Africa recognize the spiritual debt the world owes to Abraham and his descendants and that they provide a common heritage for people of Darfur, Chad, and the Central African Republic.

Today the household goods, crops, cattle, camels, and vehicles of many families in Chad and the Central African Republic have been taken to Darfur as war booty. The spoils of war in these two countries could bring more blood in Darfur if Muslims and Christians seek reprisals for these horrendous crimes, reprisals that would find justification in the books of Moses. A more spiritual approach, however, would be to seek Muslim leaders to reach their kinspeople of Darfur, more than 90 percent of whom are Muslim. These imams must urge the people to pray and ask Allah for forgiveness because they have stolen the goods of their neighbors and murdered them by the thousands. Prayer is also needed for the leaders of other countries, that they may bring peace to the heart of Africa (N'diékhor, 2003a, 2003b; Soudan, 2002).

International Diplomacy Needed to End the Violence

In addition to this spiritual approach to the horrors of Darfur, diplomatic and political solutions are also necessary. In important ways, these must be combined. To this purpose, the efforts of Libya, which tried to solve the crisis of Darfur and its sub-region, should be commended. The European Union's plan to send their forces into Chad and the Central African Republic to help the surviving victims is also helpful. Apparently, however, these two efforts have not yet convinced the protagonists of the sub-region to end the fighting — nor can they, so long as Idriss Déby continues to weave his webs of intrigue from N'Djaména (BBC News, 2006; Henshaw, 2008).

Unfortunately, Libya's efforts to help the region may be stymied by people's memory of former strongman Khadafi's previous actions. Many rebel leaders (that is, those who oppose the current leadership of Chad and the Central African Republic, Déby and his henchmen) may not trust Khadafi. In fact, Khadafi's previous actions may have earned the region's distrust:

- In 1993, Khadafi reconciled Déby with his brother in-law, Abbas Koty. Koty trusted that reconciliation and returned to N'Djaména. Presidential Guards of Déby's palace came to Koty's residence and killed him (U.S Department of State, 1994).
- In 2003, Khadafi initiated a special peace approach between Déby and Patassé, the elected president of the Central African Republic. They met in Niamey, Niger, for reconciliation during the regional meeting of CEN-SAD. At the moment when Khadafi "reconciled" Déby and Patassé, Déby's mercenaries were overthrowing Patassé's government (Madonet, 2004; Benamsse, 2003).
- In 2006, Khadafi was able to reconcile political opponent and defense minister Mahamat Nour with Déby and (in the Central African Republic) Abdoulaye Miskine with Déby's supporter, François Bozizé. Today Mahamat Nour is still hiding out in Libya's embassy in Chad from Déby's mercenaries. And Miskine was rejected by his followers and at the same time by Bozizé, despite any agreement.

Libya's recent peace efforts, then, were never likely to bring the war in Darfur to an end. It remains to be seen what Libya will be able to accomplish after reconstituting itself in the post–Khadafi era.

Ironically, in addition to the reasons provided above, part of the problem in Chad and the Central African Republic is democracy itself. In the history of Libya, there is no democracy. What advice could Libya give to Chadian rebels and opposition leaders who are fighting against Déby's totalitarian regime? How could "strongman" Khadafi's successors convince Chadian rebels not to oppose Déby's attempt to alter the country's constitution to keep power for the rest of his life? Can a post–Khadafi ruler ever convince Déby to renounce his constitutional revisions and step down? That is the only way that rebels and opposition leaders will stop fighting Déby. Can the former rebels and now rulers of Libya persuade Déby to stop supporting the rebels of Darfur who are putting down the opposition against him, showing off his power in neighboring countries, and bringing him wealth? It would be a miracle for one dictator to advise another dictator to take a step toward democracy (Sheer and Jackson, 2005), and it remains to be seen whether Libya itself becomes more democratic after the fall of Khadafi.

As for the promised presence of European forces in the sub-region to put down the Darfur conflict, this approach would be more likely to work if other countries in Europe could advise France to back out. France needs to remove all its forces from Chad. Other troops who have not been involved in the atrocities in Africa must lead the peace mission. Withdrawal of French troops would help convince the protagonists of the sub-region to trust the European forces and cooperate with them for a common cause (Baldauf, 2008; Verschave, 2000).

Diplomatic and political success in the heart of Africa will require the United Nations to accept even more responsibility. This world body must involve itself directly in the problems of the sub-region by thinking about the map of peace that is suggested here and then trying new strategies. The first step should be to gather all information about the international corporations, including oil companies, who are helping the different groups of rebels and the regimes of Sudan, Chad, and the Central African Republic in their business of genocide (Engdahl, 2007; Verschave, 2000, pp. 56–59, 66–67, 371–395, 419–421).

Once the United Nations has this information, a second step could be taken. The United Nations should then take collective action to influence international corporations. Currently oil companies especially tend to hire and arm mercenaries to defend their interests. Mercenary forces then "stabilize" local governments friendly to the operations of those companies (Verschave, 2000). The United Nations must craft policy to ensure that the effect of international commerce is not genocide but peace and prosperity for Africa. To that end the list of recommendations in Gary and Reisch (2005) makes a good start. Gary and Reisch provide 19 major recommendations for oil companies (including the ExxonMobil-led consortium and EnCana); international financial institutions (the World Bank, the IMF, and the International Advisory Group); key donors (the United States, France, and the European Union); the current regime in Chad; Chad's Petroleum Review Oversight and Control Committee; and both local and international human rights organizations and other civil societies, to end the horrors that oil development has brought to Chad. Nine recommendations were made earlier by Nguiffo and Breitkopf (2001) to wrest oil wealth from corrupt officials and provide it to the people as agreed before the Chad-Cameroon pipeline was constructed. Such recommendations and the evidence behind them can be a starting point for policy decisions.

The third step is to recognize that the entire sub-region of Africa is paralyzed because of the actions of Déby and al-Bashir. This needs to be clearly communicated not only to the world but also to these two war criminals themselves. The United Nations itself must gather its courage to lead negotiations in the region, negotiations inclusive of all rebel and opposition leaders and civilian leaders as well as those currently recognized as government officials. Also invited to participate at those conferences should be the civil rights and humanitarian organizations delegated by the United Nations to end the sufferings of the people.

Each country's case must be studied and resolved individually, in accordance with the causes of its internal problems.

Chad

In Chad, President Déby has ensured a constitutional change that permits him to stay in power for the rest of his life. He is opposed by almost all the political leaders and civil rights organizations in his country. Many former friends and even his relatives have raised up rebel groups against his regime. All of those groups mention Déby's assaults on Chadian democracy as their main argument for his removal from power. Déby's regime a few years ago revised the constitution after his second five-year term in power, giving him power for the rest of his life, and yet at the same time both Déby and the French ambassador in Chad claim the improvement of "democracy" in that country (*L'Observateur*, 2005).

Leaders of all groups opposed to Déby's regime ask for inclusive peace talks. Would this not be a good time for the United Nations to seize this opportunity and host peace talks among all the warring groups (and their victims) in Chad? Unanimously, those who fight against the regime of Déby have said they are fighting for democracy and are ready to negotiate with the regime to create a government based on real democracy. Although their claims must be evaluated carefully, their talk of democracy provides a good opportunity to end the genocide in Darfur.

Instead of letting the peace talks be led by Libya, which has no experience of democracy, the United Nations itself must help Chad on its journey to democracy. For the interests of the sub-region, the United Nations can claim itself as a warrantor of peace talks and find an African country with some experience of democracy (such as South Africa or the Benin Republic) to host the talks.

Why is it so important that the United Nations play the role of mediator during the period of negotiation and reconciliation? It may be difficult for opposition leaders to demand that Déby step down. That is, it may be difficult to bring it about that Déby actually does step down. He might justifiably claim that his departure from power would result in a maelstrom of civil conflict among opposing forces, each claiming to be doing the work of democracy. But the United Nations might insist on a kind of power sharing for the period of transition, structured in such a way that Déby could accept this option. Alternatively there may appear one individual qualified to take the reins of government for the period of transition who could continue to lead the country after transparent and democratic elections.

Under the expected shared power arrangement, Déby would appoint some ministry offices, and others would be appointed by opposition groups. When key ministries are no longer under the control of Déby and his armed groups, those currently in rebellion against Déby could be more confident and have more trust in Déby's good faith. Civil rights organizations might agree on a candidate to be named to the ministry of internal affairs, a rebel group might take responsibility for the ministry of defense, and Déby's party might retain leadership of external affairs.

After that agreement, they could look for a plan of gathering all rebels in Chad for disarmament before the election. Because rebel leaders have pledged that they carry arms in the cause of democracy, once their participation in government is assured, they will have to lay down their weapons. And because the United Nations would guarantee peace at the peace talks, rebel leaders could be reassured that Déby would not risk all in an assassination plot against them when they arrive in N'Djaména, as he did against Koty, Kétté Nodji, Laoukeïn, and many others.

Because the peace conference must be inclusive, all groups of rebels will be involved and will be disarmed. No more Chadian rebels will have any reason to be in Sudan, if the cause of Chadian rebels is to claim democracy for Chad, as they say. If the rebels of Chad accept disarmament, there will likewise be no need for the regime of Chad to keep helping the rebels of Sudan or to allow rebels of Sudan to maintain a base of operations in Chad. In fact, the United Nations would be able to draw soldiers from government and rebel troops to form unified forces to patrol the borders and keep the peace until free and democratic elections can be held.

At the same time as the United Nations works for peace in Chad, it should "wage peace" in the other two countries, as well. The solution to Darfur requires not only bringing democracy to Chad and cooling the simmering resentments in that country, but also drawing Sudanese and Central African Republicans together with their rebel groups for peace talks overseen by the United Nations.

Sudan

Rebels of Darfur have accused Sudan's regime of not developing their region. This was, they said, the main cause of the initial rebellion in Darfur.

Other sources disagree (Hoile, n.d.; Masud, 2004). Rather than responding with promises of development, al-Bashir recognized that there was more to the rebels' demands than a desire to compete economically with other regions of the country. He reacted strongly with military force against the rebels, just as he continues to attack South Sudan. Suspecting neighboring Chad's President Déby of supporting the rebels with the equipment and troops al-Bashir himself had given Déby to wrest power from the previous regime and make himself president of Chad, al-Bashir diplomatically asked Déby for the return of those troops. According to al-Bashir, Déby's failure to return the wayward forces was the main cause of the war in Darfur. This necessitated that al-Bashir arm against the rebellion not only the Arab Chadians and Sudanese (now known as the Janjawiid) but also the oppressed Chadian refugees who took shelter from Déby in Sudan. Today, Darfur's war becomes even more complicated than these simple beginnings (N'Diékhor, March 31, 2003).

We believe that with the involvement of the United Nations, all factions of rebels, the Janjawiid, and the government of Sudan could meet and find a way to achieve the goals of all three groups. In case the protagonists do not agree on some of the issues, the United Nations might find some experts in these areas to help work out a solution appropriate for the peoples of Sudan and South Sudan and their vast resources. On the assumption that all rebel factions in Darfur and the government of Sudan commonly agree on a schematic for peace, the United Nations might then claim itself as warrantor of that agreement and strictly supervise the peace agreement until the target is reached.

Once a peace agreement has been achieved among Janjawiid leaders, the rebel leaders, and the government of Sudan, the signators of that peace agreement should try to gather their forces for a mass disarmament. At that point, we believe all Chadian rebels would leave Sudan and return to Chad for their disarmament. All Sudanese rebels would leave Chad and return to Sudan's side of the Darfur border for their disarmament as well.

The Central African Republic

At this point, there is no decision that the puppet ruler of the Central African Republic, General Bozizé, can make without Déby's agreement. It was Déby who uprooted the democratic government in Bangui to install Bozizé in the palace. Bozizé's security is thus in the hands of Déby. There is nothing Bozizé could do to bring about peace in his country, even if he wanted to (Mas, April 19, 2006).

Once the United Nations has been able to convince Déby to accept shared governance in Chad, it might well ask Bozizé to begin negotiating with rebels in his country. Such negotiations would need to be inclusive of all political and military groups. The rebels and political parties would be eager to welcome the idea. The Central African Republic's problem will be easy to solve once the United Nations has dealt with the issues in Chad and Sudan. Let us assume that Déby allows Bozizé to hold inclusive peace talks with leaders of those who oppose him. The rebel leaders will gather their forces and disarm them according to their peace agreement. The UN should be the warrantor of that peace agreement, as in Chad and Sudan.

When the United Nations is successful with this strategy, these three countries with their governments of reconciliation will form a Special Brigade to control their borders. Sudan will form its amalgamated brigade with Janjawiid, rebel, and National Army forces. Chad will form its brigade from rebels and national military forces. The Central African Republic would use the same strategy to create a select new force from the many groups now in opposition to each other. At that point the three brigades of the three countries would join together to ensure the security of their borders until their countries complete the final process of transition to democracy or at least internal peace. The United Nations would need to provide security and supervision to ensure the effectiveness of this strategy.

Instead of sending European forces to arouse local suspicion of their motives, the UN could send its forces with the mediators to follow the evolution of the peace agreement of each country. The UN forces might be equipped with radar and other devices to patrol the borders and secure them from penetration by non-allied troops. The major part of the work would be not the UN's involvement but rather the integration of each country's forces. People of each area know their neighbors and can more effectively and inexpensively patrol their area. There is nothing the United Nations can do without the willingness of the people themselves, but most people in these countries desire peace.

In the worst-case scenario, if one of the governments or rebel groups refuses to participate in this strategy offered by the UN, the Security Council would be empowered to take appropriate action against any regime or group of rebels to end the genocide in the sub-region. At that point, all Security Council members would likely reach consensus on the right action to take.

Appendix A

Interview of Hassan Fadoul Kitir by *Alwihda*[*]

March 16, 2001

Translation of the interview from French into English is provided by Ésaïe Toïngar. The interviewers are not identified on the website, except that one reports for Chadian Internet news source *Alwihda*, AL, and the other for the French newspaper *Jeune Afrique*, JA.

AL: *Why do you want to testify today? What are the reasons that have motivated you to do so?*

HFK: In reality I have made that decision for the simple reason that the book entitled *Black Silence* has prompted questions about counterfeiting money, suggesting that from the beginning it was I who initiated the flow of illicit money — by cargo planes — into Chad. Therefore, I believe it would be in my best interest to testify at the trial. However, there are other circumstances that do not allow me to seize the opportunity to fully express myself.

AL: *Can you tell us exactly what happened?*

HFK: Indeed, at that time I was advisor to President Idriss Déby. Just after I was named to this cabinet post, I was asked by Déby to go to Argentina on counterfeiting business. Thus I traveled there. When I was assured of the possibility of procuring counterfeit funds, I returned to Chad and gave the details to the president. The plan involved a group of individuals who

---

[*]Courtesy of *Alwihda*, used by permission.

conspired to "mint" the currency of Bahrain, if we would pay them $2 million U.S. to buy the special paper for that currency. Flying on the presidential airplane, I traveled to Johannesburg to give the money to that group. But a few days later they sent a message saying that the cost of transportation would be an additional $300,000—and that cost would be on our charge. Again, I took the additional fee to Mr. Louan Bacquis, representative of the Ciccone Company in South Africa. From that point three cargo loads of counterfeit bills were immediately scheduled. Once we were informed about the shipping dates, we set forth plans for receiving them. The first shipment was intercepted in Niger and the airplane stowed in Niamey [in Niger]. We were able to receive the second and third shipments in Chad. Then part of those two shipments, $2,800,000, was exchanged in Kano, Nigeria. Each box contains 2,000 Bahrain dinars. A check of more than $4 million U.S. was given to us with the name of President Idriss Déby on it. We gave the check to Idriss Déby and he took it to the Banque du Developpement du Tchad [BDT]. Before the [Nigerian] check was approved, we withdrew one billion CFA, but it turned out that the check [that we had deposited], from a London bank, was without sufficient funds. At that point, the president told me that people had been investigating us. Thus, he told me, I had to take precautions [and step down from my position] in the cabinet until we got a solution to this crisis in the following months.

AL: *What kinds of precautions were you asked to take?*

HFK: It was to try to create confusion, by saying that President Déby did not know anything about this matter. But it was his circle that was involved in the counterfeiting plans from the beginning. Then, on August 5, 1998, he signed a document that officially ended my political appointment.

AL: *Do you mean that he wants to make you bear the burden of responsibility?*

HFK: Yes, exactly. He wanted a simple solution, so that in the end I would bear the burden of responsibility.

AL: *So you have been used as a scapegoat?*

HFK: Yes, that is the right word. Since that day, up to my visit to Paris [today], no one has made a gesture of thanks to me. Thus I've taken this initiative to tell the truth. I pretended to be sick in order to make my trip here possible. Upon arrival in France, I received the result of my checkup (indicating there was no illness), then I went to the police station at Nanterre (a suburb of Paris).

AL: *Did you anticipate that French authorities would be waiting to interrogate you upon your arrival? Or were you surprised when the authorities confronted you?*

HFK: Ah, no! I had mentally prepared myself since leaving Chad. So I was waiting for the police to arrive at the airport.

AL: *So it was not Déby that sent you to France?*

HFK: Ah, no! If I have been firm in my own decision to explain what happened ... it is because he gave instructions to denounce me to the [French] police.

AL: *Let's go back to when your problem of counterfeiting took place. At that point, were you prepared [to come clean], or only from the time you were dismissed by Déby?*

HFK: Ah, no! I was dismissed a long time ago. I wanted to speak out since my dismissal on August 5, 1998, which ended my official functions. But from that date up to July 2000, when I was nominated as the chief of the Department of Abéché, I was not seen or heard.

AL: *In other words, you went to the police of your own accord?*

HFK: No! While I was finishing up with my medical checkup, I was preparing myself to go to the [French authorities]. At that time an anonymous letter had been posted to the Paris District Defense, directly addressed to the prosecutor, stating my full Parisian address (starting with my district, apartment level, and room number). Subsequently, the prosecutor gave orders to Interpol to arrest me. They came early in the morning. I told them they were late; I had been waiting for them since the airport.

AL: *Were you in France earlier [since this counterfeiting charge]?*

HFK: The first time I arrived in France was on October 22, 2000. After that, I went back to Africa and then returned to Paris on November 21, 2000.

AL: *So when were you arrested?*

HFK: I have never been arrested!

AL: *Never been arrested?*

HFK: Never!

AL: *But the police came and looked for you, and your story was heard by a judge.*

HFK: I had a hearing. It took about nine hours, and then I left.

AL: *You have not been placed in custody?*

HFK: I was placed in custody and then released on forfeit of 100,000 FF [French francs].

AL: *You paid the amount of 100,000 FF?*

HFK: Yes, 100,000 FF.

AL: *And after that did you have to return to custody?*

HFK: No! After November 12, 2000 — on the 13th — they told me I was done and asked me to go and see the prosecutor.

AL: *What was Déby's reaction, when he heard about your detention?*

HFK: First of all, to come to France was not easy.

AL: *Why?*

HFK: For a long time I wanted to come to France, but there was no way.... Every time I tried, I was categorically rebuffed by President Déby. Finally I decided to present my passport to the French embassy, which gave me the visa. Even on my trip to France, Déby sent two people to dissuade me because he was certain that my trip would implicate him.

AL: *But you were confronted by Interpol and your name circulated [indicating the information was in France even before you arrived]?*
HFK: I well understood, and that was why I purposely did it.
AL: *Was your life threatened in Chad?*
HFK: Not at all ... but I was not rewarded for the unspoken business of the counterfeit trafficking.
AL: *Did that upset you?*
HFK: No! But what bothered me was the anonymous letter that denounced me and evidently came from the president of the Republic.
AL: *Wow! From the president of the Republic himself ... and to the French authorities!*
HFK: Of course. And I seized those circumstances to unburden myself.
AL: *What was President Déby's interest in denouncing you to the French authorities?*
HFK: Simply put, he wanted to leave me standing all alone. It was a way for him to say that it was he who had sent me to justice and that he had nothing to do with the illicit affair, without acknowledging that I am a mere executor.
AL: *What was the role of Pedro [one of the persons involved] in that affair?*
HFK: Pedro was someone whom we used at the last minute. It was only when the operation blew up, and President Déby did not want the names of those who were involved from the beginning to surface.... It was as if he had given a diplomatic passport to Pedro to go to Paris. Pedro told President Déby that we could launder the rest of the counterfeit money in London. The presidential airplane took him [Pedro] to Niamey, where he left for Paris via Air Africa, to continue on to London. But Pedro was arrested in Paris with the counterfeit money.
JA: *What? [An exclamation by our colleague from* Jeune Afrique News, *who is surprised.]*
HFK: Yes! The police arrested him at the moment he was exchanging the counterfeit money in question.
JA: *I have a stupid question to ask: Did you accept this mission without question? Was it natural for you to become involved with counterfeit money?*
HFK: No, we are simple executors; a president of a republic is free to direct his people. He can tell you not only to make some counterfeit money but even, on occasion, to kill. The life of human beings is more significant than counterfeit money.
AL: *What was the money to be used for?*
HFK: Idriss Déby is greedy, especially when there is an ongoing war or an approaching election. He absolutely must have money through different ways. There was not only the use of counterfeit Bahraini money, but in 1996 we used counterfeit money in CFA to finance the electoral campaign.
JA: *How much?*

HFK: Five billion CFA.
JA: *Five billion in counterfeit CFA to finance the campaign?*
HFK: Yes, and now he has started again.
AL: *Counterfeiting again to finance the next campaign?*
HFK: Yes.
AL: *Do they make the money in Chad or somewhere else?*
HFK: Yes, in Chad.
AL: *Do they have machines and all other necessities?*
HFK: Yes! But the problem is that the counterfeit CFA bills, made in the Palace of the President, all have the same serial number and keep the same serial numbers no matter the quantity. Even one or two billion CFA's have the same serial number. Despite that, we manage to use them. For example, if there is a source of external assistance to finance our elections, we keep the genuine money and give the counterfeit money to our illiterate citizens.
AL: *Are you saying it is the same number on each bill?*
HFK: Even if we make ten billion of them, it is quite obviously the same serial number, but it is difficult for the average citizen to know that.
JA: *But it is visible!*
HFK: Not for an illiterate person.
AL: *Can you tell us anything about the videotape shown by Yorongar, on the massacre of Ouaddaï in 1994? How that happened? Was Déby involved?*
HFK: It was really horrific and inhumane. To tell you the truth, as a member of the government I was the president of the delegation that went that very day to investigate. It was the most horrible massacre that I have ever seen. There were 104 civilians dead. The people of Déby's tribe, as you may know, have long been hostile toward the people of Ouaddaï. I wrote my report to President Déby, detailing the massacre, but it was ignored. There is no doubt Déby is directly involved in that problem.

To prevent further violence, the following day we took measures to avert bloodshed in Abéché and N'Djaména. Unfortunately, those measures did not stop the forces of the president from shooting civilian protestors, killing 315 people in N'Djaména.
AL: *So Déby was personally involved?*
HFK: You have to understand that nothing can be done in Chad without President Déby's instructions — especially to kill, arrest, violently rob, or counterfeit currency. The leader is confused about the difference between the common good and his own private welfare. I positively confirm that we cannot talk about the massacres in the region of Ouaddaï (Abéché, Gniguilim, and many other villages), or the regions of the South (Moundou, Doba, and so on) without mentioning his name.
AL: *I want to ask you a little bit of a stupid question. You know a lot about the regime and about Déby himself, so are you not afraid?*
HFK: It is a matter of choice. Being afraid of Déby would lead to what? Isn't

it death? But what you have to know is even without Déby, we are going to die one day. So for me, I think there is a problem of conscience and also of history — in the sense that even if we die, our children will at least know the truth.

AL: *So that means you are liberating your conscience?*

HFK: Yes, that is it.

AL: *Why did you wait so long before taking action? You have been serving that government for seven years.*

HFK: Not only seven years. I have been his companion since Biltine. I have known him well for 30 years!

AL: *So is it not the loss of your role in the government that caused you to express this position today?*

HFK: First of all, I took that position in Abéché for my soul and conscience. I was chief of the department of the region. About two and a half years ago the department was divided. You know that Ouaddaï today is not like before. Adré and Dar-sila became prefectures. So before this, Abéché had monthly revenues between 80 and 90 million [CFA] but this last July produced only 500,000 CFA. Because the goods coming from Sudan are cleared through customs in André and Tiné, those from the North are cleared through customs in Kalaït, and those that get out from Abéché are cleared through customs in N'gueli, Abéché is disappearing. Government salaries, beyond the functional budget, go up to 68 million CFA. In the month of August, despite a tax we had only one million CFA [with which to pay salaries].

I think decentralization that only focuses on elections is going to make Abéché like Ati [the poorest prefecture in the North]. Despite all that ... they have sub-divided even more areas. Take for example Guerri; as a sub-division, they do not even have water. The government of Déby has created a post in Guerri, Am-dam, Abougoudam ... and so on.

AL: *Since that happened, did you take a position against Idriss Déby, your companion of 30 years? So you belong to the opposition to Déby? Or what is your position?*

HFK: Idriss Déby and I "grew up in the same forest," even during the time of Hissène Habré. At that time, I was nominated to the post of first councillor in the chargé d'affaires office in the embassy of Chad in Baghdad. We served in the UNIR (Union National pour l'Independence et la Revolution) with a lot of pride. At that period we did not know sadistic cynics. Suddenly a message arrived calling me to N'Djaména. It was related to the war with Libya. You know Saddam Hussein had tried his best to help President Habré [in his fight against Libya]. We flew with one of [Hussein's] sons on a special airplane with money. The following day, I greeted the president [Habré], and he said, "Mr. Hassan, I heard while you were in Baghdad you planned a rebellion similar to Ouaddaï."

I said, "Mr. President, you say some horrible things! I have never had meetings with anyone in Baghdad to harm our country."

He said to me, "No! No! There is evidence."

The following day, I decided to leave and join Déby in rebellion.

When we make decisions, we have to weigh the consequences. The problem cannot be presented in terms of "companion of 30 years." I could even say if it was my father who did not honor his commitments to his people, and thought only of his own personal interests, family, and clans, then he would have to be dealt with. You know, [to Déby] the administration of the country becomes purely and simply a matter of clan, and the country becomes a familial business. Worse yet, we blur the distinction between public property and personal property.

AL: *When did you develop that sentiment?*

HFK: Frankly, since Abéché, where I saw the hate that Déby fosters.

AL: *We noticed today that the entire opposition is reorganizing itself. For example CMAP and CPAL are trying to sign an accord, CMAP/CPAL. Beyond that, we have heard that you had contact with Mr. Hissein Kotty [executive secretary of CMAP]. Can you let us know your position with those organizations?*

HFK: It is shameful that I find the opposition in the same condition as in 1998. When I left Adré in 1988, I came to Paris to make a statement at International France Radio (RFI) and *Jeune Afrique* before I left for Cotonou. In Cotonou, there were a multitude of rebel factions that did not understand each other. I knew right away that those people could not disquiet Habré's sleep. Six months later, fortunately Goukouni arrived in Cotonou, and he was able to convince me to fight Habré. So he advised me to approach Libya. In fact, my personal intention was to go back to Algeria, where I attended college. But finally we decided to go to Tripoli, to the rebel faction leaders there, and they asked me the same questions: "What do you want to do, Mr. Fadoul; do you have your own political/military party or do you want to join others?" I told them I was not interested in having or joining a party. However, I told them I would make a modest contribution to fight Hissène Habré.

And I noted the very same situation today. The FNTR on the one side and the CNR on the other, those brothers are not working together.

Yes, I have met many of their leaders, but up to now I have yet to make my decision. With all the problems that I have endured, I left N'Djaména despite the fact that Déby is personally targeting my family. I know I have yet to take a position. I do not know which to select.

You know, to remain just an observer while President Déby continues massacring people, it does not make sense. Yet creating my own party or joining the party of Mister X—walking around with him, traveling from hotel to hotel, and spending money does not accomplish anything, either.

AL: *So what do you want to do?*

HFK: Ah! There are many methods we can use to fight. The world is changing, and so too are the things in the world. This is no longer the period of Habré.

AL: *And if it is no longer the period of Habré ... can you give us one or two examples of formulas or methods?*

HFK: Ah! The world today has become very small. Let us take the example of Pinochet.

AL: *Can we say that by starting with this [counterfeiting] trial, Déby opens his own trial?*

HFK: That problem can be seen under many forms. Do not delude yourself. Chadians have many possibilities. In a sense, each of us must not only testify against Déby but must strive to go beyond that vision. That means they can lodge a complaint against Déby for his crimes against humanity.

AL: *I come back to your problem of counterfeiting money. Do you think you will be found innocent?*

HFK: I have told the judges all I know about the counterfeiting occurring since December 2000, despite all the threats to me and my family still in Chad.

AL: *Throughout this trial and your involvement in the counterfeiting scheme, we feel the presence of politics. Do you not think this might influence the speed of the trial that is under way and may even in some way turn against you? You know we have the impression that a judge who wanted you to be able to testify has now changed his mind.*

HFK: The important thing is that there is either influence or refusal. The public was present and noted that I wanted to testify but was not allowed.

AL: *Do you think that your testimony is inadmissible?*

HFK: In principle, whatever the circumstances are, those who have knowledge of the root of the problem should be allowed to testify.

AL: *What are Déby's defense attorneys afraid [you will testify to]?*

HFK: For them, what is important is money.

AL: *Do you think your testimony could impede the speed of the trial?*

HFK: It needs to be revealed.

AL: *Do you think your presence distressed Déby's lawyers?*

HFK: Vergès was really embarrassed. This proved that he was not expecting my testimony. When we first arrived for the testimony, his first reaction was to say, "Ah, no! M. Fadoul cannot testify."

When I wanted to argue the importance of my testimony to another lawyer, he also said, "M. Fadoul cannot testify." The judge nearly allowed me to be sworn in. However, after a recess, he apparently received a phone call. As a result he changed his mind.

AL: *Whom are you talking about?*

HFK: About M. Vergès. [He seems to have misunderstood AL's questions asking who he thought had made the call to Justice Vergès.]

JA: *So, you think he received a phone call?*

HFK: Yes, I think so, but anyway we were not in the room at that time.
AL: *To clarify the problem, are you willing to write a book or take Déby to the International Criminal Court?*
HFK: I do not think the work of only one person can yield a tangible result. If there is a common willingness of all our brothers to end this alarming situation, then one day we will.
AL: *Are you making allusion to the oppositions that are outside of Chad?*
HFK: To all brothers that do not appreciate Déby's nepotism.
JA: *Did you leave a family there?*
HFK: Yes.
JA: *Are you married? Do you have children?*
HFK: I am polygamist. I have four wives and ten children.
JA: *Are your children in Chad?*
HFK: Yes!
JA: *Are you worried about them?*
HFK: Oh! Even at the time of Hissène Habré, it was the same. Being a person of faith, I leave my children in the hands of Allah. Now it is the same thing, despite the negativity and cruelty of Déby.
AL: *But at this moment they are safe?*
HFK: Ah! The government has cut off the electricity to their houses and taken away their cars.
JA: *Will you go back to Chad?*
HFK: Ah, no! [Laughs.] Never ... no way.
JA: *Do you want to bring your family here or leave them there?*
HFK: Who will allow the family of Fadoul to escape from Chad? So I do not think of bringing my family here.
AL: *During your trip in Africa, did you feel threatened? You have already spoken of Déby's cruelty. Where did he try to kill you or abduct you?*
HFK: Before I left Paris, I was harassed several times. But once I was heard and released on bail, [Déby] changed his tactics. He called me many times to persuade me to return to Chad. But knowing Idriss Déby and his tantrums, I preferred joining the opposition.
AL: *What do you think about President Idriss Déby's willingness to take you to court?*
HFK: Déby is in an awkward position to pursue me for evildoing. The problem with counterfeiting dinars was that [Déby] was the one who led the team. He paid two million U.S. dollars, and we took it to Johannesburg. [Part of this sentence was erased from the record at HFK's discretion.] We took a regular flight on Air Africa from N'Djaména to Abidjan to give $300,000 [in three round trips] to the representative of CHYCONE in Africa. I am actually in possession of a copy of a check for four million U.S. dollars, given in Kano, Nigeria, by an agent of the currency exchange, with Déby's name on it.

The check was taken to the Chadian Bank of Development [BDT]—

and you know the result. I have to tell you that after the check (for which there were insufficient funds) was sent to London, Déby himself arranged with Idriss Ousman to return the $1 billion CFA to the BDT. You have to know that they turned to the other countries who are friends of Chad to obtain that amount.

So I have to affirm that Déby is not in a good position to harass me ... and I am waiting for him with open arms. I am in Paris to finish with my trial. (Laughs.) I am asking myself, "Who will pursue whom?"

He is someone that I have known more than 32 years, and he is covered in crimes and massacres. He will not take the risk of doing that. Otherwise his world will start to unravel. But I know that that strategy is a simple trick to put to sleep the people on the streets of Chad. He wants to let the poor people think that he is innocent!

However you have to know that Chad is a sovereign country. We cannot bring two cargo planes packed with foreign currency into our country without the knowledge of customs officers, police officers, National Agents of Security (ANS), or even the army. It is absurd to say that the entire security structure of Chad failed to notice the cargo planes! It is also irresponsible for Déby to let Chadians believe that he did not know anything about the counterfeiting and that Hassan Fadoul did — that Hassan Fadoul alone is able to bring two cargo planes of counterfeit money into N'Djaména, load them, and be in charge of them. This is not possible. It is unthinkable. I suppose he would argue that I used his special airplane behind his back?

AL: *Déby denied cooperating with you in the counterfeiting scheme. Do you insist on implicating him?*

HFK: Déby denied having killed even one person. I would say that it has taken courage for me to recognize what has been done, and I have a clear conscience. Now it is his turn to do the same, if he is courageous. The people of Chad are waiting for the truth from [Déby]. We took the counterfeit money to the bedroom, at his villa, where he had put Nwamba. Déby gave him a diplomatic passport. When he saw the sample bills, Déby could not wait. That is why he called all his friends, like Brahim Maïnassara (ex-president of Niger), who was able to intercept the first cargo for his own use. Maïnassara was anxious to send his special advisor on an airplane to Dubai, with an enormous amount of counterfeit money [to exchange for the valuable currency of Dubai]. Unfortunately, he was intercepted and questioned because of the information that came from the Central Bank of Bahrain. That is why the special advisor of the president of Niger was arrested and the presidential airplane [of Maïnassara] was provisionally seized [in Dubai].

AL: *Apparently last March the 32 soldiers assumed to be supporting you were accused of a coup [against Déby] and were executed. Can you confirm that?*

HFK: Idriss Déby executes people every day and we cannot be surprised. It is a pleasure for him to execute, kill, and humiliate people. He is a student of Habré, and that is why he has to be pursued in the name of justice, just as Habré was. If Déby killed his brother-in-law and friend, Abas Koty, it is not strange that he would execute others. Surely he will pay the price one day. Moreover, he is not the only one, and we must accuse of crimes not only him but his entire tribe or clan. Many are those who are implicated in the affair of Koty and others.

AL: *Togoïmi phoned you. Do you want to join his movement, the MDJT?*

HFK: Togoïmi called me twice. He did not ask me to join the Movement for Democracy and Justice in Chad, and I did not commit to his movement. I have known Togoïmi a long time, which means since [Habré's] National Union for Independence and Revolution (UNIR), all the way to [Déby's] Patriotic Movement of Salvation (MPS).

AL: *Hissène Koty said you are one of the founders of CNR. Are you now a member of CNR?*

HFK: Yes, I am a founding member of CNR. However, first I have to finish with my problems at the court, and then my position will be known. Then we will be able to face a common enemy, Idriss Déby. I will answer the question of membership next time.

AL: *Allegedly you had a three-way meeting last week [with Ahmat Yacoub and Hissein Koty]. What was it about?*

HFK: It is only normal to discuss the various responsibilities of the politico-military opposition in order to pull together a common strategy.

AL: *The opposition may be waiting for your financial assistance. What do you think?*

HFK: Where would I get money? I am now in the opposition, and I do not think I am able to finance a group of rebels.

AL: *In the newspaper* N'Djaména Hebdo, *at the end of March, it was published that the French service of DGSE is taking care of you, that you are living in the hotel Belle Étoile and receiving FF 300 per day.*

HFK: [Apparently surprised that this information was published by *N'Djaména Hebdo*, he turns to Hissène Koty next to him and asks where that hotel is located. Koty smiles and answers that he does not know and that he himself is surprised at this accusation.] It is a pure fabrication, and I do not know where they get that news. I came to Paris last March to contribute to the trial of Verschave. It was also an opportunity for me to liberate my conscience for the first time and to release the heavy burden that I have borne for more than two years. DGSE has not contacted me or put me up in a hotel. All this is a manipulation of Déby, because he is a specialist in this kind of manipulation. However, it is not forbidden to be in touch with DGSE. He himself took power through a DGSE agent, whom he met for the first time in Amsterdam in 1989. Déby should not be surprised if I contact the DGSE very soon.

AL: *In the same newspaper,* N'Djaména Hebdo, *they say you had a diplomatic travel order from President Déby when you arrived, yet the French embassy in Chad refused your visa the first time you applied. Isn't that so?*

HFK: It is not true. I immediately received a one-year visa that same day, allowing 90 days of residency [in France]. I must add that I do have a diplomatic passport.

AL: *The newspaper* Le Journal Progrès *was skeptical of your first interview with Alwihda last March. What do you have to say?*

HFK: It is normal. The mission and role of Mahamat Hissène, editor of *Le Journal Progrès*, is to defend Idriss Déby. It is a newspaper that we, MPS, created. I was in charge of financing that project, under the direct instruction of Idriss Déby, when I was cabinet director in 1992. Then in 1993, when I was minister.... [Mahamat Hissène] has to continue assuming his small-minded responsibilities despite free expression. *Le Journal Progrès* is financed by Déby; everybody knows that. It is the voice of MPS.

AL: *Hassan Fadoul, you laundered money for the MPS. Are you telling us that during the time of Hissène Habré you didn't put your hands on one billion CFA? Then, over the last ten years with MPS, you are telling Chadians that you have not taken the opportunity to fill your pockets? Haven't you taken advantage of counterfeit bills too? Surely Déby is not the only one who has benefited in that way?*

HFK: Indeed, when I was with Idriss Déby, I traveled to many neighboring countries and met with the heads of state — Bongo [of Gabon], Boigny [of Ivory Coast], Yadema [of Togo], Libya, Sudan — to bring to Idriss Déby more than 23 billion CFA. I was naïve and did not know that life would turn out like this. Even all the personal gifts that I have received, I gave them to Déby. Actually, he stole them from me. He is mean spirited. He is always interested in what someone else has. With Déby one cannot wear anything better than he has. He is interested in furniture, cars, and even good-looking clothes. He was a friend, and I know him well. He instructs his people to go and loot. As an example, Bouegues gave us 3 billion CFA [for Déby], and they gave me 100 million CFA [as a transaction fee] in front of Mayodine Sallah, who was the financial minister at that time. Once we arrived in N'Djaména, I gave Déby the details of our trip, and he took the 100 million CFA payment that was intended for me.

Appendix B

Chad Discovers Oil

This letter to French president Georges Pompidou from the president of Chad, Francois Tombalbye, in September of 1969 marks the beginning of Chad's troubles, for without oil wealth to squabble over, there would not be a power struggle in Chad today. No one would supply warlords and militias if there were no hope of great wealth from Chad's rich resources.

Earlier, French petroleum companies had explored Chad and notified President Tombalbye that unfortunately Chad was lacking in such resources. They did set aside some tracts of land for future exploration but indicated that no country in the world was so poor in natural resources as Chad (Aubert, Brana, & Blum, 1998; Béguy, 2002; Djimrabaye, 2005).

Tombalbye must have understood that in fact below Chad's land was a rich and deep oil basin that the French might want to keep as a private oil reserve for their own country's use in the future. Their lack of interest in immediate development may have masked a hunger to use Chad's resources after they had exhausted other sources of oil. Tombalbye made arrangements to accept Conoco's offer to assess Chad's reserves (Aubert et al., 1998; Béguy, 2002; Djimrabaye, 2005). Conoco indicated that significant resources were available for development, and Tombalbye courteously communicated this information to the French president, expressing his regret that Pétropa had been unable to find oil after the effort and expense of their exploration.

The text of the first four paragraphs of President Tombalbaye's letter reads roughly as follows:

Le Président de la République

DAH

Fort-Lamy, le 5 SEPTEMBRE 1969

No 90 /PR/CAB.

Monsieur le Président,

    Fidèle à l'amitié traditionnelle qui lie nos deux pays, j'ai l'honneur de vous faire part du projet qui préoccupe actuellement le Gouvernement Tchadien et moi-même : la recherche des hydrocarbures liquides ou gazeux au TCHAD.

    Nous venons de recevoir une demande de Permis de recherches d'hydrocarbures dans le Bassin du Lac Tchad et dans la Dépression du Chari (fosse de Doba), émanant d'une société Américaine, la CONTINENTAL OVERSEAS OIL COMPANY.

    Je précise, Monsieur le Président, qu'à l'exception de la fosse de Doba où l'ORSTOM (Office de Recherche Scientifique et Technique d'Outre-Mer) a effectué des études préliminaires très superficielles, aucune société Française n'a entrepris des recherches dans ces deux régions. Comme je le signalais plus loin pour des considérations stratégiques et aussi pour respecter les accords FRANCO-TCHADIENS dans de tels domaines spécifiques je tiens tout particulièrement à vous en informer.

..../...

The President of the Republic of Chad
                Fort Lamy (N'Djaména), September 5, 1969
No 90/PR/CAB
Mr. President,
    Mindful of the traditional friendship that ties our two countries, I am privileged to inform you about a project that currently preoccupies the government of Chad and myself: The search for liquid hydrocarbons in Chad.
    We have just received a request for a license permit to search for hydrocarbons in the Basin of Lake Chad and in the Depression of Chari (the pit of Doba), emanating from an American company, the Continental Overseas Oil Company [Conoco].

- 2 -

Le gouvernement Tchadien et moi, aurions vivement souhaité qu'une telle entreprise fût menée par des organismes français. Malheureusement l'exemple de Pétropa dans le Tibesti où cette Société, après des recherches qui lui ont coûté tant d'argent n'a rien trouvé, n'inciterait pas d'autre Sociétés françaises à intervenir au Tchad. C'est à la lumière de tous ces éléments si haut signalés que le Gouvernement Tchadien et moi-même avons cru devoir accepter cette demande qui à notre avis ne manquerait pas de susciter l'émulation d'autres compagnies.

Veuillez agréer, Monsieur le Président, l'assurance de ma très haute considération.

F. TOMBALBAYE

S. E. Monsieur Georges POMPIDOU
Président de la République Française
Palais de l'Elysée

-PARIS-

To be clear, Mr. President, with the exception of the pit of Doba where the ORSTOM (Office de recherché Scientifique et Technique d'Outre-Mer) has made very superficial preliminary studies, no French company had searched in these two regions. As I have mentioned above for strategic consideration and also to respect our FRANCO-CHADIAN agreements in such specific areas I particularly have to inform you about it.

The government of Chad and I would highly wish that such an initiative should be undertaken by French companies. Unfortunately, the example of Pétropa in the Tibesti, after that company's search that cost it so much money discovered nothing, does not encourage other French companies to step in in Chad. It is in light of all these elements mentioned above that the Government of Chad and I believe we should accept this request, which in our opinion would not fail to stimulate the emulation of other [French oil] companies.

Please accept, Mr. President, the assurance of my highest regards.

F. Tombalbaye

H. E. Mr. Georges Pompidou
President of the French Republic
Elysée Palace
-Paris-

Appendix C

Groundbreaking Ceremony at Komé Oil field

These are the remarks by Callisto Madavo, World Bank vice president for Africa, at the Komé groundbreaking ceremony on October 18, 2000, as reported on the Esso (2000–2003) website:

Your Excellency, President Déby, Your Excellency, President Biya, Distinguished Guests, Ladies and Gentlemen:

A Proud and Historic Moment

This is a proud day for Chad and Cameroon. It is also a proud day for the World Bank. As the Vice-President for Africa, I am pleased to represent our President Mr. James Wolfensohn at today's groundbreaking ceremony. He has asked me to convey his warmest congratulations to all of you on this occasion and to express his continued personal interest in this extraordinary project. As an African, too, I am heartened by the sheer size of this private investment at the heart of our continent—which needs to attract much more international capital if we are to realize our development dreams. And I can almost feel the burden of those thirty years you have been waiting here in Chad—since this oil was first discovered—being lifted from your shoulders now. For all these reasons, we feel privileged to be at your side at this historic and promising moment.

Partnership and Purpose

The preparation of this project has involved a high degree of partnership and purpose, first, on the part of the two governments and the Consortium and, secondly, between them and the international official lenders (including the World Bank and the International Finance Corporation). But it has also involved the efforts of many individuals, local communities and non-government organizations within the two countries and overseas. And, in its final form, it represents a consensus on the part of the international community as a whole, expressed in the discussions of the World Bank Group's Board, that this was an opportunity which should not be missed.

Some have regretted the controversy which surrounded this project. But we feel that the international debate was necessary and valuable, and that the project is sounder as a result. Having to give clear answers to tough questions—even when we were confident that the project design should speak for itself—was a useful discipline. And it allowed Chadians and Cameroonians outside Government to understand the risks and benefits of the project better. The best way to celebrate our achievements so far will be to implement the project with the same seriousness and openness.

Together, we need to demonstrate that petroleum resources can be used to lift our people out of deep poverty, while protecting the environment and respecting the rights of communities and individuals. Together, we can encourage other private investors to consider projects in Africa which will bring them good returns but also—with imaginative public policy and good government—improve African society at large. And, together, we can show how a partnership between governments, multinational companies, multilateral financial institutions, and local communities can benefit everyone. The world is watching this experiment closely and we should take advantage of that attention. In fact, I would like to see us transform what was a controversy into a model of intelligent and open project implementation.

In a sense, it is even more important that we live up to the high standards we have set for ourselves—as we take the project design from the drawing boards and our offices into the countryside. New information and new challenges await us, and we need to respond to these in ways which will draw on the widest range of advice. Quite apart from the physical construction, how the two governments manage their resources and the natural environment before the oil starts flowing will be key to raising public confidence in the project and lowering concern about how the oil money will be used.

The Task Ahead

Oil production is still three years away. But, during that time, we have a major task ahead of us to strengthen the public institutions necessary for protecting the environment and ensuring that the new revenues will be used directly to reduce poverty. You can count on the World Bank Group's support in meeting that challenge. We are at the start—not the end—of a journey which will make this project not just a connection between two countries or a route to world markets but also a pipeline to a better life. For this to be achieved on both sides of the border, there will need to be continuous dialogue, rapid response (when problems arise) and the full participation of everyone concerned.

The success of the partnerships underlying this project will be expressed not in the rates of oil production, nor in the levels of eventual revenues for the two countries, but in firm conviction that all voices have been heard and a belief by all Chadians and Cameroonians that this project belongs to them. I salute the Government of Cameroon's decision to manage the oil revenues in a way which will be understandable to its people. And I wish the two governments, the private investors, and all the men and women who will be involved in project implementation the same boldness, ingenuity and determination which have led to this historic day.

Thank you.

Following the speech by Madavo were these remarks by Tom R. Walters, president, Esso Chad, at the Komé Groundbreaking Ceremony on October 18, 2000:

> *Good Afternoon, Your Excellency, President Déby (Chad), Your Excellency President Biya (Cameroon), Vice President Madavo (World Bank), Distinguished Ministers from Chad and Cameroon, Distinguished Members of the Diplomatic Corp, World Bank Representatives, Prefets, Sous-Prefets, Canton and Village Chiefs, Ladies and Gentlemen:*
>
> *I want to welcome you on behalf of ExxonMobil, Esso Chad, and our co-venturers, Petronas and Chevron.*
>
> *I am both proud and excited to be here today—a day all of us have long strived for over the past several years.*
>
> *We are here to celebrate our accomplishments and define our upcoming challenges, as construction begins on a project that is important for the Consortium sponsors, as well as for the countries of Chad and Cameroon and the World Bank Group.*
>
> *The year 2000 has been a remarkable one for the Chad–Cameroon Oil Development and Pipeline Project.*
>
> *In April, changes were announced to the Consortium of co-venturers responsible for development of the project. Both Petronas, the National Oil Company of Malaysia, and Chevron Corporation, of the United States, officially joined the Project at that time. They are represented here today and will be joining me at the microphone later. I want to express Esso's sincere appreciation for the dedication they have shown to the project. You have been committed and contributing partners from the outset and we look forward to a long and beneficial relationship in this endeavor.*
>
> *Also in April, the Consortium expressed our commitment to Chad and Cameroon and to this project. Our objective was to move forward as quickly as possible, and we have.*
>
> *As all of you know, on June 6th, the World Bank Board of Directors overwhelmingly approved their participation in the Project—truly a great day for Chadians and Cameroonians. I echo the words of Bank President Wolfensohn when he stated that this project reflects an unprecedented collaborative effort between the Bank Group, the Consortium and the two governments. On behalf of the Consortium, I wish to express my congratulations and my sincere appreciation to you, President Déby, and to all those who have worked so diligently for so long to make this milestone a reality.*
>
> *The Bank's decision to approve their participation was important for two reasons. First, it validated the Project's environmental and socioeconomic assessment and mitigation plans. It speaks volumes for the careful planning that has gone into this project over the past eight years. And second, it has opened the door for Chad and Cameroon to move forward in their fight against poverty—providing a foundation for the countries to grow and develop to the benefit of the citizens and for generations yet to come.*
>
> *The Consortium has long had the objective to conduct the project in accordance with appropriate standards for environmental protection and respect for*

local citizens. We have been focused on that objective and through a collaborative process with the World Bank, have developed a project plan that is responsible and leading edge. Here in Chad, a Compensation and Resettlement Plan has been developed to support (the limited number of) local farmers required to relocate their homes. This will come through a program of compensation and construction of new compatible replacement housing. These initiatives have benefited from the direct input of local citizens through a consultation effort, unmatched in Africa, and likely, in the world.

The success we have experienced reflects the dedication, perseverance, and cooperation of all of you (the World Bank, and the governments and citizens of Chad and Cameroon). I congratulate Mr. Madavo and the World Bank Organization for their tireless effort to support this project, in the spirit of cooperation between the public and private sector. Certainly, your President, Mr. Wolfensohn, has shown strong conviction and leadership as the Bank assessed its participation, all the time knowing that the Project represents an opportunity to create a brighter future for this country.

I also congratulate Mr. Abderhamen Dadi, who has long represented Chad in Project negotiations, and Mr. Adolfe Moudiki, who has done the same for Cameroon. Both gentlemen have been instrumental in moving the project forward with a vision of what this can mean to each country's development. The future for the Project begins today. It's clear the challenges will continue as we move forward with project implementation. Indeed the eyes of the world are on this world-class project, and we must be focused and vigilant in the execution of our plans. Make no mistake, I have great confidence in our collective abilities to deliver.

Let me summarize some of our key near-term activities: We are now mobilizing project and contractor staff to complete detailed engineering designs; we are restarting previously suspended major contracts; line pipe is now being manufactured at mills in Europe; and near year-end, we will commence road and bridge work in Cameroon and Chad following the end of the regional rainy season.

During the construction phase and the subsequent operation phase, we will honor our commitments and pursue the Project with the same degree of transparency and dedication brought to it so far. Ongoing dialogue will be maintained with local populations, and the required mitigation will be implemented to help ensure benefits as planned.

The country of Chad will benefit beyond the direct project revenues through many near-term infrastructure upgrades coincident with project construction. Such improvements include many kilometers of road upgrades and construction of the new bridge at the Mbere River. Both will improve market accessibility. In addition, priority will be given to Chadian businesses for contracts involving construction supplies and services when offered at competitive terms. As well, local citizens will receive preference for labor positions.

Next year will see full-scale activity with pipeline installation in Cameroon plus field facilities construction and well drilling here in Chad. There is much to do, but I can assure you we are up to the task. Above all, we will complete our work safely. There will be no higher priority for the Consortium and our contractors.

In conclusion, we know that profound poverty is an unfortunate reality in much of Africa. Its alleviation requires private investment, collaboration and responsible governmental policies. The Chad–Cameroon Project embodies all these elements. It offers great hope to the people of these two countries and we are proud to be involved now and in the future.

Appendix D

World Bank News Report

June 6, 2000

On June 6, 2000, the World Bank issued a news report announcing the Chad–Cameroon pipeline deal. Leading with the humanitarian purposes of the project, the report goes on to describe the project planning process and a few of the World Bank's concerns. Note that this report contains no process to halt the project should regime leaders in Chad and Cameroon fail to employ project funds to benefit the environment and the poor.

The Board of World Bank Group today overwhelmingly agreed to support the Chad–Cameroon Petroleum Development and Pipeline Project — an unprecedented framework to transform oil wealth into direct benefits for the poor, the vulnerable and the environment. In addition to the financing, the package of support includes a first-of-its-kind program to direct new revenues to support economic and social development programs in Chad, which is one of the world's poorest countries.

The project, which is expected to cost $3.7 billion, will develop the oil fields at Doba in southern Chad and construct a 1,070 km pipeline to offshore oil-loading facilities on Cameroon's Atlantic coast. The sponsors are ExxonMobil of the U.S. (the operator, with 40 percent of the private equity), Petronas of Malaysia (35 percent), and Chevron of the U.S. (25 percent). Depending on world oil prices, the project could yield up to $2 billion in revenues for Chad and $500 million for Cameroon over the 25-year production period.

Almost all the $3.7 billion investment will be private. The World Bank Group will provide $93 million on IBRD terms ($53.4 million for Cameroon and $39.5 million for Chad) to finance the governments' equity share in the project and a $100 million loan from International Finance Corporation (IFC) to the joint-venture pipeline companies. In addition, IFC will mobilize up to $300 million in syndicated loans from commercial banks. The remaining funding will be provided by the oil companies themselves, commercial bank loans supported by export credit agencies, and possibly project bonds.

James D. Wolfensohn, President of the World Bank Group, while acknowledging the international debate surrounding the project, expressed strong support for it:

"The Chad–Cameroon project reflects an unprecedented collaborative effort between the Bank Group, the consortium of private companies and the two governments. While some may still have doubts, I believe that the hard work of specialists from the Bank Group, the private companies and the two countries, combined with the strong participation of civil society within Chad and Cameroon and around the world, have made this a better, stronger project. The real challenge is about to begin. We intend to pursue it, with our partners, with the same openness and thoroughness we have brought to the process so far."

This project represents an unparalleled opportunity for creating a much brighter future for Chad. At present, the country cannot afford to provide the minimum public services necessary for ensuring a decent life for its people. In four years' time, the pipeline would increase annual Government revenues by 45–50 percent per year over current levels and allow it to use those resources for poverty-reducing investments in health, education, environment, infrastructure and rural development.

In addition to the IBRD and IFC investments in the pipeline project, the Board approved two projects to help strengthen Chad's and Cameroon's capacities for environmental management and monitoring of the petroleum sectors. These would be supported by US$23.7 million and US$5.8 million equivalent credits from the International Development Association (IDA), the World Bank's lending arm for the poorest countries.

An International Advisory Group consisting of independent international experts will monitor the projects, with particular attention to social and environmental safeguards, and will report to Mr. Wolfensohn. Their findings will be discussed by the Senior Management and Board of the Bank Group and then made public.

Additional information on the project, including arrangements for protecting the environment and ensuring the proper use of the oil revenues, is attached.

The Chad–Cameroon Petroleum Development and Pipeline Project Background Information

Why the Project?

Chad is one of the poorest countries in the world. About 80 percent of its 7 million people — or 5.6 million people — live on less than $1 a day. Chad also has very high infant mortality rates, limited access to basic social services, and extremely poor nutrition levels. Without oil, and despite recent growth of 5 percent a year, it could well take 35 years to double Chad's per capita income.

Ninety percent of the country is desert or semi-arid. Its very narrow economic base and lack of skilled people limit the opportunities for growth in most sectors. This project provides Chad with a unique opportunity to lift itself out of its extreme poverty. The additional revenues could remove the bottlenecks that constrain growth and create opportunity for the next generation of Chadians.

However, natural resource "booms" are difficult to manage. Drawing on its global knowledge, the Bank Group is seeking to ensure that the country's new wealth will be invested responsibly, for the well-being of all Chadians.

The project would increase Government spending on key economic and social services. Rather than displace social sector projects, the pipeline would support implementation of World Bank and other donor projects in these sectors by generating additional revenues to finance critical Government expenditures, such as teachers' salaries.

Why Now?

Petroleum was discovered in southern Chad 30 years ago, and the country has been waiting anxiously ever since for the right combination of international prices and private interest to develop the resource. Chad is not the only country with untapped petroleum reserves. Exploration is underway throughout the continent to find new oil sources — which could prove cheaper and more accessible. If Chad does not seize this opportunity, it may well pass the country by.

More needs to be done to build capacity within Government and society to participate fully in project implementation. This will start immediately and continue for at least the four years before oil revenues start to flow. Until the oil is developed, poverty will remain deep and widespread. For example, each year 1 in 5 children die before the age of five. Although the project by itself will not eliminate early childhood deaths, it is certain that revenues from the pipeline — linked to improved basic health and education programs — will save a large number of these young lives in the future.

Managing the Oil Revenues

Chad and the Bank Group have applied the lessons of international experience to the proposed management of the oil resources. In fact, the Government has already taken unusual steps to target most of the oil revenues to poverty reduction and to ensure public oversight of the use of these resources.

On December 30, 1998, Chad's Parliament approved a law that sets out the Government's poverty reduction objectives and details arrangements for the use of the revenues. Under the law, 10 percent of the royalties and revenues will be held in trust for future generations, 80 percent of the remaining funds will be devoted to education, health and social services, rural development, infrastructure, and environmental and water resource management, and 5 percent will be earmarked for regional development in the oil-producing area (over and above its share of national spending). There will be annual published audits of the petroleum accounts, regular public expenditure reviews by the Government and the Bank, and special arrangements for channeling and accounting for the funds.

In addition, the law created an oversight committee to monitor the use of the oil revenues. This committee will include representatives of the Government, Parliament, the judiciary and civil society. A related IDA capacity-building credit will support the work of the oversight committee, as well as strengthen Chad's general accounting office and the dissemination of information about government expenditures.

In Cameroon, increased revenues from the project will be less significant: only 3 percent of the national budget, compared with 45–50 percent in Chad. Public disclosure of the use of oil revenues is already part of the Bank and IMF's economic reform program in the country.

Protecting the Environment

Any large project of this nature entails risks for the natural environment. From the start, the environmental risks of this project were seen to be significant but manageable. Numerous issues were identified, but in all cases adequate measures have been designed to deal with them. There was considerable work in studying alternative routings and induced — not just direct — impacts. National experts, Bank Group specialists, and consortium personnel walked the entire pipeline route to double-check data from aerial surveys. These analyses were summarized in a 19-volume Environmental Impact Assessment and Management Plan, the first draft of which became available in June 1998. The final version was made public in June 1999 and additional information regarding the oil spill response plan was made available in October 1999. These documents were the subject of regular exchanges of views with local and international NGOs. Those discussions were aimed at ensuring that the project planners were studying the full range of potential risks and applying the appropriate standards of environmental protection.

Following 18 months of analysis, significant changes were made to the proposed right-of-way. As a result, the project will have only a minor net effect on the natural and human environments. The pipeline will be buried, rather than above-ground. For most of the route, it follows existing infrastructure. No one will need to be resettled along the 1,070 km route — although a maximum of 150 families (probably many fewer) may be displaced where the oil itself will be produced. Construction may interrupt farmers' access to their land, but during a brief period. They will be compensated fully for lost income and lost fruit trees.

The final route complies with World Bank safeguard policies, including those on Environmental Assessments, Natural Habitats, Indigenous Peoples, Cultural Property, Resettlement, and Forests. Only a small amount of tropical forest (10–15 sq. km.) will be lost as a result of the construction. To compensate for this, two large new national parks (approximately 5,000 sq. km.)

have been created in Cameroon, and will be managed for better biodiversity conservation in those areas.

Human Rights

Chad has had a troubled history. However, the country has made progress since the early 1990s towards a more inclusive and stable political environment. A democratic process and a program of national reconciliation have been launched. Opinions differ on how significant this progress has been. Military incidents in southern Chad two years ago and the temporary imprisonment of a parliamentarian from the project area created obvious concern. But everyone agrees — inside and outside Chad — that the success of the project will be enhanced by the free expression of community views. In itself, the preparation of the pipeline project has been a training ground for public debate. More information has been made available about this project than any other activity in the country. In addition, seminars organized by non-government organizations (NGOs) over the last three years have allowed local NGOs, traditional village authorities and farmer organizations to speak out about the project. These exchanges have improved the project — and also contributed to strengthening the voices of civil society.

HIV/AIDS

HIV infections are still relatively low in Chad, which has taken a proactive approach to controlling the disease. In Cameroon, the rate is rising and effective action at the national level is only starting. The project sponsors are coordinating with the national HIV/AIDS programs in both countries to ensure that the project does not adversely affect the surrounding communities or workers. The project will provide health education and immunizations to workers. Condoms will be made available at subsidized prices. Medical teams, including emergency medical technicians, will be on site during construction to provide treatment when needed and to supervise health and sanitation conditions in the construction camp.

Consultations

Public consultations on the project started in 1993. The initial aims were to share project information with the affected communities; determine project land needs; and establish a framework for reducing adverse impacts. Consultations since 1998 have focused extensively on the draft Environmental Impact Assessments studies and draft Environmental Management Plans. Information on the project has been widely disseminated, and hundreds of public meetings have been held in local languages. The World Bank country offices and local staff have been actively involved in improving the quality of the consultation process, and in helping to build the capacity for constructive engagement of local NGOs. In addition, Washington-based staff have participated in some of these consultations or facilitated discussions between the parties. The consultation process will continue during project implementation.

APPENDIX E

Dreaming of a Kingdom of Zaghawas*

"I fear that Chad will one day lose its sovereignty"— Interview with Maurice HelBongo by Isolda Agazzi for InfoSud

Thursday, February 21, 2008

Adoum Maurice HelBongo (2008)— In the wake of a failed rebel attack three weeks ago, the Chadian capital of N'Djaména is feeling the effects of a clampdown on opposition leaders, activists and reporters — this as authorities scour the city for any remaining rebels.

Calls are being made for the release of Ibni Oumar Mahamat Saleh, head of the Party for Liberty and Development; Ngarlejy Yorongar of Federation Action for the Republic; and former president Lol Mahamat Chouanow — now leader of the Rally for Democracy and Progress. Concerns have also been expressed about Wadel Abdel Kader Kamougué of the Union for Renewal and Democracy, whose whereabouts are unknown, rights watchdog Amnesty International said Wednesday.

The strike on N'Djaména was launched January 31 by an alliance of three rebel groups hoping to topple President Idriss Déby. After several days of fighting, government troops assisted by France were able to repel the rebels, but not before some 160 civilians were killed and tens of thousands made into refugees. Chad accuses neighbouring Sudan of backing the rebels — while Khartoum claims that Déby's government is aiding insurgents in the western Sudanese region of Darfur.

Another opposition leader, Maurice HelBongo, told correspondent Isolda

*Courtesy Isolda Agazzi/InfoSud

Agazzi* that current events threatened Chad's survival as a nation. HelBongo lives in Switzerland but maintains close links with the country of his birth and knows some of the rebels involved in the recent attack.

Isolda Agazzi (IA): *Who are the rebels that attacked N'Djaména, and what do they want?*

Maurice HelBongo (MB): Mahamat Nouri, Timane Erdimi, and a certain Abdelwahid (Aboud) whom I don't know personally. Mahamat Nouri was a minister for former president Hissène Habré and for Idriss Déby, and he is very well known in the country. He is a Goran—the same ethnic group as Hissène Habré—and he is also the brother-in-law of Idriss Déby. As for Erdimi, he is the nephew of Déby. For a long time, he was his chief of staff and directed his policies for years.

With this past, I doubt that they can suddenly become democratic. What they want above all is power and money. And since Chad has become an oil producer, there is lots of money. Déby is not at all worried about promoting a policy of development; he only wants to fill his pockets and those of his clan.

IA: *Is a democratic transition possible in Chad?*

MB: It is possible, but not with Déby! During the national conference† in 1993, which lasted three months, we did excellent work; but as we pushed for democracy Déby tried to put an end to it, as he clearly saw what was obvious: that all Chadians—from the south and the north—were excited by our discussions. Even the nomads on their camels were glued to their radios! We spoke of "three months of democratic celebration...."

In spite of this, I still hope that we will be able to implement our recommendations sooner or later, even if all the main opposition leaders—who have always refused to take power forcibly—have been detained.

IA: *What role does Sudan play?*

MB: As in Sudan, the north of Chad is Muslim and the south Christian and Animist. Since the independence of Chad, our northern brothers have twisted political problems, presenting them as ethnic and religious divisions. I have always said that this was a false problem, but northern officers went to Sudan and other Arab countries to say that the problems of Chad are religious in nature. Sudan has a strong influence on Chad, and it is even worse today with the racist government in power in Khartoum.

IA: *Does the conflict in Darfur risk spreading throughout the region?*

MB: As soon as Khartoum made peace with rebels in the south, it hurriedly

---

*Isolda Agazzi is a journalist at InfoSud, a news agency based in Geneva. This interview is published under an agreement between InfoSud and IPS.

†The Sovereign National Conference, held after Habré was ousted from power, established a transitional government headed by Déby.

turned towards Darfur—where the residents are also Muslims, but black. Idriss Déby helped stir up the conflict in Darfur.

He's of the Zaghawa ethnic group that lives along the border between Chad and Sudan, and in Darfur. This ethnic group has always been neglected by Khartoum. Before taking power in N'Djaména, Déby promised to help the Zaghawa of Darfur if he became president; and persistent rumours, that I can't verify, even say he promised them that he would build a Zaghawa kingdom in Darfur. It is he who raised up these people against Khartoum.

IA: *Are you saying that everything would be going well between Khartoum and the Sudanese Zaghawa were it not for Déby?*

MB: No, not at all; don't put words in my mouth. One thing is certain: that this region of Darfur has always been neglected by Khartoum, before Idriss Déby come to power. This supposes that sooner or later there would have been problems, even without Déby.

IA: *What role does—or should—France play?*

MB: France's role has always been very negative. I'm speaking of the government and not of the French people. Even the parliament does not really know what goes on. At the Elysée* there's a unit that manages African affairs in a very opaque way. France does not want democratic governments in Africa; it prefers corrupt leaders.

IA: *Even now?*

MB: Of course; if not, why would the French government support Déby? ... It completely supports Déby, widely known to be a despot.

IA: *How do you see the future of your country?*

MB: The problem has not been solved. The rebels are still there, and it's not impossible that they'll return. And I fear chaos taking hold in Chad. The south is completely marginalized; it's still in the grip of utter misery that is in the process of spreading to the north as well. And all Chadians could be the losers.

In the end the country could be shared between its powerful neighbours: Cameroon, Nigeria, Libya and Sudan. I fear that if this continues Chad will one day lose its sovereignty.

---

*The Elysée Palace, in Paris, is the official residence of the French president.

References

Abbé Yambassa. (2002, February). *Contre-offensive victorieuse des rebelles congolais.* Retrieved from http://www.google.com/search?hl=en&q=abb%C3%A9+Yambassa

ABS-CBN News. (2009, July 8). *ICC prosecutor wants Sudan's Beshir for genocide.* Retrieved from http://www.abs-cbnnews.com/world/07/08/09/icc-prosecutor-wants-sudans-beshir-genocide

ADES. (2004, March 21). *Newsletter.* Association pour le dévelopement social et économique de Yemi. N'Djaména, Chad.

Adoum, D. (2008). *Nous refusons l'embarquement.* Retrieved from http://tchadnews.info/joomla/index.php?option=com_content&task=view&id=57&Itemid=1

Adusei, Lord Aikins. (2009, May 18). *Is the ICC targeting Africa and the third world countries?* Retrieved from http://www.americanchronicle.com/articles/view/102788

African Union. (2003, January 15). *Communiqué of the eighty-ninth ordinary session of the central organ of the mechanism for conflict prevention, management and resolution at ambassadorial level.* Addis Ababa, Ethiopia. Retrieved from http://www.africa-union.org/news_events/Communiqu%E9s/Communique_20_Eng15jan03.pdf

AfriquEducation. (2006, May 16–31). Quand Idriss Déby planque 100 milliards de francs CFA au Camerooun; un parti [politique] courageux en France condamne fermement la politique de Chirac au Tchad. *AfriquEducation*, No. 204. Retrieved from http://www.afriqueeducation.com/archive/sommaire/index.php?id=204

Afrique-Express. (2001, May). Elections présidentielles au Tchad. Retrieved from http://www.afrique-express.com/archive/CENTRALE/tchad/tchadphotos/elections-tchad.htm

Afrique-Express. (n.d.). *Biography of Idriss Deby Itno.* Retrieved from http://www.afrique-express.com/archive/CENTRALE/tchad/tchadbios/deby.htm

Agence France-Presse. (2002, December 29). *Libya: News and views.* Retrieved from http://www.libya-watanona.com/news/news1202/1202nwsc.htm

Agence France-Presse. (2008, February 27). *Au Tchad, Sarkozy obtient une "enquête internationale" sur les opposants.* Retrieved from http://afp.google.com/article/ALeqM5hMIvyuMCEzpEMtwBa-ghvCNQXqcA

Agence France-Presse. (2009, March 29). *Kadhafi et l'UA fustigent la CPI en soutien au président Béchir.* Retrieved from http://www.google.com/hostednews/afp/article/ALeqM5hW0zz91luwPhfY6AeqSL9ngeWVZA

Ahmat, Cherif. (2006, April 26). *Qui sont ces rebelles Centrafricains du FUC?* Retrieved from http://www.cnrdutchad.com/formation.html#redFuc

AI Index. (2007, November). *Uganda: Arrest now.* Amnesty International. (AFR 59/008/2007. Retrieved from http://www.amnestyusa.org/document.php?id=ENGAFR590082007&lang=e

Ali, Mahamat. (1999). Personal communication. High Commissioner for Refugees, Lagos, Nigeria.

Ali-Dinar, Ali B. (1998, November 6–12). *Central and eastern Africa: IRIN weekly round-up*, 46–98. Retrieved from http://www.africa.upenn.edu/Hornet/irin_111 398.html

Ali-Dinar, Ali B. (Ed.). (1999, June 17). *IRIN-CEA Update 695.* United Nations Office for the Coordination of Humanitarian Affairs Integrated Regional Information Network for Central and Eastern Africa. Retrieved from http://www.africa.upenn.edu/Hornet/irin695.html

AllAfrica.com. (2009, March 9). *Rwanda: President Paul Kagame's interview with Jeune Afrique.* Retrieved from http://allafrica.com/stories/200903260212.html?page=3

Allazam, Albissaty Saleh. (2006, October 12). *Introduction sur la nature du pouvoir d'Idriss Déby.* Retrieved from http://www.tchadactuel.com/documents.php?2006/10/22/24-introduction-sur-la-nature-du-pouvoir-du-president-deby

Alwihdactualité. (2001, March 23). *Deby peut être poursuivi pour crime contre l'humanité.* Retrieved from http://maxpages.com/tchad/alwihda15

Alwihdactualité. (2001, April 19). Retrieved from http://maxpages.com/tchad/alwihda 16

Alwihdactualité. (2003, October 27). *Carrefour 12. (La liberté d'expression est un droit).* Retrieved from http://maxpages.com/tchad/carrefour12

Amnesty International. (1996, May 20). *Chad: Cases for appeal.* AI Index: AFR 20/05/96. Retrieved from http://www.amnesty.org/en/library/asset/AFR20/005/1996/en/dom-AFR200051996en.html

Amnesty International. (1997). *1997 annual report for Chad.* Retrieved from http://www-secure.amnesty.org/en/library/asset/AFR20/012/1997/en/163f47d6-e8ea-11dd-a3f5-0b60099daafd/afr200121997en.html

Amnesty International. (1998, March 19). *Extrajudicial executions/Fear for safety.* (AI Index: AFR 20/03/98). Retrieved from http://www.amnesty.org/en/library/asset/AFR20/003/1998/en/dom-AFR200031998en.pdf

Amnesty International. (2001, October 16). *Chad: The Habré legacy.* (AI Index: AFR 20/04/01). Retrieved from http://asiapacific.amnesty.org/library/pdf/AFR200042001 ENGLISH/$File/AFR2000401.pdf and http://www.amnesty.org/en/library/info/AFR20/004/2001/en

Amnesty International. (2003, November 6). *Execution/Fear of imminent execution.* Retrieved from www.amnesty.org/en/library/asset/AFR20/001/.../afr200012003en.pdf

Amnesty International. (2009, September). *Broken homes, broken lives.* (AFR Index: AFR 20/005/2009). Retrieved from http://www.amnesty.org/fr/library/asset/AFR 20/005/2009/fr/e6532246-114b-416d-9451-b705bdac2c56/afr200052009en.pdf http://thereport.amnesty.org/eng/regions/africa/chad

Amnesty International. (2013, October 23). *Chad: Repressive tactics against government critics must come to an end.* Retrieved from http://www.amnestyusa.org/news/news-item/chad-repressive-tactics-against-government-critics-must-come-to-an-end

Amnesty International Urgent Action Bulletin. (1997, November 4). *At least 80 people killed in Moundou, others arrested.* (AI Index: AFR 20/12/97). Retrieved from http://www.hartford-hwp.com/archives/35/327.html

ARDHD. (2001, May 31). *Chad alert: Fraud and attempted hold-up electoral, accurate, abuse and torture.* Association pour le Respect des Droits de l'Homme à Djibouti. Retrieved from http://www.ardhd.org/francais/bulletin/bulns11.htm

Arieff, A., R. Margesson, and M. A. Browne. (2009, July 14). *International Criminal Court cases in Africa: Status and policy issues.* Congressional Research Service. Retrieved from http://www.fas.org/sgp/crs/row/RL34665.pdf

Arieff, A., R. Margesson, M. A. Browne, and M. C. Weed. (2011). *International Criminal Court cases in Africa: Status and policy issues.* CRS Report for Congress. Retrieved from http://www.fas.org/sgp/crs/row/RL34665.pdf

Aubert, M.-H., P. Brana, and R. Blum. (1998, November). *Rapport d'information n° 1859 sur le rôle des compagnies pétrolières dans la politique France-Afrique.* Retrieved from http://www.assemblee-nationale.fr/rap-info/i1859-02.asp

Baldauf, S. (2008, February 6). *France backs Deby, may intervene in Chad.* Retrieved from http://www.csmonitor.com/2008/0206/p04s03-woaf.html

Bangui-Rombaye, A. (1999). *Tchad: Élections sous contrôle.* Paris: Harmattan.

Banhoudel Mékondo, Frédéric. (2008, February 26). *Ressources pétrolières et réalisations: Qui a accès à l'information?* Centre d'etudes et de formation pour development (CEFOD). Retrieved from http://www.cefod.org/spip.php?article1748

Bardet, P. (2008, February 10). *Idriss Déby, un criminel contre l'humanité soutenu par la France.* Retrieved from http://toulouse.indymedia.org/article.php3?id_article=18645

Barthélémy, A. (1998, May). Frémissements ... Bien sûr, la .... *Billets d'Afrique,* No. 58. Retrieved from http://survie-france.org/IMG/doc/58.doc

Bast, A. (2006, August 3). Genocide in Darfur: The case of Minni Minnawi. *New York Inquirer.* Retrieved from http://nyinquirer.typepad.com/nyinquirer/2006/08/genocide_in_dar_10.html

BBC News. (2006, November 22). *No deal in Africa's Darfur talks.* Retrieved from http://news.bbc.co.uk/2/hi/africa/6168496.stm

BBC News. (2007, May 2). *ICC issues Darfur arrest warrants.* Retrieved from http://news.bbc.co.uk/2/hi/africa/6614903.stm

BBC News. (2008, March 4). *Trench to encircle Chad's capital.* Retrieved from http://news.bbc.co.uk/2/hi/africa/7277830.stm

BBC News. (2008, September 10). *End to World Bank's Chad oil deal.* Retrieved from http://news.bbc.co.uk/2/hi/business/7608163.stm

BBC News. (2009, March 4). *Warrant issued for Sudan's leader.* Retrieved from http://news.bbc.co.uk/2/hi/africa/7923102.stm

BBC News. (2011, March 11). *Charles Taylor's Sierra Leone war crimes trial closes.* Retrieved from http://www.bbc.co.uk/news/world-africa-12701803

Béguy, Ramadji Angèle. (2002, September). Quelques dates de l'histoire du pétrole tchadien. *T&C* [Chad & Culture], 209–210. Retrieved from http://www.cefod.org/spip.php?article189

Békoutou, Daniel. (1992). *11 journalists killed in 1992/Motive unconfirmed.* Retrieved from http://www.cpj.org/deadly/1992_list.html#unconf

Békoutou, Daniel. (2000, April 11). *Hunting the dictator.* Retrieved from http://www.cpj.org/Briefings/2000/Bekoutou/bekoutou.html

Bénadji, Hubert. (2003, November 10–12). Exécutés pour vraiment servir d'exemple? *N'Djaména Hebdo,* No. 718.

Benamsse, Joseph. (2003, March 16). Rebels attempt coup in Bangui. *The Independent.* Retrieved from http://www.independent.co.uk/news/world/africa/rebels-attempt-coup-in-bangui-600767.html

Bérassidé, Guidingar. (1993, July 8). La spirale de la violence. *N'Djaména Hebdo,* 89, pp. 4–5.

Bétreau, Eric. (2008). *L'Arche de Zoé, les dessous de l'affaire d'états: Ma vérité.* Paris: Plon.

Billets d'Afrique.com. (1996, July). *Fraud in the elections in Chad.* Retrieved from http://survie.org/IMG/doc/36.doc

Bloomfield, Steve. (2007, April 30). Darfur: War without end. *The Independent.* Retrieved from http://www.independent.co.uk/news/world/africa/darfur-war-without-end-446777.html

Boisbouvier, Christophe. (2004, April 25). *Envahissants "libérateurs."* Retrieved from http://www.jeuneafrique.com/jeune_afrique/article_jeune_afrique.asp?art_cle=LIN2 5054envahsrueta0

Boisbouvier, Christophe. (2008, February 10). La bataille de N'Djamena: Jeune Afrique. Retrieved from http://www.jeuneafrique.com/jeune_afrique/article_jeune _afrique.asp?art_cle=LIN10028labatanemaj0

Bolloré, V. (1998, September 24). Le dernier empereur de l'Afrique [The last emperor of Africa]. *La Lettre du Continent,* No. 313.

Boulada, Jean-Prosper. (2003). *Situation politique au Soudan, au Tchad, et éclairages de la situation dans le Darfour.* Retrieved from http://www.ialtchad.com/dossierbou ladasoudan-tchad.htm

Brody, Reed. (2001). The prosecution of Hissène Habré— an "African Pinochet." *New England Law Review, 35*(2), 321–335.

Cameroun Link.net. (2006, May 26). Detournements: Idriss Déby fait passer 100 milliards au Cameroun. *Cameroun Link.* Retrieved from www.camerounlink.net/fr/ news.php?nid=22947&kat=1&seite=288

Cash, Audrey C. (2009). *Oil revenue management, the deliverance of priority-sector development projects and the role of non-governmental organizations (NGOs) in Chad.* Retrieved from http://www.devstud.org.uk/aqadmin/media/uploads/4ab8ef8504 659_SA2-cash-dsa09.pdf

Catholic World News.com. (2008, February 5). *Chad rebels plan to expel missionaries.* Retrieved from http://www.cwnews.com/news/viewstory.cfm?recnum=56422

CED/FoE-Cameroon, Milieudefensie and FoEI. (2001, June). *Chad elections: Towards a "petro-dictatorship"?* Retrieved from http://www.foei.org/en/publications/pdfs/ promises.pdf

Cherif, Ahmat. (2006, April 26). *Qui sont ces rebelles Centrafricains du FUC?* Retrieved from http://www.cnrdutchad.com/formation.html#rebFuc

Chitour, Chems Eddine. (2009, March 9). And the others? *Watching America.* Retrieved from http://watchingamerica.com/News/23401/and-the-others/

Le Citoyen. (1998, September 22). Affaire des faux dinars [The affair of the counterfeit dinars: Revelations continue]. *Le Citoyen (Niamey).*

Coalition to Stop the Use of Child Soldiers. (2008). *Child Soldiers Global Report 2008: Chad.* Retrieved from http://www.child=soldiers.org/global_report_reader.php? id=97

Commission de l'Immigration et du Statut de Réfugié du Canada (CISR). (2000, February 17). *Extended response to request for information.* Retrieved from http://www2. irb-cisr.gc.ca/fr/recherche/cnd/ref/index_f.htm?docid=58&cid=0

Clottey, Peter. (2009, March 30). Defiant Bashir in Doha ahead of Arab summit Monday. *Voice of America News.* Retrieved from http://www.voanews.com/english/Africa/ 2009-03-30-voa3.cfm

Cohen, Herman. (2006, July-August). Deby must go for the sake of Chad and Sudan. *Journal of International Peace Operations, 2*(1), 19.

Collelo, Thomas (Ed.). (1988). *Chad: A country study (political dynamics).* Washington, DC: GPO for the Library of Congress, 1988.

Collins, James E. (2007). *Lessons from Chad: Ethnic conflict and economic reorganization in post colonial cultural landscapes.* San Marcos, TX: Texas State University.

Committee to Protect Journalists. (1998, December 31). *Country report: Chad.* Retrieved from http://www.cpj.org/attacks98/1998/Africa/Chad.html

Cornwell, Richard. (1999). Africa Watch Chad: Fuelling the flames (Divisions between the warlords and the intervention of neighboring States and external powers during the cold war). *African Security Review, 8*(5). Retrieved from http://www.iss.co.za/pubs/ASR/8No5/AfricaWatch.html

Correau, Laurent. (2006, April 21). *Implications croisées*. Retrieved from http://www.rfi.fr/actufr/articles/076/article_43201.asp

Correau, Laurent. (2008, August 8). *Goukouni Weddeye, tel qu'il se raconte*. Retrieved from http://www.rfi.fr/actufr/articles/104/article_70216.asp

Country reports on human rights practices for 2004. (2005). *Report submitted to the Committee on Foreign Relations, U.S. Senate, and the Committee on International Relations, U.S. House of Representatives, by the Department of State*. Retrieved from http://www.internationalrelations.house.gov/archives/109/99700.pdf

Couvé, Philippe. (2002, August 7). *Accrochage meutrier à frontalier Tchad-Centrafrique et début de ballet diplomatique*. Retrieved from http://www.sangonet.com/ActualiteC10/Accrochage2jmeurtreTC.html

Daoud, Bourma Ahmad. (2008, July 8). *Tchad: Que reste t-il du pouvoir monarchique de Deby?* Retrieved from http://makaila.over-blog.com/article-21077540.html.

Daoud M. (2002, December 19). La rocambolesque filière africaine (The fantastic African industry). *Radio France Internationale.*

Darfur revisited: The international response. (2007). *Hearing before the United States Senate Committee on Foreign Relations, September 28, 2005*. Retrieved from http://www.access.gpo.gov/congress/senate

Darmian, Jean-Marie. (2007, November 5). *Les coulisses de l'exploit* [Behind the scenes of exploit]. Retrieved from http://www.darmian.net/article-13563999.html

Debos, Marielle. (2008). Fluid loyalties in a regional crisis: Chadian "ex-liberators" in the Central African Republic. *African Affairs, 107*(427), 225–241. Retrieved from http://afraf.oxfordjournals.org/cgi/content/abstract/107/427/225

Dédjébé, Service Pierre. (2003, March 20–23). Le jeu diplomatique de la France devient un peu obscur, il n'est pas transparent. *N'Djaména Hebdo*, No. 660, p. 2.

De Waal, Alex. (2008, May 21). *Why military intervention in Darfur will not work*. Retrieved from http://news.bbc.co.uk/2/hi/africa/7411087.stm

Dika, Pierre-Paul. (2005). *Institut de documentation et de recherche sur la paix*. Retrieved from http//:www.institutidrp.org

Djimrabaye, Renodji. (2005, September). *Petrole et dette: Cas du Tchad* [Oil and debt: The case of Chad]. Retrieved from http://www.oilwatch.org/2005/documentos/deuda_tchad_fra.pdf

Djonabaye, Dieudonné. (2002). *Tchad—Youssouf Togoïmi: La mort d'un rebelle. Radio France International*. Retrieved from http://www.rfi.fr/actufr/articles/033/article_18166.asp

Dougueli, Georges. (2008, July 2). *Tchad: 72 morts lors de l'arrestation d'un "gourou" jihadiste*. Retrieved from http://www.jeuneafrique.com/fluxafp/fil_info.asp?reg_id=0&art_cle=47298

Doumnandé, Ramadji. (2006, December 25). *What is the international community missing in Darfur crisis?* Retrieved from http://www.ramadji.com/index.php?option=com_content&task=view&id=153&Itemid=2

Doyle, Mark. (2003, January 1). "Blood Diamond" scheme begins. *BBC News World Edition*. Retrieved from news.bbc.co.uk/1/hi/world/africa/2619663.stm

Dumas, Roland. (2005, June 14). *Tchad: histoire secrète d'une négociation*. Retrieved from http://www.mitterrand.org/spip.php?article234

Dumont, René. (1966). *False start in Africa*. New York, NY: Praeger. (*L'Afrique noire est mal partie*, 1962)

Les En-dessous d'une affaire de gros sous [Hidden truth of the big-money affair]. (1993, July). *N'Djaména Hebdo, 89*, pp. 7–8.

Engdahl, F. William. (2007, May 20). *Oil in Africa*. Retrieved from http://www.engdahl.oilgeopolitics.net/Geopolitics_Eurasia/Oil_in_Africa/oil_in_africa.html

Eolas. (2006, June 6). *Vous reconnaissez avoir fait le ménage, c'est honnête!* Retrieved from http://www.maitre-eolas.fr/2006/06/06/363-vous-reconnaissez-avoir-fait-le-menage-c-est-honnete

ESSOChad. (2000, June 6). *World Bank group approves support for Chad-Cameroon petroleum development and pipeline project*. Retrieved from http://www.essochad.com/Chad-English/PA/Newsroom/TD_NewsRelease_060600.asp

ESSO Exploration and Production Chad. (2000–2003, October). Speech by His Excellency Mister Idriss Déby, president of the Republic of Chad, head of state, at the official Doba oil valve opening veremony — Komé, October 10, 2003. Retrieved from http://www.esso.com/Chad-English/PA/Newsroom/TD_Speeches.asp

Feingold, Russell. (2007). Statement. *Senate Foreign Relations Subcommittee on African Affairs Hearing on Chad and the Central African Republic: The Regional Impact of the Darfur Crisis*. Retrieved from http://feingold.senate.gov/statements/07/03/20070320.htm

Feingold, Russell D., Landrieu, Mary L., Lieberman, Joseph I., Leahy, Patrick J., and Dodd, Christopher, J. (2008, August 5). *Letter to the Honorable Condoleezza Rice, Secretary of State*. Retrieved from http://www.rfkcenter.org/node/223

Le Figaro. (2008, February 27). *Au Tchad, Sarkozy discutera du sort des opposants*. Retrieved from http://www.lefigaro.fr/international/2008/02/27/01003-20080227ARTFIG00012-sarkozy-au-tchad-pourla-grace-de-l-arche-de-zoe.php

Fisher, Jonah. (2006, July 29). Cracks emerge in Darfur peace deal. *BBC News*. Retrieved from http://news.bbc.co.uk/2/hi/programmes/from_our_own_correspondent/5224098.stm

Flint, Julie, and Alex de Waal. (2003). *Darfur: A short history of a long war*. London, UK: Zed Books.

Flint, Julie, and Alex de Waal. (2008). *Darfur: A new history of a long war*. London, UK: Zed Books.

France24. (2008, June 13). *Chad rebels announced a fresh offensive against the government*. Retrieved from http://www.france24.com/en/20080613-chad-rebels-call-peace-mediation-or-new-offensive-chad

Friends of the Earth. (2001, June 18). *Friends of the Earth requiring suspension of the oil project Chad–Cameroon*. Friends of the Earth International. Retrieved from http://www.amisdelaterre.org/Les-Amis-de-la-Terre-demandent-la.html

Fund for Peace. (2007, September 28). *Country alert: Chad*. Retrieved from http://www.fundforpeace.org/web/index.php?option=com_content&task=view&id=257&Itemid=403

Gagnon, Georgette. (2008, March 19). *Central African Republic: Chadian army attacks, burns border villages*. Human Rights Watch. Retrieved from http://hrw.org/english/docs/2008/03/19/carepu18312.htm

Gagnon, Georgette. (2008, April 2). *Chad: Thousands left homeless by forced evictions*. Human Rights Watch. Retrieved from http://hrw.org/english/docs/2008/04/02/chad18416.htm

GAO. (2002, June). *International trade: Critical issues remain in deterring conflict diamond trade*. United States General Accounting Office Report to Congressional Requesters. Retrieved from http://www.gao.gov/new.items/d02678.pdf

Garro, Helle. (2008, December). *Does humanitarian space exist in Chad?* Humanitarian Practice Network. Retrieved from http://www.odihpn.org/report.asp?id=2974

Gary, Ian. (2008). *Oil and gas revenues, funds and state budgets: Minimising leakages and maximizing transparency and accountability in the hydrocarbon value chain*. United Nations Development Programme (UNDP) Discussion Paper 6: Fuelling Poverty Reduction. Retrieved from http://www.un.org.kh/undp/knowledge/publications/

discussion-paper-6-fuelling-poverty-reduction-selected-papers-international-oil-and-gas-conf-eng

Gary, Ian, and Nikki Reisch. (2005, February). *Chad's oil: Miracle or mirage? Following the money in Africa's newest petro-state*. Bank Information Center and Catholic Relief Services. Retrieved from http://crs.org/publications/list.cfm?sector=26

Gay, B. Marion. (2009, July 6). *La saga des vrais-faux dinars de Bahraïn*. Retrieved from http://www.bakchich.info/La-saga-des-vrais-faux-dinars-de,08206.html

Genova, Windsor. (2008, February 5). *Amnesty International USA calls for release of detained Chad opposition leaders*. Retrieved from http://www.allheadlinenews.com/articles/7009941492#ixzz0MULOYguQ

Gounoumoundjou, Zacharie. (2004). *Histoire de la démocratie en République Centrafricaine: Des origines au coup d'état du 15 Mars 2003: 1946–2003*. Bangui, CAR.

Grignon, François. (2008, May 25). Congo ex-rebel chief Bémba held for war crimes. *Agence France Presse*. Retrieved from http://www.france24.com/en/20080525-congo-ex-rebel-chief-arrested-war-crimes-dr-congo

Haggar, Bichara Idriss. (2003). *Tchad témoignage et combat politique d'un exilé*. Paris: L'Harmattan.

Hancock, Stephanie. (2007, May 9). *Chad signs deal to demobilise child soldiers*. Retrieved from http://www.alertnet.org/thenews/newsdesk/L09132002.htm

HelBongo, Adoum Maurice. (2008, February 20). *Q&A: I fear that Chad will one day lose its sovereignty: Interview with Maurice HelBongo*. Retrieved from http://ipsnews.net/news.asp?idnews=41280

Henderson, D. H. (1984, April 2). *Conflict in Chad, 1975 to present: A central African tragedy*. Marine Corps Command and Staff College, Marine Corps Development and Education Command, Quantico, Virginia. Retrieved from http://www.globalsecurity.org/military/library/report/1984/HDH.htm

Henshaw, A. (2008, February 26). Darfur: Little hope five years on. *BBC News*. Retrieved from http://news.bbc.co.uk/2/hi/africa/7263663.stm

Herz, Virginie. (2008, March 18). *Carnet de route au Tchad* [Log book in Chad]. Retrieved from http://www.france24.com/fr/20080315-carnet-route-tchad-reportages&navi=AFRIQUE

Heurtaut, Diane. (2006, June 4). *Justice: Six mois avec sursis pour le fils du président tchadien*. Retrieved from http://tfl.lci.fr/infos/france/0,,3306664,00.html

Hoile, David. (n.d.). *Darfur Information — page 1*. Retrieved from http://darfurinformation.com/darfur-in-perspective/page-1.asp

Human Development Report. (2010). *Human development index — 2010 rankings*. Retrieved from http://hdr.undp.org/en/statistics/

Human Rights Watch. (2007, January). "They came here to kill us": Militia attacks and ethnic targeting of civilians in eastern Chad. *Human rights Watch, 19*(1A). Retrieved from http://hrw.org/reports/2007/chad0107/

Human Rights Watch. (2007, July 16). *Chad: Government keeps children in army ranks*. Retrieved from http://www.hrw.org/english/docs/2007/07/13/chad16388.htm

Human Rights Watch. (2008, July 14). *Darfur: ICC moves against Sudan's leader*. Retrieved from http://www.hrw.org/node/74138

Idriss Déby Itno. (n.d.). *Biography*. Retrieved from www.afrique-express.com/archive/CENTRALE/tchad/tchadbios/deby.htm

International Criminal Court (ICC). (2009, March 4). *ICC issues a warrant of arrest for Omar Al Bashir, President of Sudan*. ICC Press Release. Retrieved from http://www.icc-cpi.int/menus/icc/press%20and%20media/press%20releases/icc%20issues%20a%20warrant%20of%20arrest%20for%20omar%20al%20bashir_%20president%20of%20sudan?lan=en-GB

International Criminal Court (ICC). (2009, June 15). *Pre-trial chamber II commits Jean-*

Pierre Bémba to trial. (ICC-CPI-20090612-PR420). Retrieved from http://www.icc-cpi.int/NR/exeres/852AE61D-E05C-489A-9172-E6F68D87F182.htm

International Criminal Court (ICC). (2009, July 14). *Trial of Thomas Lubanga Dyilo: The Office of the Prosecutor finishes its case presentation.* (ICC-CPI-20090714-PR437). Retrieved from http://www.icc-cpi.int/NR/exeres/E10A622B-3115-4C05-B8A2-EA83DC2827D8.htm

International Criminal Court (ICC). (2009, September 24). *Trial of Germain Katanga and Mathieu Ngudjolo Chui to commence.* (ICC-CPI-20090327-PR402). Retrieved from http://www.iccnow.org/?mod=drctimelinekatanga

International Crisis Group. (2006, June 1). Chad: Back towards war? *Africa Report,* No. 111. Retrieved from http://www.crisisgroup.org/home/index.cfm?id=5993&l=1

International Crisis Group. (2007, December 13). Central African Republic: Anatomy of a phantom state. *Africa Report,* No. 136. Retrieved from http://www.crisisgroup.org/home/index.cfm?id=5259&l=1

International Crisis Group. (2009, April 15). Chad: Powder keg in the east. *Africa Report,* No. 149. Retrieved from http://www.crisisgroup.org/home/index.cfm?id=6055&l=1

International Federation of Human Rights. (2000, July). *Rapport hors série de la lettre mensuelle de la Fédération Internationale des Ligues des Droits de l'Homme,* No. 295, p. 23.

International Federation for Human Rights. (2004, September). Chad — Death penalty: Ending a moratorium, between security opportunism and settling of scores. *International mission of investigation, report 404.* Retrieved from http://www.unhcr.org/refworld/pdfid/46f146ce0.pdf

IRIN. (2004, December 21). *Chad: Children sold into slavery for the price of a calf.* Retrieved from http://www.irinnews.org/report.aspx?reportid=52490

Jaillard, Nicholas. (2007). A qui profite le petrole du Tchad? *Cameroon InfoNet.* Retrieved from http://wmedia.cameroon-info.net/mm/cin_watch_video.php?m_uid=38649414946177C3F10296

JeuneAfrique. (1994, October 14). Retrieved from http://survie-france.org/article.php3?id_article=353x

JeuneAfrique. (2009, March 11). Mandat d'arrêt contre Béchir: délégation de la Ligue et de l'UA à New York en mars. Retrieved from http://www.jeuneafrique.com/Article/DEPAFP20090311T142206Z/

Juliard, J. (1998, September 9). La France et le Tchad divorcent, mais les apparences sont sauvées [France and Chad divorce but save face]. *Le Canard enchaîné.*

Kahn, Gabriel. (2003, February). *Contre-offensive victorieuse des rebelles congolais.* Retrieved from http://www.google.com/search?hl=en&q=abb%C3%A9+Yambassa and http://www.rfi.fr/actufr/articles/038/article_20584.asp

Kaloga, Inah. (2007, November 4). French journalists accused in Chad child row return home. *CNN.* Retrieved from http://edition.cnn.com/2007/WORLD/africa/11/04/chad.children/index.html

Kashagama, Dan. (2003, March 17). Is the African Union government complicit in the C.A.R. coup d'état? *African Front.* Retrieved from http://www.africanfront.com/page777.php

Katala, Maurice, and Maluza Wasiluadio. (2009, March 10). Declaration of AIPD-GL and CIRAC on the international arrest warrant on the President Omar al-Bashir of Sudan. *UN Watch.* Retrieved from http://blog.unwatch.org/wp-content/uploads/2009/03/ngos-on-icc-sudan-warrant.pdf

Kayangar, Abbas. (2008, February 6). *La situation est grave au Tchad.* Retrieved from http://librafrique.com/index2.php?option=com_content&do_pdf=1&id=161

Kebzabo, Saleh. (2005, December). Réflexion de Saleh Kebzabo, député, leader de l'UNDR, sur le régime d'Idriss Déby. *Afrique Express*. Retrieved from http://www.afrique-express.com/archive/CENTRALE/tchad/tchadbios/kebzabo-Deby.htm

Konto, Adoum Mahamat. (2004, May 6). *Dans toute vos déclarations le problème de la sécurité nationale occupe la 1ère place*. Retrieved from http://www.yorongar.com/article.php3?id_article=41

Koumba, Golndo-Mogne. (2003, September 21). Terreur et peur sur N'Djaména. *N'Djaména Hebdo*, No. 703, p. 3.

Kpatindé, Francis. (1999, June 8). Youssouf Togoïmi: "Négocier avec Déby? Ceux qui ont essayé sont morts!" *JeuneAfrique*. Retrieved from http://www.jeuneafrique.com/jeune_afrique/article_jeune_afrique.asp?art_cle=LIN08066youssstromt0

Kpatindé, Francis. (2000, February 17). *Issue papers, extended responses and country fact sheets*. Retrieved from http://www.irb-cisr.gc.ca/en/research/ndp/ref/index_e.htm?docid=59&cid=0

Lacey, Marc. (2006, April 21). Family feud complicates revolt over Chad's leader. *New York Times*. Retrieved from http://www.nytimes.com/2006/04/21/world/africa/21chad.html

Lanne, Bernard. (2004). Recent history. In K. Murison (Ed.), *Africa South of the Sahara* (33rd ed.), pp. 218–221. London, UK: Routledge.

Laoukoura. (1994). Personal correspondence.

Larché, Jérôme. (2007). Revue humanitaire n° 17 — Islam et solidarité.

La Lettre du Continent. (1998, August 23). Un intermediaire avec des vrai-faux dinars de Bahrein [A middleman with the true-counterfeit dinars of Bahrein]. *La Lettre du Continent*, No. 310.

La Lettre du Continent. (1998, September 24). Faux dinars de Bahrein [Counterfeit dinars of Bahrein]. *La Lettre du Continent*, No. 313.

Loalngar, N. Maxwell. (2006, June 7–13). Editorial: De la ratatouille au sommet.

Machira, Polycarp. (2008, July 16). AU voices opposition to indictment of Bashir. *The Citizen* [Dar es Salaam]. Retrieved from http://allafrica.com/stories/200807160422.html

Madina, Alphonse. (1994). Personal communication after his discharge from military service.

Madjirangar, F. K. (1991, January 26). Paysans-éleveurs: Pourquoi une cohabitation difficile? *N'Djaména Hebdo*.

Madj-kida, Klaïngar. (2003, September 18–21). Insécurité permanente à Béboro. *N'Djamena Hebdo*, No. 703, p. 6.

Madonet, Georges. (2004, January). Idriss Deby, nouveau patron de l'Afrique Centrale? *AfriqueEducation*, Nos. 147–148.

Maldong, Léon. (2003, March 13–16). Le Géneral Bozizé serait-il revenue au Tchad. *N'Djaména Hebdo*, No. 658, p. 8.

Malitti, Tom. (2008, February 5). *Chad's capital quieter but rebels threaten new assault; France ready to intervene if needed*. Retrieved from http://www.newser.com/article/d8uka67o0.html

Manga, Ibangolo Maïna. (2006, September 13). *Assassinat du Président du Collectif et Associations des Jeunes (Camojet) Adoum Abakar Moustapha*. Retrieved from http://www.lale-online.com/actualites-tchad__assassinat_adoum_abakar__13092006.html

Marchal, Roland. (2006). Chad/Darfur: How two crises merge. *Review of African Political Economy, 33*(109), 467–482. doi:10.1080/03056240601000879

Mas, Monique. (2006, April 14). Entre Khartoum et N'Djaména, le Darfour les forces armées tchadiennes ont été soutenues par des rebelles du Darfour [Chadian forces have been supported by the rebels of Darfur]. Retrieved from http://www.rfi.fr/actufr/articles/076/article_43067.asp

Mas, Monique. (2006, April 19). *Rebelles d'hier à demain*. Retrieved from http://www.rfi.fr/actufr/articles/076/article_43155.asp
Masud, Enver. (2004, August 7). *Sudan, oil, and the Darfur crisis*. Retrieved from http://www.twf.org/News/Y2004/0807-Darfur.html
May, Roy, and Simon Massey. (2001, March). The 1996 and 1997 elections in Chad. *Electoral Studies, 20*(1), 127–135.
Mayadi, Ngarteri Mathias. (1996, November). Déby, entre Mobutu et Tchador. *Survie*. Retrieved from http://surviefrance.org/article.php3?id_article=353&var_recherche=Mayadi+
Meunier, Marianne. (2010, February 2). *Faux dinars et vrais Escrocs*. Retrieved from http://www.jeuneafrique.com/Article/ARTJAJA2563p024.xml1/.
Meynier, Roger. (2008, February 8). Tchad: une dictature qui dure grâce au soutien français. *Lutte Ouvrière*. Retrieved from http://www.lutte-ouvriere-journal.org/?act=artl&num=2062&id=37
Michailof, Serge, Markus Kostner, and Xavier Devictor. (2002, April). Africa Region Working Paper Series 246, No. 30, Post-Conflict Recovery in Africa. *An Agenda for the Africa Region*. Retrieved from http://www-wds.worldbank.org/external/default/WDSContentServer/WDSP/IB/2002/09/07/000094946_02082104034280/Rendered/PDF/multi0page.pdf
Miskine, Abdoulaye. (2002, June 11). Le chef rebelle tchadien Abdoulaye Miskine casé au Togo après avoir été décoré Commandeur de l'Ordre du Mérite Centrafricain. *Togo Confidentiel*. Retrieved from http://www.togo-confidentiel.com/texte/Politique/Abdoulaye_Miskin_au_Togo.htm
La mort d'Adouma marquée-t-elle la fin d'une histoire de sous? (2003, November 16). *Ndjaména Hebdo*, No. 719, p. 6.
Moussa, Nadjita. (1996, December 22). Personal communication. Koussouri, Cameroon.
Musualuendu, Albert Buyamba. (n.d.). *Kabila pille, Kabila dévaste, Kabila ravage Mbuji-Mayi* [Kabila is pillaging, Kabila is devastating, Kabila is ravaging Mbuji-Mayi]. Retrieved from http://www.congonline.com/Forum1/Forum05/Buyamba01.htm
Nadingar, Alladoum. (2006, June 8–11). Brahim Déby, conseiller immature. *N'Djaména Hebdo*, No. 956. Retrieved from http://www.tchadactuel.com/presse.php?2006/06/10/225-brahim-deby-conseiller-immaturendjamena-bi-hebdo-n-956-du-8-au-11-juin-2006
Nadoum, Bour. (2008, February). Personal correspondence.
Nadoum, Bour. (2009, June). Personal correspondence.
Nadoumngar, Judé. (2009, December). Personal communication.
Nako, Madjiasra. (2003a, June 29). Haro sur les vendeurs d'enfants du Mandoul. *N'Djaména Hebdo*, No. 688, p. 5.
Nako, Madjiasra. (2003b, June 29). Les esclavagistes qui séjournent dans le Mandoul n'ont qu'à bien se tenir. *N'Djaména Hebdo*, No. 688, p. 6.
N'Diékhor, Daniel Ralongar. (2003, March 31). La rébellion du Darfour menace-t-elle les relations Soudano-Tchadiennes? *N'Djaména Hebdo*, No. 663, p. 5.
N'Diékhor, Daniel Ralongar. (2003a, April 16). Foire de pillards à Moundou [Thieves' market at Moundou]. *N'Djaména Hebdo*, No. 667, p. 3.
N'Diékhor, Daniel Ralongar. (2003b, April 16). Pillage délibéré ou butin de guerre? [Deliberate pillage, or spoils of war?]. *N'Djaména Hebdo*, No. 667, p. 4.
N'Diékhor, Daniel Ralongar. (2003, September 21). Insécurité permanente à Béboro [Permanent insecurity in Béboro]. *N'Djaména Hebdo*, No. 703, p. 6.
N'Diékhor, Daniel Ralongar. (2003, October 5). Le commanditaire de l'assassinat de Acheik sous les verrous. *N'Djaména Hebdo*, No. 707.
N'Djibo, Nobo. (March 23, 2004). La récurrence des conflits intercommunautaires, et la tragédie humaine qu'ils provoquent ont amené aussi bien les hommes politiques,

la société civile à réagir, en [...]. Retrieved from http://www.yorongar.com/article.php3?id_article=40
Nékim, Jean-Claude. (1993, July 8). Les en-dessous d'une affaire de gros sous [The hidden truth of the matter of a large sum of money]. *N'Djaména Hebdo*, No. 89, pp. 7–8.
New Internationalist Magazine. (2001, October). *Omar al-Bashir's legacy*. Retrieved from http://www.thirdworldtraveler.com/Zeroes/Omar_al-Bashir.html
Ngarmbassa, Moumine. (2008, July 2). Chad's Deby rejects peace meeting with Sudan leader. *Reuters*. Retrieved from http://www.reuters.com/article/latestCrisis/idUSL02442894
Ngarnim, Idriss. (2005, September 27). Qui sont les vrais assassins de l'homme d'affaire Soudanais, Acheik Ibn Oumar? Retrieved from http://www.ialtchad.com/forumactualitesuite.htm
Nguiffo, Samuel, and Susanne Breitkopf. (2001). *Broken promises: The Chad Cameroon oil and pipeline project; Profit at any cost?* Center for the Environment & Development and Friends of the Earth International. Retrieved from http://www.ciel.org/Publications/chadcam_broken_promises.PDF
Niang, Issa. (2006, October). Crise au Darfour: La rébellion tchadienne accuse Ndjaména de tirer les ficelles [Crisis in Darfur: A Chadian rebel accuses N'djaména of being puppeteer]. *Walf Fadjri*.
Nolutshungu, Sam C. (1996). *Limits of anarchy: Intervention and state formation in Chad*. Charlottesville, VA: University of Virginia.
L'Observateur. (2005, July 27). Sombres perspectives pour la France au Tchad. *L'Observateur*, No. 340. Retrieved from http://www.pressafrique.com/m237.html
Open Society Justice Initiative. (n.d.). *The trial of Charles Taylor*. Retrieved from http://www.charlestaylortrial.org/trial-background/who-is-charles-taylor/#four
Ouango, Prince Hervé. (2006a, October 3). Contenu du message 344038. *AfricaTime*. Retrieved from http://www.africatime.com/dynamique/Forum/affiche.asp?num=344038&grp=201295&IdSujet=17&IdPays=4
Ouango, Prince Hervé. (2006b, October 3). *Jean Pierre Bemba, un danger pour l'Afrique Centrale ... !* Retrieved from http://groups.yahoo.com/group/Great-Lakes/message/3727
Oulatar, Yaldet Bégoto. (1998, August 28). La poisse est elle arrive? [Has calamity arrived?] *N'Djaména Hebdo*.
Oulatar, Yaldet Bégoto. (2003, March 20–23). La chute. *N'Djaména Hebdo*, No. 660, pp. 1–3.
Partnership Africa Canada. (2003, January 10). *Diamonds in the Central African Republic: Trading, valuing and laundering*. Retrieved from http://www.reliefweb.int/rw/rwb.nsf/db900sid/ACOS-64CGJP?OpenDocument
PBS. (2009, September 8). *ICC prosecutor makes case against Sudan's president*. Retrieved from http://www.pbs.org/newshour/bb/africa/july-dec09/icc_09-08.html
Philp, C., and F. Gibb. (2009, January). Thomas Lubanga becomes first to stand trial for war crimes at the ICC. *The Times*. Retrieved from http://www.timesonline.co.uk/tol/news/world/africa/article5586688.ece
Polgreen, Lydia. (2005, December 13). Chad backs out of pledge to use oil wealth to reduce poverty. *New York Times*. Retrieved from http://query.nytimes.com/gst/fullpage.html?res=9902EEDA1E31F930A25751C1A9639C8B63&sec=&spon=&pagewanted=all
Polgreen, Lydia. (2008, February 12). Deby survives, but dissidents' peril grows. *New York Times*. Retrieved from http://www.nytimes.com/2008/02/12/world/africa/12chad.html?_r=1&oref=slogin
Posthumus, Bram. (2000). *Can the cycle of war be broken?* European Centre for Conflict

Prevention (ECCP). Retrieved from http://www.conflict-prevention.net/print.php?id=56

PressAfrique. (1994-2004). *Politique africaine de la France au Soudan (1994-2004).* Retrieved from http://www.pressafrique.com/m11.html

Prunier, Gérard. (1999, October). L'Ouganda et les guerres Congolaises. *Politique Africaine, 75,* pp. 43-59. Retrieved from http://www.politique-africaine.com/numeros/pdf/075043.pdf

Prunier, Gérard. (2007, March). Sudan: Genocide in Darfur. *Le Monde Diplomatique.* Retrieved from http://www.exacteditions.com/exact/browse/373/399/2074/3/1

Prunier, Gérard. (2007, September 7). *Chad's Tragedy.* Open Democracy. Retrieved from http://www.opendemocracy.net/article/democracy_power/africa/chad_tragedy and http://www.globalpolicy.org/component/content/article/198/40253.html

Prunier, Gérard. (2008, February 19). *Chad: Between Sudan's blitzkrieg and Darfur's war.* Global Policy Forum. Retrieved from http://www.globalpolicy.org/security/issues/chadcar/2008/0219chadprunier.htm

Prunier, Gérard. (2008, March 5). Chad: Caught in the Darfur crossfire. *Le Monde Diplomatique.* Retrieved from http://mondediplo.com/2008/03/05chad

Que lumière soit faite sur la mort de Neldé. (2003, November 26). *N'Djaména Hebdo,* No. 722, p. 8.

Radio Nederland Wereldomroep (RNW). (2008, June 27). *ICC: Confirmation of charges in Kantaga case.* Retrieved from http://static.rnw.nl/migratie/www.rnw.nl/internationaljustice/icc/DRC/080627-ICC-redirected

Reuters. (1987, March 23). Chad is said to capture strategic Libyan air base. *New York Times.* Retrieved from http://query.nytimes.com/gst/fullpage.html?res=9B0DE1DA163DF930A15750C0A961948260

Reynolds, Paul. (2007, June 4). Charles Taylor: The trial begins. *BBC News.* Retrieved from http://news.bbc.co.uk/2/hi/6707551.stm

Rolley, Sonia. (2008, April 22). Quand N'Djaména se barricade. *Liberation.* Retrieved from http://www.liberation.fr/transversales/grandsangles/322455.FR.php

Rosen, Isaac. (n.d.). *Hissène Habré: Biography and much more.* Retrieved from http://www.answers.com/topic/hiss-ne-habr

Rota, Madelène. (1991). Personal communication to author.

Rwanda News Agency. (2010, December 8). *Is the ICC prosecutor Africa's only hope for justice?* Retrieved from http://www.rnanews.com/regional/4534-is-the-icc-prosecutor-africas-only-hope-for-justice

Sangonet News Service. (2003, March 15). *Les rebelles reprennent les villes détenues par les loyalistes et leurs alliés du MLC de Bémba, puis pénètrent samedi 15 mars 2003 dans la ville de Bangui (le film de la journée).* Retrieved from http://www.sangonet.com/ActualiteC14/rebellion_repriseV_bangui15ms03.html

Sarkozy, Nicolas. (2007, July 26). *Allocution de M. Nicolas Sarkozy, Président de la République, prononcée à l'Université de Dakar.* Retrieved from http://www.elysee.fr/elysee/elysee.fr/francais/interventions/2007/juillet/allocution_a_l_universite_de_dakar.79184.html

Sheer, Julie, and John Jackson. (2005, September 4). Some of the key events in Moammar Kadafi's rule. *Los Angeles Times.* Retrieved from http://www.latimes.com/news/nationworld/world/la-fg-uslibyachrono4sep04,0,980049.story?coll=la-tot-promo%20target=_blank

Simpson, Chris. (1999, June 23). Africa DR Congo: What price peace? *BBC News.* Retrieved from http://news.bbc.co.uk/1/hi/world/africa/376633.stm

Slackman, Michael, and Robert Worth. (2009, March 30). Often split, Arab leaders unite for Sudan's chief. *New York Times.* Retrieved from http://www.nytimes.com/2009/03/31/world/africa/31arab.html?_r=2&ref=africa

Soudan, François. (2002, December 2). Sous la tente de Kaddafi. *Jeune Afrique*. Retrieved from http://www.jeuneafrique.com/jeune_afrique/article_jeune_afrique. asp?art_cle=LIN15122souslifadda0

Soudan, François. (2009, March 9). Tutu, Kagamé et le cas El-Béchir. *Jeune Afrique*. Retrieved from http://www.jeuneafrique.com/Article/ARTJAJA2513p003-004.xm 10/-CPI-Paul-Kagame-Omar-el-Bechir-mandat-d-arret-international-Tutu-Kagame-et-le-cas-El-Bechir.html

Soudan, François. (2003, March 23). La chute de l'Ange. *Jeune Afrique*. Retrieved from http://www.jeuneafrique.com/jeune_afrique/article_jeune_afrique.asp?art_cle=LI N23033lachuegnale0

Survie. (1996, November 7). *N'Djamena: Deby between Mobutu and tchador*. Retrieved from http://survie.org/publications/les-dossiers-noirs/dossier-noir-no3-france-tchad/article/n-djamena-deby-entre-mobutu-et

Takirambudde, Peter. (2007, July 16). *Chad: Government keeps children in Army ranks*. Retrieved from http://www.hrw.org/en/news/2007/07/15/chad-government-keeps-children-army-ranks and http://www.hrw.org/english/docs/2007/07/13/chad16388.htm

Talbot, Chris. (1999, May 14). *Congo war drags on—Uganda and Chad pull out*. Retrieved from http://www.wsws.org/articles/1999/may1999/cong-m14.shtml

Tanner, Victor, and Jérôme Tubianna. (2007). Divided they fall: The fragmentation of Darfur's rebel groups. *The Small Arms Survey*. Geneva, Switzerland: Graduate Institutes of International Studies.

Tchadactuel. (2007, May 9). *Nouri/Arabie saoudite: Quels liens et pour quels objectifs*. Retrieved from http://www.africatime.com/tchad/nouvelle.asp?no_nouvelle=325334&no_categorie=

Tchadoscopie. (1996, June 1). *Tchad: la "métropole" sans boussole*. Retrieved from http://www.tchadoscopie.com/pages/Tchad__la_metropole_sans_boussole-492327.html and http://survie.org/publications/les-dossiers-noirs/dossier-noir-no3-france-tchad/article/tchad-la-metropole-sans-boussole

Tedga, Jean Paul. (2008, February). *AfriquEducation*, No. 246, February 15–29.

Teluu. (2011, July 3). *International Criminal Court: An instrument of neo-colonialism*. Retrieved from http://alft-teluu.blogspot.com/2011/07/international-criminal-court-instrument.html

Tempest, Matthew. (2008, March 20). Journalist barred from Chad. *The Guardian*. Retrieved from http://www.guardian.co.uk/media/2008/mar/20/afp.chad

Le Temps, No. 482. Retrieved from http://www.tchadactuel.com/presse.php?2006/06/11/227-editorial-de-la-ratatouille-au-sommetle-temps-n-482-du-7-au-13-juin-2006

Toïngar, Ésaïe. (2006). *A teenager in the Chad civil war*. Jefferson, NC: McFarland.

Tran, Phuong. (2007, May 15). Chad schools try to stop child soldier recruitment. *Voice of America*. Retrieved from http://www.voanews.com/english/archive/2007-05/2007-05-15-voa4.cfm?CFID=59950077&CFTOKEN=49007633

Transparency International. (2010). *Corruption Perceptions Index 2010*. Retrieved from http://www.transparency.org/policy_research/surveys_indices/cpi/2010/results

Tuquoi, J. (1999, June 28). L'affaire de faux dinars of Bahrein. *Le Monde*.

UNHCR. (2009, July 16). *Freedom in the World 2009—Chad*. Freedom House. Retrieved from http://www.unhcr.org/refworld/docid/4a6452c6c.html

United Nations. (1998, July 17). *Rome statute of the International Criminal Court*. Retrieved from http://untreaty.un.org/cod/icc/statute/99_corr/cstatute.htm

United Nations Security Council. (1997, November 6). *Press Release 6439. Acting under Chapter VII, Council extends mandate of monitoring mission in Central African Republic for three months, from today*. Retrieved from http://www.un.org/News/Press/docs/1997/19971106.SC6439.html

Uriz, Genoveva Hernández. (2002, November 2). *The application of the World Bank standards to the oil industry: Can the World Bank Group promote corporate responsibility?* Retrieved from http://www.brooklaw.edu/students/journals/bjil/bjil28i_uriz.pdf

U.S. Department of State. (1992). *Background notes, May 1992.* Retrieved from http://dosfan.lib.uic.edu/ERC/bgnotes/af/chad9205.html

U.S. Department of State. (1994). *Chad human rights practices, 1993.* Retrieved from http://dosfan.lib.uic.edu/ERC/democracy/1993_hrp_report/93hrp_report_africa/Chad.html

U.S. Department of State. (1996). *Chad human rights practices, 1995.* Retrieved from http://dosfan.lib.uic.edu/ERC/democracy/1995_hrp_report/95hrp_report_africa/Chad.html

Useem, Jerry. (2002, April 15). *Exxon's African adventure: How to build a $3.5 billion pipeline—with the "help" of NGOs, the World Bank, and yes, chicken sacrifices.* Retrieved from http://money.cnn.com/magazines/fortune/fortune_archive/2002/04/15/321403/index.htm

Valdiguié, L. (1998, September 30). The mystery of counterfeit dinars of Bahrein. *Le Parisien.*

Verschave, François Xavier. (2000). *Noir silence.* Paris: Les Arènes.

Verschave, François Xavier, and Laurent Beccaria (Eds.). (2001). *Noir procès.* Paris: Les Arènes.

Vincent, Faustine. (2008, February 28). Visite polémique de Nicolas Sarkozy au Tchad. *Monde.* Retrieved from http://www.20minutes.fr/monde/215916-Monde-Visite-polemique-de-Nicolas-Sarkozy-au-Tchad.php

Voice of America. (2007, January 12). *Defining Sudan-Chad relations.* Retrieved from http://www.voanews.com/english/archive/2007-01/Chad2007-01-14-voa17.cfm?renderforprint=1&textonly=1&&TEXTMODE=1&CFID=117844993&CFTOKEN=60544386

Voice of America. (2007, August 7). *Chad's rebels and government continue peace dialogue.* Retrieved from http://www.voanews.com/english/archive/2007-08/2007-08-07-voa49.cfm?moddate=2007-08-07

Voice of America. (2009, October 27). *Defining Sudan-Chad relations.* Retrieved from http://m.voanews.com/a/553219.html

Waging Peace. (June 6, 2008). *Briefing report.* Retrieved from http://www.wagingpeace.info/files/20080606_WagingPeaceReport_ChildrenSoldiers.pdf

Workman, Daniel. (2007). Most corrupt trade nations. *International Trade.* Retrieved from http://internationaltrade.suite101.com/article.cfm/most_corrupt_trade_nations

World Bank. (2006). *The Chad–Cameroon petroleum development and pipeline project.* Retrieved from http://web.worldbank.org/WBSITE/EXTERNAL/COUNTRIES/AFRICAEXT/EXTREGINI/EXTCHADCAMPIPELINE/0,,contentMDK:20516071~menuPK:843292~pagePK:64168445~piPK:64168309~theSitePK:843238,00.html

Yorongar, Ngarlejy. (1999, September 29). *Décès tragique du militant des Droits de l'Homme au Tchad: Néhémie Benoudjita, par empoisonnement.* Retrieved from http://www.ardhd.org/francais/liberte/lib001.htm#3009TCHAD

Yorongar, Ngarlejy. (2000, May 17). *La Liberté (34).* Retrieved from http://www.ardhd.org/francais/liberte/lib034.htm#1705TCHAD

Yorongar, Ngarlejy. (2000, August 11). Letter to James Wolfensohn re: Massacres des populations du site pétrolier par des hélicoptères de l'armée nationale tchadienne (ANT). L'Association pour le Respect de Droits de l'Homme a Djibouti (ARDHD). Retrieved from www.ardhd.org/francais/bulletin/bul010.htm#2308TCHAD

Yorongar, Ngarlejy. (2003). *Tchad: Le procès d'Idriss Déby.* Paris: Harmattan.

Yorongar, Ngarlejy. (2004). *Un baril de pétrole tchadien pour plusieurs barils du sang des Tchadiens* [A barrel of Chadian oil for many barrels of Chadians' blood], Articles 19 & 20. Retrieved from http://www.yorongar.com/article.php3?id_article=65

Yorongar, Ngarlejy. (2004, August 19). *Lettre au Premier minister*. Retrieved from http://www.yorongar.com/spip.php?article48

Yorongar, Ngarlejy. (2004, August 20). *Les auteurs des récents massacres de Bao et de Maïbogo jouissent d'une remarquable impunité*. Retrieved from http://www.yorongar.com/article.php3?id_article=49

Yorongar, Ngarlejy. (2004, November 18). *Lettre au ministre de l'administration du territoire assurant l'intérim du ministre de la sécurité publique*. Retrieved from http://www.yorongar.com/spip.php?article68

Yorongar, Ngarlejy. (2004, December 3). *Un baril de pétrole tchadien pour plusieurs barils du sang des Tchadiens. (Tome I: Flagrantes violations répétées de la constitution et des droits de l'Homme: état des lieux)*. Retrieved from http://www.yorongar.com/article.php3?id_article=65

Yorongar, Ngarlejy. (2004, December 9). *A propos des menaces ouvertes proférées contre le Député Fédéraliste Mahamat Adoum Konto: Interpellation du Premier ministre*. Retrieved from http://www.yorongar.com/article.php3?id_article=73

Yorongar, Ngarlejy. (2006, March 25). *Courrier au Premier Ministre Pascal Yoadimnadji*. Retrieved from http://www.yorongar.com/spip.php?article107

Yorongar, Ngarlejy. (2007). *Letter to His Excellency Ban Ki-Moon, general secretary of the United Nations: How Idriss Deby created the bloody rebellion of Sudanese Darfur on December 1, 2003, in Tiné-Chad*. (Published June 9, 2008.) Retrieved from http://www.bbc.co.uk/news/world-africa-12701803

Index

Abacha, Sani 27–28
Abakar, Abdul Allah 66
Abakar, Koki Sougui 27
Abatcha, Ibrahim 71
Abaye 112
Abbas, Maldom Bada 9, 20
Abbas, Youssouf Saleh 79
Abbud, Ibrahim 69
Abdallah, Djirdi 66
Abdallah, Khamis 137
Abdallah, Soubiane 18, 25
Abdelaziz, Abbas 68
Abderahim, Saleh 38
Abderaman, Abakar 112
Abderamane, Moubarak Bakhit 59
Abéché 32, 67, 111, 113, 131, 158
Abidjan 40
Abu Gamra 64
Action Internationale Pour la Paix et le Development (AIPD) 163
Acyl, Mahamat 73–74
Advanced Financial Corporation in Chad (AFCORP-Tchad) 89
Agadaye, Djamal Adoum 28
Aganaye, Bintou 29
Aguid, Hassan 111
Aguid, Saleh 66
Ahmat, Adouma Ali 58–63, 89
Ahmat, Hisseine 138
Albaye, Nosso 111
Algeria 125, 148, 163
Ali, Mahamat 105
Allahbarem, Edouard 104
Allazam, Albissaty Sateh 11, 65
Alliance des Démocrates Résistants (ADR) 137–138

Alyo, Akim 105
Amnesty International 28, 59
Amtiman 131
Angola 48, 161
Aouzou 72, 77, 139
arbatachar 23
Argentina 42–43
Armed Forces Revolutionary Council (AFRC) 155
Asngar, Dobian 49, 54–55, 158

Bahar, Ahmed Mohamed 68
Bahrain 39, 42, 44, 162
Baltimore, Alain 24
Banque des États de l'Afrique Centrale (BEAC) 41
Bao 104
Barclays 43
Barka, Mahamat Ben 55
Bashar, Abdallah Abakar 66
Bashir, Omar Hassan el- 1, 7, 53, 58, 62–63, 68, 74–76, 84–88, 90–92, 95–97, 140, 142, 144–145, 152–153, 155–168, 171
Batadjana 111–113
Batha 113
Bebo Pen 102
Beboudja 49, 53, 104–105
Beidi, Joseph 15, 21, 23
Béïndi, Félix Ngakoutou 5–7, 32, 46, 72
Békôdô I 103
Belgium 43, 155, 163
Benin Republic 29, 169
Bénoudjita, Néhémie 3
Bessané, Robert 104
Bidi, Néatobeye 16
Bidi, Valentin 37

Bissou, Mamadou 9, 21
Biya Yaoundé, Paul 42, 132
Bockarie, Sam 155
Bodo 23, 99, 103–104
Bolloré (industrial holding group) 157
Bongo, Oumar 78, 132
Bongor 22
Borkou-Ennedi-Tibesti 72, 139–141
Bossangoa 135
Bosso 112
Bouteflika, Abdelaziz 125
Bouygues (industrial holding group) 157
Boy, Youssouf 41–42
Bozizé, François 122–129, 131–132, 134–135, 137–138, 156–157, 160, 167, 171–172
Brahim, Fadoul Salet 112
Brahim, Mahamat Salet 111–112
Bunda, Abdul Allah 66]
Bureau des Recherches Pétrolières 45
Burkina Faso 43, 119
Bush, George W. 66, 106, 154
Businga 159

Cameroon 10, 29, 41–42, 47–50, 52, 55–56, 73–75, 80, 82, 96–97, 104, 126, 131–133, 158, 168
Camous (Kodadingar) 98
Canada 14, 39
Caring for Kaela (CFK) 163
CEMAC (Economic and Monetary Community of Central Africa) 125–126, 129–130, 132, 134, 136
Central Africa 1–2, 6, 39, 58, 67, 92, 119–121, 166
Central African Republic 6, 55, 67–68, 75, 90–91, 93–94, 96, 102, 104, 115–138, 145, 151, 155, 157–158, 160–172
Chad Petroleum Company 58–59
Chadian Association for the Promotion and Defense of Human Rights 49
Chadian National Union (UNT) 71
Chaibo, Bichara 28
Chari-Baguirmi 113
Chevron Oil 46–48
China 85, 160, 162, 165
Chirac, Jacques 1, 30, 52, 157
Choua, Abakar 112
Choua, Lol Mahamat 81, 91, 126
Chui, Mathieu Ngudjolo 153–154
CNR (National Council for Recovery) 22
CNSM (High National Military Council) 72–73
CODOs 75, 115–118
Collège de Contrôle et de Surveillance des Ressources Pétrolières (CCSRP) 49–50, 55

Commission Électorale Nationale Indépendante (CENI) 79
Commité de Sursaut National Pour le Development (CSNPD) 27, 116–117
Community of Sahel and Saharan States (CEN-SAD) 125–126, 129–131, 133–134, 156, 162, 167
Congo Republic 1, 54, 91, 93, 102, 130, 158–159
Conoco Oil 46, 123
corruption 28, 45, 49–50, 54–55, 77–83, 135, 149, 168
CotonTchad 10–11, 41, 99, 135
counterfeiting 11, 39–44

Dadjos 137
Dagdagou 112
Danyo, Merci 24
Daoud, Miriam 113
Dar Tama 111
Darfur Liberation Front (DLF) 68–69
Darmian, Jean-Marie 6
Déby, Brahim 29–30
Déby, Timane 69
Déclaud, Djérabé 2
Democratic Republic of Congo 1, 75, 96, 120–121, 128, 131, 135, 154–156, 158–159, 162
Digui, Bichana 23
Dillah, Ferdinand 104
Diredj, Dr. 69
Djama, Mahamoud Bechir 89
Djamous, Hassan 20, 75, 92
Djamtato 10
Djar, Al Nabbi Bahraddine 6
Djato 13–14
Djekoula, Dominique 24
Djépatamia, Alfred 104
Djerou, Tidjani Salim 65
Djibouti 3, 133–134
Djibril (Col.) 66
Djibrine Dassert 19
Djimé, Togou 60
Djimlelngar 105
Djiraïbé, Delphine 49, 51, 53–54
Djonabaye, Dieudonné 3
Doba 8, 46, 57, 97, 99, 103, 105, 124–125, 128
Dogui, Demou 37
Dougia 73
Doumbogo 105
Doumran, Alain 24
Doumro 116–117
Dremi 36–37

Egypt 5, 72, 75
Ehemir, Néné 138

Elf Oil 47–48, 50, 79, 157
Elysée Palace 157
Emmanuel 82
England 163
Épervier Plan 31
Equatorial Guinea 124, 126, 130
Erdémi, Timan 9, 11, 142, 146, 151
Erdémi, Tom 9
Esso, Exxon/Mobil 46–48, 52, 57, 128–129, 168
European Union 1, 15, 29, 79, 163
European Union Forces (EUFOR) 145

Fada 6, 111, 113
Fadil, Mahamat 26, 28
Faki, Moussa 96–97
Fakki, Ali Mahamat 66
FANT (Chadian National Army) 9
el Fashir 95
FIDH (International Federation for Human Rights) 42, 53, 62
FNI (National Integrationist Front) 153
Forces Armées du Nord (FAN) 73
France 1–2, 5–6, 8, 13, 28–29, 31–34, 39–45, 47–48, 53, 60, 70–72, 74, 77–79, 86, 96, 119, 125, 128–133, 136, 139–141, 144–147, 150–153, 157, 160–164, 168
FranceAfrique 132, 144, 146, 157, 161–163
Front d'Action pour la République Fédérale (FARF) 24, 26
Front de Liberation Nationale Tchadienne (FROLINAT) 7, 24, 71, 73
Front de Libération Tchadienne (FLT) 7, 70–72
FRPI (Patriotic Resistance Force in Ituri) 153
FU/ADT (United Front for a Democratic Alternative in Chad) 11

Gabon 54, 78, 126, 130, 132
Gali, Sy Koumbo Singa 3
Galium 32
Garang, John 75, 85, 87
Garfa, Mahamat 95
Gassi, Tahir 89
Germany 28–29
Gillé, Rosalie 111
Gombo, Jean-Pierre Bémba 120–121, 125, 128–135, 155–156, 161–162
Goré 25, 116, 131, 158
Gounoumoundou, Zacharie 133
Goz Beïda 32, 67, 137
Grah, Armand 40
Grand d'Esnon, Jérôme 79
Guéra 20, 71, 112, 123, 128–129, 137, 141
Guet, Goukouni 27

Gouverment d'Union Nationale de Transition (GUNT) 19, 74

Habré, Hissène 6–9, 14, 18–20, 22–23, 27–28, 32–33, 46–47, 63, 72–75, 77, 86–88, 92–95, 97, 107, 117, 140–143
Hadj, el- 81
Hadjiraï 19–21, 92, 94–95, 141
Haggar, Bichara Idriss 14, 158
Hamat, Taher 36–37
Hamdan, Col. 79–80
Hamit, Mahamat 111
Haroun, Abderamane Hamid 59
Haroun, Ahmed 155
Hemchi, Brahim 111
Hissein, Abderahim Mohamed 68
Hissène, Djiddi 33–38
Hollande, François 2

Ibedou, Younous 95–96, 138
Ibrahim, Khalil 13, 65
Independent National Election Commission (INEC) 79–81
International Committee for the Respect of the African Charter on Human and Peoples' Rights (ICRAC) 163
International Criminal Court (ICC) 152–164
International Monetary Fund (IMF) 168
Iran 87–88
Issa, Mahamat Adam 16, 59
Itno, Daoussa Déby 65
Ivory Coast 39–40

Janjawiid 56, 65, 68, 76, 85, 94–106, 140, 149, 155, 171–172

Kabadi, Haroun 11
Kabila, Joseph 128–129
Kabila, Laurent Desiré 1, 96, 119, 128, 133, 156
Kabo, Bourkou Louise 15–16
Kagamé, Paul 153, 161
Kamogué, Abdel Kader 7, 16
Kanem 113
Kanembou 81, 158
Kano 73
Karang-Karang 35
Kassiré Coumakoï 81
Katanga, Germain 153–154
Kebzabo, Charles 91, 126
Kebzabo, Saleh 14, 19
Kerim, Ngarou 19
Kétté, Nodji Moïse 21, 23, 27, 54, 115–118, 170
Khadafi, Muammar 7, 19, 22, 77, 120–122, 129–131, 146, 153, 167

Khartoum 7–8, 53–76, 85–87, 91, 144
Kitir, Hassan Fadoul 1, 42–44
Kodadingar (Camou) 98
Koddi 20
Kolingba, André 117, 134
Komé 47–48, 57, 78, 104
Kony, Joseph 154
Kosheib, Ali 155
Kotiga, Alphonse 73
Koty, Abbas 22–23, 141, 167, 170
Koulamallah 151
Koumandoh, Jackson 82
Koussouri 29, 41, 131
Kribi 48

Labadri, Yahya 27
Lagos 19, 73, 80–81
Laïna, Loum Hinaïssou 16
Laonoji, Desiré 24
Laoubélé, Dangdé 16
Laoukeïn, Bardé Friston 24, 27, 115–117, 170
Liberia 154–155, 159
Libreville 132
Libya 6–7, 18–19, 22, 27, 44, 72, 74–75, 77, 86–87, 92, 94, 120–122, 125–126, 129–134, 139–141, 143, 146, 153, 166–167, 169
Lisan, Ahmet Tagod 65
Lossimian, Naïmbaye 15
Loussouba, Pascal 159, 161
Lubanga, Thomas 156
Lukwiya, Raska 154

Madjiri 123
Mahamat, Ahmat 95
Mahdi, Sadiq al- 75
Maïbogo 102
Maïnassara, Baré Ibrahim 26, 42
Malabo 124
Mali 2, 118–119, 163
Manang, Sam 36
Mandoul 102, 109–111
Mangalmé 71
Maro 125
Mathias 24
Maxime, Kouladoumbaye 2, 12–13
Mbaïnaïbey, Gaston 25, 158
Mbikou 104
Mianbé, Mbaïlaou 14–17
Miandoum 57, 124
Michailof, Serge 49–50, 57
Middle East 73, 161, 163
Minnawi, Minni Arkou 66, 106
Miskine, Abdoulaye 102, 124–125, 130–131, 167; *see also* Nadingar, Martin Koumtamadji

Miskine, Idriss 19–20, 74
Mission d'Intervention et de Surveillance des Accords de Bangui (MISAB) 118–119, 122
Mittérand, François 31–32
Mobutu Sese Seko 1, 96, 119–120
Mohamed, Anwar Ahmed 69
Mongo 131, 137
Morin, Hervé 146
Moukoïgué 111
Moundou 8, 18, 21, 24–26, 68, 104–105, 112, 116
Moungar, Fidèle Abdelkarim 33, 35–37
Moursal 13, 17, 23
Moussa, Col. 79–81
Moussa, Nadjita 118
Moussoro 27, 112
Moustapha, Adoum Abakar 28
Mouvement Patriotic du Salut (MPS) 19–23, 79–82, 120
Movement for Democracy and Development (MDD) 28, 116
Movement for Democracy and Justice in Chad (MDJT) 26–27, 40, 116–117, 158
Movement for Justice and Equality (MJE) 65–66
Movement for Liberation of Sudan (MLS) 66, 137
Movement for the Liberation of Congo (MOC) 128, 133
Moyen Chari 46–47, 102, 104
Musa, Ahmed Hassan 71–72, 87
Muslim Brotherhood 7, 71

Nadingar, Martin Koumtamadji 124
Nadoum, Bour 31–38
Nadoumngar, Judé 82–83
Nahor 124
Nassara, Maïna Bal 26
Nassour, Mahamat Ali Abdallah 65
National Security Agency of Chad 22
Ndeïdoum, Léon 104
N'Djaména 6–13, 15–18, 20, 22–28, 31, 38, 89, 91, 95, 97, 99–103, 108, 113, 116, 119, 127, 131, 137–138–144, 150, 158, 166, 170
N'djébété (Dr.) 124
Ndoh, Grabé 105
Ndolé, Ngarelnan 102
Nelde 61–62
Ngak 81
Ngarbaroum, Demtita 9, 32
Ngarboubou (Col.) 19–20
Ngarteri, Archbishop Mathias 79
Ngororo, Nadjita 19
Ngudjolo, Matthieu 153–154
Nguesso, Denis Sassou 78, 161

Niamey 42, 130–132, 134, 167
Niger 26, 28, 39, 42, 44, 78, 80, 111–112, 130–132, 163, 167
Nigeria 19, 21–22, 27, 43–44, 47, 73, 79–81, 87, 131, 154, 163
Nigué, Hassan 111
Noël, Laoukeïn 15
Noïngar, Paul 111
Nour, Mahamat 86–87, 113, 167
Nourene, Abdallah Mohamed 68
Nouri, Mahamat 86–87, 96, 142, 146, 151

Occidental Logone (Logone Occidental) 16, 24–25, 32, 117, 131
Odhiambo, Okot 154
Oil 2, 7, 30, 45–63, 65, 76, 78–9, 85, 89, 91, 97, 106, 123–125, 128, 130, 147–148, 151, 157, 162, 168
Ongwen, Dominic 154
Oriental Logone (Logone Oriental) 23–25, 32, 46–47, 50, 103–104, 109, 117, 124, 128, 131
Otti, Vincent 154
Ouaddaï 22, 32, 68, 71, 85, 95, 100, 141, 158
Oulatar, Yaldet Bégoto 3
Oumar, Issa 36–37
Ousman 112

Pakistan 87–88
Paris 20, 29–30, 39, 43–44, 83, 125, 131
Pasqua, Charles 157
Patassé, Ange Felix 67, 91, 93, 96, 102, 115–138, 151, 156, 160, 161, 167
Pazangué 128
Petroleum Review Oversight and Control Committee 168
Petronas Oil 48
Ping, Jean 153
Pipeline 47–56, 58, 97, 124, 151, 162, 168
Pompidou, Georges 45
Portugal 163
Presidential Guard 15–17, 22–25, 34–36, 60, 67, 119, 149, 167

Quesnot, Christian 31

RaFAD, Rassemblement des Forces Armées Démocratiques 11
Rémadji, Irène 113
Revolutionary United Front (RUF) 155
Rice, Condoleeza 77
Richard, Alain 119
Rome Statute 152, 157–159
Royingam, Robert 33–34, 37
Rwanda 118, 120, 153, 161

Salah, Abdallah 68
Salamat 46, 141
Saleh Annadif 17
Saleh, Ibni Oumar Mahamat 2
Salet, Adoum 104
Sallah, Mayodine 32
Sangar 103
Sankoh, Foday 155
Sarh 47, 105, 123, 127, 131
Sarkozy, Nicolas 1, 151
Satom 148
Saudi Arabia 44, 59, 87, 96
Sedigui 46–48
Senegal 11, 75, 118–119, 153
Sesay, Issa 155
Shell Oil 46–48
Sidick, Abba 72
Sierra Leone 67, 133, 155
Sillou, Basile 132
SNER (National Society of Road Maintenance) 89
Somalia 1
Souleymane, Ibrahim 68
Soumaïne, Daoud 122–123, 131
South Africa 39, 169
Sudan People's Liberation Army (SPLA) 75, 85, 87

Tahir (Ambassador) 81–82
Tanja 133
Taylor, Charles 146, 154–155, 159–161
Teguil, Ali 27
Tiné 10, 32, 64, 67–68
Togo 28, 125, 131, 133
Togoï, Adoum 19
Togoïmi, Youssouf 26–27, 44, 53, 117, 158
Tokinon, Pierre 116
Tombalbaye, François Ngarta 5–7, 45–46, 70–72, 91

Uganda 75, 154
Ukraine 148
Union Générale des Fils du Tchad (UGFT) 71
United Front for Change and Democracy (FUCD) 138
United Kingdom 5
United Nations 19, 102, 111, 126, 146, 149, 151–152, 157, 161, 163, 165, 168–172; African Union Mission in Darfur 145; High Commissioner for Refugees 2; International Covenant on Civil and Political Rights 59
United States 5–6, 18, 25, 32, 39–41, 45–47, 49–50, 64–66, 74, 77, 96, 106, 121, 133, 138, 154, 163–164, 168
UNT (Chadian National Union) 71

Vatankah, Tchanguis 3
Verschave, François-Xavier 44, 77–78, 158–9, 163

Wade, Abdoulaye 153
Wardougou, Daoud 29
Washington, D.C. 25, 49, 51–52
Weddeye, Goukouni 7–8, 18, 72–74, 144
Wolfensohn, James 50–55
World Bank 47–57, 78, 124, 149, 151, 168
Woulingar, Djassam Thomas 111

Yaoundé, Paul Biya 42, 132
Yoadoumnadji, Pascal 37
Yogueadé, Augustine 113

Yomi 102
Yorongar le Moïban, Ngarlejy 6, 11, 22, 25, 44, 49, 53, 62, 83, 91, 96, 109, 111–113, 126, 130–131, 150, 169
Youdeiman, Joseph 32
Youssouf 79, 81
Yusuf, Acheik Ibn Oumar 58–62, 76, 95

Zaghawa 9–20, 30–31, 33–34, 36, 38, 61, 63–68, 74–76, 78, 84–85, 88, 90, 92–96, 107, 109–111, 113, 116, 120, 129, 132, 137, 140–142, 151
Zaire 96, 119–121
Zène, Mahamat 111
Zougoulou, Adoum 104